Political Initiation in the Novels of Philip Roth

Political Initiation in the Novels of Philip Roth

Claudia Franziska Brühwiler

BLOOMSBURY
NEW DELHI • LONDON • OXFORD • NEW YORK • SYDNEY

BLOOMSBURY INDIA
Bloomsbury Publishing India Pvt. Ltd
Second Floor, LSC Building No. 4, DDA Complex, Pocket C–6&7,
Vasant Kunj, New Delhi 110070

BLOOMSBURY, BLOOMSBURY ACADEMIC INDIA and the Diana logo are
trademarks of Bloomsbury Publishing Plc

First published 2013
This paperback edition first published 2014
First published in India 2023

This edition published with permission from Bloomsbury Publishing Plc,
50 Bedford Square, London, WC1B3DP, UK

Library of Congress Cataloging-in-Publication Data
Brühwiler, Claudia Franziska.
Political initiation in the novels of Philip Roth/Claudia Franziska Brühwiler.
pages cm
Based on the author's dissertation (doctoral)–Swiss Institute for International
Economics and Applied Economic Research (SIAW-HSG) of the
University of St. Gallen Switzerland.
Includes bibliographical references and index.
ISBN 978-1-4411-5321-0 (hardcover: alk. paper) 1. Roth, Philip–Criticism and
interpretation. 2. Political socialization in literature. 3. Political participation in
literature. 4. Self in literature. I. Title.
PS3568.O855Z59 2013
813'.54 dc23

ISBN: 978-93-54357-90-9

Typeset by Deanta Global Publishing Services, Chennai, India
Printed at Manipal Technologies Limited, Manipal

To find out more about our authors and books
visit www.bloomsbury.com and sign up for our newsletters

For Daniel
and my parents
In love and gratitude

Contents

Acknowledgments

The work on what would first be a doctoral thesis and then result in this book started at an unlikely place: at the Swiss Institute for International Economics and Applied Economic Research (SIAW-HSG) of the University of St.Gallen, Switzerland, where I was working as Professor em. Dr. oec. Heinz Hauser's teaching assistant. I am grateful to Prof. Hauser for encouraging me on my then unexpected new path that led to this book.

In Professor Dr. phil. Yvette Sánchez I found not only a wonderfully supportive supervisor, but also a good friend and professional role-model. I am likewise grateful for the help I received from my co-supervisor, Professor Dr. rer.publ. Christoph Frei, who has been a mentor from my early undergraduate years on and supported my doctoral project from its very beginning. The whole endeavor would, however, have been much more difficult to pursue had Prof. Sánchez and I not received a generous research grant from the Swiss National Science Foundation (SNF). I thank Prof. Sánchez, Prof Frei, and PD Dr. Till Kinzel for their invaluable help in drafting the project submission to the SNF.

A research semester at the University of Notre Dame, Indiana, was crucial to my progress. There, my host advisor, Professor Catherine H. Zuckert, PhD made not only valuable suggestions for the improvement of Chapter 1, but also provided a welcoming atmosphere and a creative environment. I thank her very much for her ongoing support and encouragement.

A huge thank-you must go to Professor Aimee Pozorski, PhD, current president of the *Philip Roth Society*. She not only provided comments and suggestions concerning an article on which Chapter 7 is based, but also reviewed my book manuscript and made very helpful remarks for its improvement. Chapter 2 evolved out of a conference paper, which I presented at the National Conference 2008 of the Popular Culture Association and the American Culture Association in San Francisco. At this occasion, Grete and Otto Heinz offered their hospitality in Carmel—I thank them for their incredible kindness and the stimulating discussions.

Turning my dissertation into a book would have been all the harder had I not received wonderful advice from Professor Thomas Dumm. During my postdoctoral research stay at Amherst College in Massachusetts in the academic year 2010–2011, he regularly commented on my work and guided me through the proposal stage. I also thank Professors Ilán Stavans of Amherst College, Jennifer Burns of Stanford University, and Roland Bleiker of the University of Queensland for their advice and support.

During both my doctoral studies and my start into postdoctoral life, my friend and colleague Dr. rer.publ. Eszter Kiss-Deák always had an open ear for my concerns and worries. *Danke* for many wonderful discussions on all things academic and beyond!

At the final stage of a book stands its publisher and I am grateful to have found the support of Haaris Naqvi at *Continuum.* I likewise thank assistant editor Ally Jane Grossan and everyone else who worked behind the scenes on my manuscript and made this book possible. I also gratefully acknowledge Purdue University Press's permission to reproduce in altered form my article "Chiastic Reflections: Rash Moments in the Life of Zuckerman," published in *Philip Roth Studies* (5, no. 2: 227–39).

I am indebted to all those mentioned, but to none more than to my husband and my family. My parents, Verena and Dr. Hermann Brühwiler, have always encouraged and supported me on my way to my doctoral degree. The one who read, meticulously corrected, and criticized my work is my husband, Dr. iur. Daniel M. Häusermann. I thank him for his commitment, patience, and encouragement. It is to him and to my family that I dedicate my book, in love and gratitude.

Claudia Franziska Brühwiler

List of Abbreviations of Philip Roth's Works

Goodbye, Columbus and Five Short Stories	*Goodbye*
Portnoy's Complaint	*Portnoy*
The Professor of Desire	*Professor*
The Ghost Writer	*Ghost*
Zuckerman Unbound	*Unbound*
The Anatomy Lesson	*Anatomy*
The Prague Orgy	*Prague*
The Counterlife	*Counterlife*
The Facts: A Novelist's Autobiography	*Facts*
Deception: A Novel	*Deception*
Patrimony: A True Story	*Patromony*
Operation Shylock: A Confession	*Shylock*
American Pastoral	*Pastoral*
I Married a Communist	*Communist*
The Human Stain	*Stain*
The Dying Animal	*Dying*
The Plot Against America	*Plot*
Everyman	*Everyman*
Exit Ghost	*Exit*
The Humbling	*Humbling*
Reading Myself and Others	*Reading*
Shop Talk: A Writer and His Colleagues and Their Work	*Shop*

List of Abbreviations of Other Works of Fiction

The Autobiography of an Ex-Colored Man	*Autobiography*
The Black Album	*Album*
The Messiah of Stockholm	*Messiah*
Mona in the Promised Land	*Mona*
"My Son the Fanatic"	*"Fanatic"*
The Shadow-Line	*Shadow-Line*
Winesburg, Ohio	*Winesburg*

Prologue

So [*said the doctor*]. Now vee may perhaps to begin. Yes?

(*Portnoy*, 274)

This line, quoted from the one novel which laid the foundations of Philip Roth's fame in 1969, is in many ways fitting for this book, as it alludes to the core subject of the treatise and its ambiguities. Dr Spielvogel's remark addresses the book's main concern quite plainly: to begin—beginnings. This book will focus on political beginnings, the way that characters in Philip Roth's novels develop their political consciousness, conceive their political ideas, and define their role in society. The formula I suggest to encapsulate these developments is "political initiation," a term which unites political science, literary theory, and anthropology. Thereby, political socialization research, the branch of political science usually concerned with individual political awakenings, can take the mechanisms of self-creation into consideration that both anthropology and literary studies have unveiled.

So far, "political initiation" is not an expression commonly used in political science and theory. When searching databases for the exact term, the rare hits mainly concern biographical descriptions,[1] referring to the point in people's lives when they discover the importance of politics. In these instances, "initiation" is used metaphorically, without reference to the term's anthropological roots and further consideration of its haziness. Dr Spielvogel's quote illustrates the ambiguities of beginnings and attempts to delineate them: although he talks of beginning, he in fact closes *Portnoy's Complaint* with his, as Roth called it, punch line. Banal as it might sound that ends are linked to beginnings, this simple truth has to be borne in mind when the idea of initiation is applied to age groups usually not associated with the term.

In contrast to political science, literary theory readily adopted the term "initiation" and its ambiguities. The term commonly describes a particular type of coming of age story, the so-called initiation story, which shows an individual's awakening to adult realities. In this book, I will show how the analysis of initiation stories or initiatory elements will contribute to a political scientist's understanding of the creation, construction, or invention and evolution of an individual's political self or the failure to do so. This analysis will, however, not be reduced to the individual level: neither narrative nor political identities are formulated in a vacuum, but are embedded in a political context, which will make it necessary to thematize space and regime. The question arises as to how an individual finds his or her role in society, and how much this process depends on a fixed spatial and political framework as a point of reference. To this end, an analysis of Philip Roth's novels shows the interconnectedness of history and individual existence, since they often take American politics and history as their setting, which has repeatedly drawn the interest of political scientists. Philip Roth's novels offer a broad range of variations on the central theme, initiation, both generally and politically. Identity and self-creation can be seen as the central topics in Roth's almost entire oeuvre, with explorations ranging from the question of a secular American Jew's attitude to Israel and the country's impact on his identity in *The Counterlife* (1986) or *Operation Shylock* (1993) to the political responsibility of the artist in *The Ghost Writer* (1979) and *I Married A Communist* (1998) and to the perils of racial passing in *The Human Stain* (2000).

Philip Roth's novels have received considerable attention from political scientists, which is no surprise as his plots feature the political events, characters, and ideas. These studies can be attributed to a subfield known as "politics and literature." Similarly to its corollary in legal studies, the law and literature movement, the field combines studies by political scientists who turn to literary texts for a myriad of reasons. They, for instance, study fiction as illustrations of political phenomena, of political theories and their consequences, as political weapons, or as a means of political and moral education. In this vein, Roth's fiction prompted scholars to ponder the extent to which reading can be conducive to good citizenry,[2] the relationship of betrayal and postwar liberalism,[3] or the challenges of multiple, fractured identities in uncertain political conditions.[4] This book aims to expand the scope of the "politics and literature" movement to political socialization research. As Part I will show, political socialization research has traditionally been the domain of sociology, which has, however, met with criticism that a politics and literature approach may address.

A political scientist approaches a literary text differently than a literary scholar. He or she usually has distinct questions in mind and may focus on aspects of a writer's oeuvre that might appear of secondary importance to a literary scholar. The latter may find that focusing on plotlines and contextual aspects of Roth's novels leads to unjustly obscuring the view for other characteristics of his writing, such as his famed style, his humor and playfulness, and his many allusions and (hidden) tributes to other writers and to their works, aspects which have let the field of Philip Roth studies become "a minor (or maybe not so minor) industry."[5] Such differences in approaches and interests may therefore result in misunderstandings across disciplines. A famous example is literary scholar Sigurd Burckhardt's 1960 criticism of articles on Shakespeare written by political scientists that had been published in the renowned *American Political Science Review*:

> "They have a worthy aim: to give a great poet a voice in the great concerns of practical life. But they have not yet learned to distinguish between the poet's voice and their own, so that, though I greet the aim, I must withhold the applause."[6]

In the case of these articles, their authors did not, in my opinion, mistake Shakespeare's voice for their own, but they read his plays with other questions in mind than most literary scholars would. This book does focus on the political aspects of Roth's novels, but it does so mindful of their many other merits and takes pleasure in venturing beyond plot analyses. It thereby complements the field of Philip Roth studies by addressing a new issue—the political identity of Roth's figures—from a less common angle—political science.

The book is divided into four parts which tentatively follow the trajectory of initiations, from Roth's variations on classical initiation stories and their defining aspects to more radical outcomes and, finally, their reversal or denial. Accordingly, I outline the methodological approach and the triangle of disciplines involved in *Part I*. This leads to the anthropological concept used to grasp the development of adolescents, initiation. Subsequently, we turn to the evolution and state of political socialization research, the branch in political science concerned with the development of individual political consciousness. The concept of "initiation" will bridge the gap between political socialization research and literary studies, as the latter are, among other things, concerned with the analysis of so-called coming of age or initiation stories.

Part II is dedicated to instances in Roth's oeuvre where he followed quasiclassical patterns of initiation stories, yet departed from certain conventions and introduced broader themes. Thus is the case in the novels discussed in Chapter 2, *The Plot Against America* (2004) and *Indignation* (2008). Both delineate nearly classic initiation stories, yet likewise offer a first glimpse of motifs and themes that will be analyzed in more depth at later stages of the book, such as spatial changes, the role of rituals, and physical maturation. Moreover, both novels are exemplary of Roth's preoccupation with history and its impact on individual lives, an invitation to explore the tense relationship between historiography and fiction.

Chapter 3 introduces a less common factor that may define an individual's political development: literature. *I Married a Communist* (1998) follows young Nathan Zuckerman's political awakening under the guidance of his readings. The novel thus offers an opportunity to discuss Philip Roth's view of the relationship between the factual and the fictional, between literature and reality, and thus between literature and its potential merits for social sciences.

By this point, space will have become a recurring theme, as journeys can become an initiatory experience. The final section of Part II, Chapter 4, thematizes the relationship between space and identity, particularly the question of what significance a member of a Diaspora community attributes to his or her geographic and religious roots. In this vein, *The Prague Orgy* (1985), *The Counterlife* (1986), and *Operation Shylock* (1993) take their protagonist through sites of Jewish history in general, and of Nathan Zuckerman's family history in particular.

Part III turns to the idea of political initiation as a total reinvention or recreation of the self. Roth's protagonists constantly challenge the limits to self-creation, but nowhere with such insistence as in the novel discussed in Chapter 5. *The Human Stain* (2000) shows how a young African-American man crosses the racial divide in American society of the 1950s, how he decides not to be inhibited by racism. This story of radical self-reinvention is contrasted by stories of assimilation, whose protagonists either undergo physical transformations or suppress their heritage in their demeanor. The following Chapter explores Roth's characterization of religious and political fanatics, one of whom will indeed turn to terrorism in *American Pastoral* (1997). Roth's approach will be compared to novels by Hanif Kureishi, John Updike, and Paul Auster, whereby distinct explanatory patterns become visible. In some cases, these patterns coincide with findings in political psychology—in others, they take a rather surprising direction.

Part IV contrasts the preceding Part in that it does not contemplate a total dedication to a political cause, but the complete disengagement from political and societal issues. Age has become the preoccupation of not only Philip Roth himself, but also his elderly protagonists in *The Dying Animal* (2001), *Everyman* (2006), and *Exit Ghost* (2007). These novels close the circle that started with the child and adolescent protagonists in *The Plot Against America*: while the young protagonists were initially unable to establish a connection between their lives and political events, Roth's old men try to repress any idea that politics might affect their private lives in any way.

Part One

The Framework

1

Beginnings and Transitions in Political Science and Literature

1. Introduction: Portnoy at the threshold

> Doctor, I can't stand any more being frightened like this over nothing! Bless me with manhood! Make me brave! Make me strong! Make me *whole*! Enough being a nice Jewish boy, publicly pleasing my parents while privately pulling my putz! Enough! (*Portnoy*, 37)

If ever anyone turned adolescence into a phase of experimenting and testing the boundaries of social probity, it was Philip Roth's protagonist of the 1969 literary scandal *Portnoy's Complaint*. In a monologue, the addressee of which cannot be established unambiguously (is his psychiatrist already in the room? at its door? are we listening to soliloquy?), Alexander Portnoy lets us partake in his endless struggles on several fronts: on the one hand against family conventions and the pressures imposed by tradition; on the other hand against his own libidinal urges which practically enslave him, as he is in constant need of channeling his lusts.[1] He can neither endure his overbearing and overprotective mother Sophie, who leaves him hardly any room to explore his sexuality, nor can he witness any longer how,

> in that ferocious and self-annihilating way in which so many Jewish men of his generation served their families, my father served my mother, my sister Hannah, but particularly me. Where he had been imprisoned, I would fly: that was his dream. Mine was its corollary: in my liberation would be his—from ignorance, from exploitation, from anonymity. (*Portnoy*, 8–9)

Alexander Portnoy seeks liberation, liberation from the haunting Jewish legacy, liberation from religious and traditional rules which are, in his eyes, only a means to chain people:

> Why else, I ask you, but to remind us three times a day that life is boundaries and restrictions if it's anything, hundreds of thousands of little rules laid down by none other than None Other, rules which either you obey without question, regardless of how idiotic they may appear (and thus remain, by obeying, in His

> good graces), or you transgress, most likely in the name of outraged common sense—which you transgress because even a child doesn't like to go around feeling like an absolute moron and schmuck . . . . (*Portnoy*, 80)

Freed, he would be a man, a member of the human race—but never part of that America he hears of on the radio, the genteel world outside the confines of his Jewish heritage.[2] Yet if you cannot be part of something, you can at least exert power over it, which is exactly what Portnoy strives for in his sexual encounters with the WASP girls who surrender to his urges.[3] Still, an erotically reckless life will not help him to find his true self, nor will it heighten his self-consciousness. A journey to Israel shall finally bring him closer to his own reality[4]—a hopeless quest.

Portnoy's quest for independence sounds like the plot of a coming of age novel, though not a typical one, which eludes the category of the *Bildungsroman* in that it celebrates disobedience,[5] but respects the rules of the twentieth century *Entwicklungsroman* in that it values experience more than innocence:[6] these are but two genres which represent literature's mode of dealing with the transition from childhood to adult life, yet not the frame in which American writers place their adolescent protagonists when they embark on their journeys of maturation. The American coming of age story typically tests the national consciousness, its values, and ideals by forcing its protagonist to contrast his or her reality with the American Dream.[7] Allusively, one can witness this confrontation in Portnoy's recognition of society's latent anti-Semitism, which would always let him stand aside, and the impossibility of becoming part of the WASP ideal.

The American coming of age story focuses on processes of self-recognition rather than of a smooth development or the aspiration of an educational ideal, as demonstrated by Portnoy, who at least strives for this ultimate goal. Although the typical American coming of age story rarely covers collective rites of passage as conceived by anthropology, its essence is an initiation. In other words, it shows a

> "young protagonist experiencing a significant change of knowledge about the world or himself, or a change of character, or of both, and this change must point or lead him towards an adult world."[8]

Portnoy undergoes a process dominated by uncertainty, ambivalence, and a transitory experience. He thus shares the predicament of many Rothian protagonists, a situation which makes him a subject of anthropologist interest.

2. The anthropological concept of initiation: Society's rules challenged

If the reasoning of the Dutch anthropologist Arnold van Gennep is applied, society's rituals guide us through critical transitions:[9] during our lifetime, van Gennep argues, we pass through a series of relatively static positions, termed statuses, such as birth, puberty, parenthood, and a rise in social classes or professional hierarchies. Given their inherent uncertainty and the energy needed to pass them, these transitions between statuses are potentially contentious.[10] In order to contain these tensions, ritualistic frameworks have evolved within societies which guide the individual through these phases.

To illustrate the main intent of such ritualistic frameworks, van Gennep calls them *rites of passage*, which ideally follow three stages: separation, transition, and incorporation.[11] Yet although every rite of passage undergoes these stages, they will emphasize the phase which concerns their core characteristic. In this vein, one can say that "[f]unerals emphasize separation; births and weddings, incorporation; and initiations, transition."[12] Thereof, initiation rites are the ones which guide an individual from his life as a child in the domestic domain to the position of an adult and full member of society.[13] Mircea Eliade, a historian of religion, describes initiation as an entirety of rites and oral instructions which aim to change the religious and/or social life of the one to be inaugurated. In becoming an adult, Eliade suggests, individuals reach the end of their lives as "natural human being[s]" and are introduced to culture.[14]

Initiation thus entails both the idea of end and beginning—the end of the old and the beginning of a new self, ideas which invoke the symbolism of death and rebirth. Yet common as this association is,[15] it instills a new meaning to the process as it does not allude to a transition with its ambiguous moments when one cannot tell whether the old still prevails or the new has already begun. Instead, the image of death and rebirth conceives of initiation as a rupture, in which the old self ceases to exist so that a new one can take shape.[16] This aspect is emphasized by initiatory rites in traditional, small-scale societies, which have often developed a series of tests for the initiand, during which he will have to prove his readiness to renounce his former way of life.[17] Accordingly, these tests foresee the initiand's ritual death, followed by his rebirth, wherein the initiation rite culminates: the initiatory death marks the end of the neophytes' childhood, of both their ignorance and their innocence.

In outline, the sequence of the traditional initiation process has now become discernible and therewith the reasoning behind van Gennep's tripartite scheme of "separation – transition – incorporation": before initiands will be exposed to teachings or to an influential experience that shall prepare them for their new life, they are *separated* from their known environment, typically the family household. As a group of coeval youths, they are then put under the tutelage of elder mentors who will mark the *transition* phase by passing on the knowledge necessary for the new stage in life. During this time, the novices are not only spatially separated from their community, but they are also virtually outcasts who are, intermittently, not bound by society's rules and who can even become a danger to communal stability.[18] Only with their rebirth, their passing of the initiatory tests, will they return to the midst of society, which will *incorporate* them, yet not in their previous positions and roles, but in the realm of adults.

Although separation and incorporation are likewise integral parts of the whole initiation process, it is the phase of transition which is essential and makes mentors or instructors vital protagonists.[19] They are the ones who empower the initiands to live up to their new roles; they become their first guides toward a new life. The relationship between initiand and mentor, however, is unambiguously defined by domination, as

Victor Turner observes: "between instructors and neophytes there is often complete authority and complete submission; among neophytes there is often complete equality."[20] Already the complete submission to the mentor reveals the coercive aspect of initiation, which is then supplemented by those forms of teaching which might not be sustainable were their contents open to questioning. In a nutshell, "initiation entails indoctrination."[21] Like indoctrination in general, initiatory instruction relies on imitation and nonevidentiary teaching whose only source of authority is the position of the mentor.[22]

In the works of Philip Roth, the Jewish rites of initiation, namely the circumcision of the newly born and the Bar Mitzvah at the age of thirteen, are the only traditional rites that play a vital role. Circumcision is, however, more a rite of separation and incorporation than a classical birth ritual.[23] By circumcising the newborn boy within the first eight days of his life, his father fulfills the *mitzvah*, a commandment of God, and ensures that the child enters the *Brit Milah*, the covenant of the foreskin.[24] Should the father fail to circumcise his male offspring by himself or to assign a *mohel*, who is trained to perform circumcisions,[25] his son can still be circumcised before his Bar Mitzvah in order to avoid being "cut off from his kin"[26] for having broken the covenant. As the sanction already insinuates, circumcision is mainly an act of collective differentiation: the circumcised is visibly separated from the rest of the population and at the same time joins the ranks of his kin.[27] Alex Portnoy experiences his circumcision in this way, for although he has long felt that his "wang was all [he] had that [he] could call [his] own", yet it had been eternally marked as "property of the Jews" (35). Portnoy might hardly agree, yet circumcision is supposed to loosen the bond with the mother, as Ronald L. Grimes points out. On the one hand, women do not bear a corresponding mark of the covenant, and, on the other hand, mothers are not allowed either to hold their son during the circumcision or to witness the act at all.[28]

While circumcision only vaguely resembles an initiation rite, scholars often regard the Bar Mitzvah as a classic example, since it marks the end of childhood.[29] Yet it has increasingly been argued that the Bar Mitzvah only allows the adolescent to participate fully in religious life by studying the Torah, instead of permitting him to acquire the social status of an adult.[30] Thus, the alleged initiates do not undergo a true transformation and change in status. Anecdotes may hardly confirm this argument, nevertheless Roth's memory of his own Bar Mitzvah training underlines how little effect it had on his coming of age:

> Though I hadn't been a total failure either, and had learned enough Hebrew to read at breakneck speed (if not with full comprehension) from the Torah at my bar mitzvah, the side of my Jewish education that had made that after-school hour, three days a week, at all endurable had largely to do with the hypnotic appeal, in those environs, of the unimpeachably profane. (*Facts*, 120)

Against the backdrop of his own experience, one is hardly surprised that Roth satirizes the Bar Mitzvah instruction in one of his earliest writings. In the short story "The Conversion of the Jews" (*Goodbye*, 1959), Ozzie Freedman cannot bear the rabbinic indoctrination which should prepare him for his Bar Mitzvah, yet fails to enlighten him and instead tries to extinguish his sense of critical thinking, for:

> [w]hat Ozzie wanted to know was always different. The first time he had wanted to know how Rabbi Binder could call the Jews "The Chosen People" if the Declaration of Independence claimed all men to be created equal. Rabbi Binder tried to distinguish for him between political equality and spiritual legitimacy, but what Ozzie wanted to know, he insisted vehemently, was different. That was the first time his mother had to come. ("The Conversion of the Jews," 108–9)

In the hands of Rabbi Binder, the preparatory course has become a means of social control, against which the child thirsting for knowledge protests, or as Grimes holds with reference to the metaphorical names, "Ozzie Freedman wants to be 'free' of Rabbi Binder, who 'binds' him."[31]

Ozzie's refusal to accept the Rabbi's teachings without further questioning conveys a general risk that initiation processes entail for society. For although the transitory phase is considered to be a stage of reflection forcing neophytes to think about their society and cosmos,[32] the initiands are supposed to ultimately return to the midst of society and accept its norms.[33] They might be encouraged to break the rules of society during the initiation process, but upon their return the same rules shall prevail—and even the prior breach of rules is just another rule to be followed. Novices may ask critical questions, but these should not be as subversive as to have a lasting impact on their peers, tempting them to refuse to live according to the principles adhered by their instructors. Test the limits, but don't venture beyond them—thus goes the commandment, since initiation permits the temporary inversion of society's rules, yet never their subversion.

This provisional permission to break rules was encapsulated by Victor Turner in the notion of *liminality*. Liminality stands for a period of ambiguity or social limbo, a moment of weightlessness during which the ritual subjects

> "elude or slip through the network of classifications that normally locate states and positions in space. Liminal entities are neither here nor there; they are betwixt and between the positions assigned and arrayed by law, custom, convention, and ceremonial."[34]

The idea of liminality signifies a return to the etymological roots of passages, in that we step back from its figurative to its spatial meaning. In this vein, we can establish a parallel between the passage from one status in life to the next and the literal passage over thresholds, through doorways, across oceans, and other spaces.[35] The threshold is the archetypical liminal space, as it is not only the translation of the Latin *limen*. Moreover, it is as such

> "a transitional space or boundary, . . . a no man's land that belongs to neither the one side nor the other, but paradoxically it is also the territory of both sides—ultimately, there can, of course, be no threshold without a space on both sides."[36]

The reference to the two sides bordering with a threshold signals that liminality is etymologically not only linked to the word "threshold," but also to the Greek term for "harbor" or place.[37] This further stresses the provisional in the liminal: we cross a threshold in order to reach our destination; it helps us to assess the significance of our destination, as it marks the difference from our point of departure.[38]

Although some argue that rites of passage are mainly practiced by traditional, small-scale communities and that they are hardly present in modern societies,[39] anyone can easily list moments and festivities linked to an individual's coming of age, reaching beyond the religious sphere to a person's first casting a ballot, a debutante's entrance ball, or the participation in basic military training. But while religious rites are still initiation rites proper, many other instances that mark a transition toward adulthood are not perceived as initiatory, being devoid of any ritual. Yet the previous journey through the different aspects of initiation has revealed the notion's multiple facets, which allows the consideration of nonritualistic initiation processes. In this vein, I will consider "initiation" independently of ritualistic frameworks, as literary theorist Ihab Hassan does when he defines it as the

> "first existential ordeal, crisis, or encounter with experience in the life of a youth. Its ideal aim is knowledge, recognition, and confirmation in the world, to which the actions of the initiate, however painful, must tend. It is, quite simply, the viable mode of confronting adult realities."[40]

Bare of institutionalized rites, we can read first sexual experiences, intellectual insights that alter someone's way of thinking permanently, the first recognition of evil, and the introduction to a new ability or the acclimatization to a new environment as instances of initiation.[41] Such processes may occur throughout a lifespan—humans are, as it will become clear, transitory beings, constantly on the move from one stage to the next. Van Gennep induces us to see man not primarily as a *zôón politikón*, but as a being in need of rituals to mark the different stages in his life cycle.

3. Initiation stories: The storytelling initiand

The theme of initiation, facing adult realities, being introduced to society as an adult, has often been the concern of literature, where it takes just as many shades and forms, if not more, as in our lives. Mordecai Marcus has divided the genre of *initiation stories* or *novels* according to the degree to which an initiation succeeds: first, the classic case, a "successful" initiation so to speak, focuses on the protagonist's self-discovery, whereby the story shows him reaching maturity and understanding, or at least indicates that he will certainly reach maturity at a later stage. The second, literal in-between case takes the protagonist across the threshold of maturity and understanding, yet leaves him "enmeshed in a struggle for certainty"[42] and thus in limbo. Lastly, Marcus names the protagonist on the threshold of maturity and understanding, though not sure whether to cross it. A decision, one might add, perhaps never to be taken.

These three stages can be complemented by the typology proposed by Peter Freese, who focuses on the motifs, contexts, and goals of initiation.[43] Accordingly, he distinguishes four types which partly mirror the essence of initiation in the anthropological sense: first, the discovery of the existence of evil; second, the loss of innocence and the subsequent maturation; third, the introduction into society; and lastly, self-discovery or self-actualization. The loss of the childhood belief in the ubiquitous good does not only entail the recognition of outer evil, but also the discovery of inner evil. Although this aspect is also covered in stories of the second type, they deal less with the nature of evil, but rather with the effect of the discovery of evil on the protagonist. At first sight, the introduction into society stands apart, as it seems to cover a collective rite in contrast to the inner trials depicted in the other three types. However, it also encapsulates a mental struggle, as the novice likewise has to deal with a new environment, its unwritten rules, and possible humiliation. Finally, a writer can send his or her protagonist on a quest for the self: a quest that can notably be started by the will of the initiand alone, as is the case with Portnoy whose story, to the reader's delight and the protagonist's dismay, remains stuck in Marcus's third category.

Not even a journey can carry Portnoy beyond this stage, although he travels to Israel with exactly this hope.[44] Journeys can indeed induce or accelerate an initiation process, as they represent one particular instance when an individual, sometimes in face of hardship, has to confront unfamiliarity and otherness, which will help him define his own identity. It is therefore no coincidence that many picaresque novels, as well as some *Bildungsromane* and *Entwicklungsromane*, take the shape of a travel novel or road novel, ranging from Grimmelshausen's *Simplicissimus* and Goethe's *Wilhelm Meisters Lehr- und Wanderjahre* to Mark Twain's *Huckleberry Finn* or J. D. Salinger's *The Catcher in the Rye*. Fittingly, the pattern of a travel account usually follows a tripartite scheme, just like the stages of initiation according to Arnold van Gennep: beginning/departure (*separation*)—middle/time at destination (*transition*)—end/home (*incorporation*).[45] For Portnoy, the journey to Israel brings about a shocking experience in that his worst fear becomes true and his potency fails him when he attempts to have his second sexual initiation, namely his first intercourse with a Jewish woman. Alas, instead of having a sobering, a maturing effect on him, Israel and the incidence of failure only bring Alexander to the psychoanalyst Dr Spielvogel's mercy.

But while Portnoy's initiation failed, the novel advanced Roth's own quest for liberty:

> It was a book that had rather less to do with "freeing" me from my Jewishness or from my family (the purpose divined by many, who were convinced by the evidence of *Portnoy's Complaint* that the author had to be on bad terms with both) than with liberating me from an apprentice's literary model . . . (*Facts*, 157)

Portnoy's initiation story became the author's own initiation—not only in his quest for his own literary voice, but also at "being a scandal." Initiation is a time of transgression, and thus both Portnoy and his author disregard the expectations of a decent Jewish life, indulging in the pleasures of disobedience, frivolity, and calculated indecency.

The liminality of Portnoy's condition is further accentuated by narrative means, namely the constant evocation of thresholds. Although "fascinated by all kinds of openings,"[46] as Régine Camps-Robertson puts it, Portnoy's conflicts often unfold at the threshold of closed doors. Locked up in the bathroom to masturbate, with his mother constantly knocking at the door, his father moaning and begging for entry, and a sister commenting on the scene sardonically, the closed door not only grants comic scenes, but also constitutes a risky zone for Alexander, as it always bears the danger of discovery. Moreover, Camps-Robertson sees in the locked door the one marker of power relations in the novel, as it not only represents the means by which Portnoy's mother exerts her authority, but also the gap between Alexander's Jewish world and the Gentile dream: while his father, an agent of an insurance company, knocks in vain at goyshe, non-Jewish doors, Portnoy indulges in fantasies of *shikses*, non-Jewish women, when staring at the closed curtains of their homes. It dawns on Portnoy that he himself as well as his father will remain forever banished to the threshold, never actually crossing it.

Apart from putting readers of initiation stories at spatial thresholds, another means to accentuate liminality is to render the threshold between reader and text more visible. The reader first approaches a text via its title, which in the case of *Portnoy's Complaint* already testifies to an individual's tirade and will later be proven as epitomizing the protagonist's self-indulgence. We as readers accept the litany and the constant breach of taboos, the vulgarity of Portnoy's account, for we believe Portnoy to be in a psychoanalytical session. It is even intended and socially accepted that he shares his innermost turmoil. Yet when we learn at the end that the whole complaint might have been placed in the doctor's absence we do not know, as Debra Shostak explained,[47] whether we can trust the tale we heard before. Moreover, the title gains a comical twist when the reader is introduced to "Portnoy's Complaint" as a psychiatric condition in an encyclopedic entry by Dr Spielvogel. The title and the short fictional definition are examples of *paratexts*, a term introduced by Gérard Genette which stands for those textual elements that go beyond the core text, but are still intertwined with it—or, in reference to the original title of Genette's major treatise, texts that serve as *seuils*, thresholds, to the core text, such as titles, notes to the reader, or dedications.

Paratexts constitute only one of five instances of transtextuality,[48] a notion which encompasses all those texts and textual elements that are related to the focal text. Thereof, *intertexts* are Roth's constant companions as they allow a similarly confusing game with the reader like paratexts. As the prefix already indicates, intertextuality alludes to the relationship between two texts, which is usually established by the effective presence of another text in the focal text. In the case of *Portnoy's Complaint,* Roth constructs such a bridge to *Alice in Wonderland,* on the one hand by quoting its title literally in the chapter "Alex in Wonderland" and on the other hand by using similar motifs.[49] Both this intertextual relation and the confusing paratext, that is the fictive encyclopedic entry, accentuate the absurdity and playfulness of the novel, thus heightening our senses for Portnoy's attitude.

The threshold between us, the readers, and the text simultaneously marks the boundary between fiction, the written world in Roth's diction, and reality, the unwritten world as experienced by us. While *Portnoy's Complaint* does not offer an illustration of this, we will later encounter several instances of Roth's taking us onto a metafictional level, by metafiction meaning

> "... fictional writing which self-consciously and systematically draws attention to its status as an artefact in order to pose questions about the relationship between fiction and reality [.]"[50]

One means to do so is the metalepsis,[51] whereby the extradiegetic narrator—the "actual" author—intrudes into the written world created by himself, the so-called diegetic universe, or vice-versa, and breaks the pact with the reader.[52] This happens, for instance, in Roth's autobiography *The Facts*, when he addresses a letter to his own writer-protagonist Nathan Zuckerman who later comments on the text and remarks with a twinkle that Roth is still as much in need of Zuckerman as Zuckerman is of Roth (161). In typical Rothian manner, Zuckerman furthermore questions the factuality of the text—the fictive character thus draws the reader's attention to those gaps which can render an alleged factual account fictitious. Such narrative techniques also sensitize the reader to treat the text *per se* as a liminal space, which in the eyes of Hein Viljoen and Chris N. van der Merwe bears further creative potential:

> "The relevance of the idea of liminality for literature is not only that many texts describe and represent liminal states, persons and transformations, but also that the space of the text itself is a symbolically demarcated liminal zone where transformations are allowed to happen—imaginary transformations that model and possibly bring into being new ways of thinking and being."[53]

Ottmar Ette described adolescence as a time when the individual is sitting on a swing: neither in the air nor on the ground, but always treading upon the same again and testing the limits and boundaries that the ropes set.[54] If adolescence and the process of initiation are phases to test the limits of our swings, this subchapter has been the first chance to test the ambit of the literary swings of initiation: traveling from the classic story of initiation processes to the text as a liminal zone might appear as a strain on the ropes of our swing. Yet it is indeed this many-sidedness that renders the notion potentially fruitful for an interdisciplinary endeavor.

4. Political socialization: The swing halted in mid-air

"Confronting adult realities,"—this was how Ihab Hassan described the essence of an initiation. Both literary theory and anthropology provide the analytical tools to dissect tales of rites, moments of ambivalence, and transition. A particular aspect of adult reality, though, has only been implied. Assuming responsibility and facing the adult world may have an entirely individualistic connotation, yet already in the original sense the term referred to the individual's changing role in its community. It addresses, in other words, the individual as a *zôón politikón*. Still, political science has been slow to acknowledge the importance of those who have not yet acquired the status of citizen and voter. While political thinkers did indeed reflect on children's political education, as already Platon's treatise of the ideal State or Rousseau's Entwicklungsroman *Émile* prominently document, modern political science only discovered childhood at the end of the 1950s.

With the sociologist Herbert Hyman's book *Political Socialization: A Study in the Psychology of Political Behavior* in 1959,[55] a new field emerged which unites the findings of social psychology and of research on public opinion, electoral behavior, and political recruitment.[56] Hyman's treatise integrates findings in the quoted branches of research, whereby he develops a joint framework to analyze what he calls "political socialization." As is often the case in recent research areas, each new publication coins a new definition of the term under scrutiny, with David Easton and Robert Hess having provided a straightforward definition: they describe political socialization as the "processes through which a young person acquires his basic political orientations from others in his environment."[57] By "political orientations" they refer to the "content that is transmitted from older to younger generations in the area of politics,"[58] such as political values, attitudes, or standards of evaluation.

At the beginning, research did not venture to study the years of change and ambiguity in a person's life. Instead of ambiguity or insecurity, it was the idea of permanence that served as the overarching theme of these studies: political socialization was seen as key to political stability,[59] since the values transmitted would guarantee coherence over time. It was generally believed that what a person learns to treasure as a child is rarely abandoned as an adult.[60] Or to put it with the often quoted and later criticized words by Easton and Hess:

> Each new generation emerges upon the political scene as a *tabula rasa*, politically speaking, upon which a political system must seek to imprint its image, however varying its measure of success, if it is to persist in some form.[61]

When the political order became tested by time, the researchers' focus shifted to adolescence. The political turmoil of the late 1960s until the early 1980s no longer provoked questions on the roots of regime stability, but rather of the opposite.[62] Instead of acquiescence with the existing rules—rebellion; instead of the regulated participation of well-adjusted citizens—protests and civil unrest. These developments likewise provoked researchers to reconsider the development of political attitudes, and ultimately led to the conclusion that adolescence and young adulthood were the major turning point in an individual's political life.

Ironically, political socialization research's own adolescence marked a decisive and nearly terminal phase for the future of this research area: scientific enthusiasm subsided as quickly as it had erupted. Whereas Hyman's impetus had led to several treatises on political socialization, Cook observed already in 1985 that "childhood . . . disappeared in political science."[63] This was hardly an exaggeration, as David O. Sears proved by reviewing 1,000 articles published between 1982 and 1986 in six prominent journals on political behavior: of these, only fourteen dealt with political socialization.[64] This sharp decline at least provoked a number of articles which examined the reasons behind the abandonment of the field. Their verdict was harsh: "In summary neither political science nor psychology has shed much light on the developmental antecedents of political beliefs, attitudes, or engagement."[65] The reasons for the declining interest in political socialization have been identified on several levels: its predominant methodology, its sociological focus, and its choice of subjects. Some of these shortcomings already shine through or can easily be spotted if one consults the actual findings of political socialization research.

The critique boiled down to its harsh core, how researchers in the field of political socialization perceived the child; that is, as a malleable, moldable creature, taking whatever shape others want.[66] Consequently, considerable attention was paid to possibly influential agents. The family, it was found, is in the position to exert the most substantial influence, which several studies have been able to quantify over time,[67] letting Robert E. Lane even speak of a "Mendelian law" of politics.[68] Taking Philip Roth's childhood as an example, he would—according to his biography *The Facts* (1988)—neatly fit into the picture drawn by these findings, as he sees himself as the inheritor of his parents' "belief in the boundlessness of the democracy in which we lived and to which we belonged" (*The Facts*, 123). Although, due to its ironic undertone, one is inclined to question the statement, doubts are swiftly cast aside by Roth's earliest childhood memories, which prove national allegiance to be one of his first lessons in life:

> "In our apartment a framed replica of the Declaration of Independence hung above the telephone table on the hallway wall . . ." (*The Facts*, 21)[69]

Roth might have shared his parents' belief in its principles, their disdain for Nixon, and his father's admiration for Franklin D. Roosevelt, yet no young adult is a "simple carbon copy of his parents,"[70] as researchers M. Kent Jennings and Richard G. Niemi observed. Other socializing agents have an impact on an individual's attitudes, which might induce the adolescent to question his parents' values vehemently. Research in the 1960s, when Roth was already approaching his thirties, indeed proved that adolescents are prone to claim their independence by adopting a rebellious youth culture, to compensate for a lack of closeness between parent and child.[71] Although the writer of our interest, Philip Roth, decided to pursue his college education at Bucknell University, away from his parents' home, he did not do so in order to flee from them. Instead, his attachment to them lasted until their death. Yet to complete this minute survey of Roth's political socialization, we shall not withhold his brief flirtation with political protest against President Dwight D. Eisenhower, expressed in a short invective in a college magazine. However, his political advocacy lost quickly in fervor and was of no consequence, as Roth himself observed:

> This outburst aside, it had never occurred to me to make a case for Stevenson on the editorial page of *Et Cetera* when my first issue appeared at the height of the presidential campaign in October of 1952. The magazine had "higher" purposes,

> *literary* purposes. . . . A year later the magazine did publish a page-long "prose poem" that I'd written over the summer vacation, a monologue by an unnamed coward too prudent to speak out against McCarthyism, which provoked no response at all . . . (*Facts*, 63–4)

Naturally, Philip Roth's biographical data cannot serve to corroborate research findings in political socialization, yet the previously quoted verdict on the failure of political socialization research was hardly based on random examples contradicting the state of research. Given the substantial number of results and their repeated verification, one marvels how this devastating verdict was reached or why Richard G. Niemi and Mary A. Hepburn even conclude that "research on political socialization, as constituted in the 1970s, perhaps deserved to die."[72]

It was found that political socialization was apt at analyzing certain causal relations, but not at grasping the individual in its complexity. To achieve the latter, it had to extend its theoretical foundations and consider findings of psychological studies. Arguing in this vein, Judith Torney-Purta pleads in her study to forsake the image of the child as a simple receptor,[73] or what Roberta S. Sigel—sardonically referring to Easton and Hess—calls the

> "tabula rasa concept [which] portrays the young person as essentially passive, willingly and gullibly subject to external influence attempts, especially those of the home and the school."[74]

As an alternative, Torney-Purta advocates the adoption of a constructivist approach to development: the young person should be regarded as the constructor of his or her own knowledge "by relating what an instructor or parent says, what is read, and what is said in discussion with peers to previously established cognitive structures."[75]

Adopting a psychological approach, however, precludes the focus on children as the main research subjects, since psychological findings refute the assumption that certain attitudes developed in childhood remain stable.[76] In contrast, such an addition demands a lifespan perspective which, for instance, requires that all sources influencing a person's opinion be assessed, not only the family and other early socializing agents, but also the impact of major events, as well as individual processes that might let a person reverse his political opinions or maintain them. Obviously, such intricate connections warrant an individual approach. Consequently, Sigel recommends narrative interviews which permit the interviewees to

> "reflect on how they came to believe or act the way that they did and to inquire whether or not that behavior represents a departure from earlier patterns, notwithstanding that reliance on retrospective reports also is fraught with problems."[77]

As psychological research has identified a connection between attitude changes and transitions in the life cycle, such interviews should concentrate on those transitory phases when people's opinions undergo the most marked changes.[78] One can detect such an approach in James David Barber's seminal treatise *The Presidential Character* (1972). Though not interview based, Barber analyzes how the experiences of their youth had shaped American presidents, what pivotal moments determined their core beliefs. Barber does not speak of presidential initiation stories, yet that is what he essentially reconstructs: he retells life stories and pinpoints the turning points, transitory moments when these future leaders would develop a vision of their future selves and their roles.

5. Instead of a conclusion, a transition: Politics and literature in liminal space

Had Alexander Portnoy, beyond or within his literary existence, been subject to a survey in political socialization, the differences in the approaches to an individual's development in political science and literature would become literally visible: a questionnaire-based study of political socialization would supply us with snapshots of his life, catching him—to use Ottmar Ette's image once more—on the swings in mid-air, or when treading the ground, falling down, or trying to get into full swing again. In contrast, his life told as a story would unfold before our inner eye like a movie which would not only let us comprehend his life in context, but also, more importantly, make his coming of age appear as a sequence of events, enriched by flashbacks, and sometimes disturbed by sudden cuts. The two approaches do not just differ in the way they present Portnoy to us, they naturally choose different aspects of his life to cover. While literature shows us Portnoy in all shades, research in political socialization is not interested in the individual as such and has to focus on a person's political attitudes. While this concentration is legitimate, some aspects of an individual's political world require broadening the perspective. As a consequence, literature can be essential to introduce the individual in its entirety to political socialization research.

Collecting snapshots instead of covering lifespans is deemed, as argued earlier in this part, one of the major shortcomings of political socialization theory. In order to overcome this deficit, Sigel suggests narrative interviews which would enable researchers to cover an individual's development and stimulate his self-reflection.[79] Her proposal will be heeded, yet taken in another direction: before taking stock of individual narrations of their political coming of age, I will follow Maureen Whitebrook's approach in *Identity, Narrative and Politics* (2001) and suggest that the narrative mechanisms to be employed be studied first; that is, I propose to concentrate on the narrative creation of identity as such and the political self in particular. In other words, let the *zôón politikón* meet its inner *zôón historôn*, the storytelling being.

Whitebrook has already ventured in this direction by studying the ways in which political identity and narrative identity intermingle, exploring the modes of identity creation and their value for political thought in a number of novels, including Philip Roth's *Operation Shylock* (1993). In her terms, political identity is to be understood

> "either as a matter of (self-)awareness about the relationship of the person to the political order or as a function of inclusion in political units and as referring to certain characteristics whereby persons can be grouped for political purposes by a wide range of identificatory characteristics[.] . . . The first represents personal identity in a political context; the second is that of the political subject taken as a unit for political analysis, citizen, member of a group or nation."[80]

Similar to the critics of political socialization research, Whitebrook deplores the depersonalization that is implied by the cited understanding of political identity. As a remedy, she sees novels as means to get back to the individual level, a motivation shared by many political scientists who dedicate their research to literature.[81] Yet Whitebrook deviates from other approaches in that she links political with narrative identity.

Man is a *zôón historôn*, or as the history teacher and narrator in Graham Swift's *Waterland* (1983), a novel on the nexus of history and narrative, said:

> But man—let me offer you a definition—is *the story-telling animal*. . . . Even in his last moments, it's said, in the split second of a fatal fall – or when he's about to drown – he sees, passing rapidly before him, the story of his whole life. (47; emphasis added)

Life is also a story. Some would even go further and claim that individuals not only tell, but are indeed stories, given that our lives need the same structural elements like a narrative: a beginning, an end, a plot, a central character, et cetera.[82] French philosopher Paul Ricœur, however, points out that in contrast to a narrative *strictu sensu* whose author disguises himself as a narrator, individuals can become their own narrators and adopt different narrative voices, but they cannot become the author.[83] It is therefore more precise to speak of everyone having a narrative identity which

> "consists of stories we tell to ourselves about ourselves and the stories we *or* others tell to others, or stories that are told to others about ourselves – all the stories in which we are included[.] . . . Narrative identity is then at once subjective and intersubjective, and entails answerability and responsibility and the capacity for negotiation."[84]

Political identity is a part of our narrative identity: by following the narrative strategies we employ in formulating our political identity, we automatically witness the creation of our political self. This treatise does not intend to be a mere variation of Whitebrook's monograph, but to take a substantially different path. Its searchlight is less focused on different strategies of self-creation and their implications for political theory. It rather concentrates on an anthropological concept and literary motif, namely initiation, and tries to uncover the concept's potential for political socialization research. The initiation story is introduced as a narrative strategy to describe the creation of the self.

Political initiation is distinct from and entailed in the notion of political socialization. It can be regarded as a step in an individual's political socialization, the shape his socialization takes in that it also represents an aspect of his development aiming at a certain relationship between individual and State. In this sense, the first time a person casts a ballot, participates at a municipal convention, or joins a party can be interpreted as ritualized instances of political initiation and simultaneously as important events in his political socialization. Initiation, however, is distinct from socialization in that it often implies rupture instead of evolution, crisis instead of harmonious continuation. Although ritualized forms of initiation stress continuity in the same fashion as socialization, even these variations point out the ambiguity of transitory phases and the risks they entail. Thus they at least consider the consequences of failure. Generally speaking, political initiation stresses transitions, which potentially can recur over a lifetime, whereas socialization aims at integration and adaptation, pictured as a process which ends with puberty.

Puberty, however, is only one of the stages in life that interest Philip Roth as a writer. His novels show that moments of initiation or initiatory tests can always recur, that an individual's identity can be constantly challenged, be it by events, the individual's environment, or the territorial context—in short, that the narrative identity is persistently rewritten.

Part Two

Classical Initiation Stories

2

Political Awakenings: Classic Initiation Patterns in *The Plot Against America* and *Indignation*

1. Introduction: Thrice initiated, thrice transformed

Three youthful protagonists, three stages in life, thrice a (nearly) classic initiation: Philip Roth's political scenario novel *The Plot Against America* (2004) and his more recent novel, set in time of the Korean war, *Indignation* (2008), both cast their protagonists in phases of transition, when they are still uncertain of their identity. All three characters not only struggle with their uncertain self, but also with the political circumstances with which they are confronted. In *The Plot*, it is the only seven year-old "Philip Roth" who has to cope with the abrupt end of childhood, whereas his brother Sanford has reached a common pivotal stage at the age of twelve. The latter is equally true for *Indignation*'s Marcus whose first college years offer a conventional setting for youthful rebellion. In all three cases, the individual struggles to define himself against the background of historical and political uncertainty: the system as such faces a crisis in its self-understanding and thus forces the three young protagonists to seek their identity while caught in the tides of history.

In their stories, motifs and symbols appear that are not only pertinent to understand and interpret these particular initiation stories, but recur in other novels and short stories by Philip Roth, which will be discussed at a later point in this treatise. This section provides a first introduction to the significance of spaces, rituals, and the initiand's attitude toward his body, two themes that will be picked up later in more depth. The two novels serve, so to speak, as a threshold to further explorations, since they follow a quasiclassic pattern, yet with a Rothian twist. The discussion closes with a topic common to many novels by Roth which is, however, particularly tension-laden in *The Plot Against America*: the fictitiousness of all factual, in this case conventional, history.

2. Plots against childhood and the longing for manhood

Childhood lost: Philip

Newark, 1940. Seven year-old "Philip" has no doubts about his identity: he is a member of the "Roth" family (which is practically modeled after the author's own, including the framed Declaration of Independence on the wall), a resident of the city's Weequahic section, a child of his time—and an American, un-hyphenated.[1] Little does Philip realize in the beginning that only his parents, "his bulwarks against the world,"[2] ascertain that he can parade as "Philip, the American," instead of bemoaning his Jewish fate from the very outset. Although he senses his parents' frustrations with the Gentile world early on, he can successfully ignore their worries as part of their adult world—until the cracks in the bulwarks become too large not to take a glimpse through them. Philip's childhood idyll starts falling apart when the political idol of his father, Franklin D. Roosevelt, is challenged as incumbent President of the United States by none other than the fascist aviation hero Charles A. Lindbergh. Adulation should thus soon make room for a feeling new to the young boy:

> Lindbergh was the first famous living American whom I learned to hate—just as President Roosevelt was the first famous living American whom I was taught to love—and so his nomination by the Republicans to run against Roosevelt in 1940 assaulted, as nothing ever had before, that huge endowment of personal security that I had taken for granted as an American child of American parents in an American school in an American city in an America at peace with the world. (*Plot*, 7)

While Philip's admiration for Roosevelt was, as he says himself, "taught" by the example of his father and probably also inspired by the sensed bond due to a shared hobby, philately, he learns his hatred for Lindbergh not only by observing his parents' attitude, but also mainly by realizing what feeling this candidacy instills: "perpetual fear" (*Plot*, 1). Perpetual fear takes possession of the Roth household whose "moral center,"[3] the parents, can no longer protect the youngest family member from recognizing his otherness. The virulent anti-Semitism conveyed by Lindbergh's campaign, which increasingly appears to resonate with a hidden base feeling in the U.S. electorate, will teach the family "what it is to be Jews" (*Plot*, 255–6). The sense of being alien to a known world becomes heightened when his father takes the family to Washington, D.C., embarking on a pilgrimage to the roots of those American values they all feel fading around them. Yet instead of offering his children the desired reassurance and restoration of faith in American constitutionality, father Herman Roth has to witness his children's first lessons in anti-Semitism. He cannot prevent the family's humiliating dismissal from the hotel nor the offensive exchanges with goys. While the true motivation for these hostilities could normally have been hidden from Philip, his elder brother Sanford puts things into the right perspective and answers the frightened question "What happened?" unambiguously: "Anti-Semitism" (*Plot*, 69).

The cracks in his bulwarks against the world let Philip perceive not only the reversal of the outside world, but also the turmoil in the realm of his family. His family ceases to be a source of security, and degenerates into another confusing and destabilizing factor. For the first time in his life, Philip has to acknowledge his father's weakness, and thus loses the much cherished childhood illusion of parental invulnerability:

> It was the first time I saw my father cry. A childhood milestone, when another's tears are more unbearable than one's own. . . . A new life began for me. I'd watched my father fall apart, and I would never return to the same childhood. (*Plot*, 113)

The loss of one illusion is closely followed by another, tightly linked to the idea of invulnerability, as David Brauner observes, namely the assumption of infallibility.[4] Philip has to witness how his father's mantric belief in the Abraham Lincoln's Gettysburg Address, his 1863 proclamation that every man was created equal, is repeatedly disproved by reality. His trust in his father's superior knowledge crumbles. The boy's development of his own sense of criticism can thus be traced against his dissociation from his father's standpoint—the more Philip himself thinks about the events around him, the less he relies on his father's opinion. The man who tells him to distrust the one American office Philip previously had been taught to hold in highest esteem, this teacher of suspicion loses for himself the trust of his disciple:

> Since what Uncle Monty said to him about Lindbergh was exactly what Rabbi Bengelsdorf had told him—and also what Sandy was secretly saying to me—I began to wonder if my father knew what he was talking about. (*Plot*, 125)

Philip loses all the points of reference he could so far rely on—his family, his environs, his America. Earlier than expected, he is forced to construct his own viewpoint; he had "never before had to grow up at a pace like this" (*Plot*, 172).

Still Philip maintains his naïveté in instances where a more sobered view would have been helpful: when his father should move to a post in Kentucky, a move inspired by the Organization of American Absorption (OAA), Lindbergh's program for the assimilation of Jewish families, Philip seeks the help of his aunt who has successfully arranged herself with the new regime. He thereby prompts the relocation of a neighboring family, the recently fatherless Wishnows. While the Roth family stays behind in Newark, the Wishnows are forced to leave Newark, a move which will later prove fatal for Seldon Wishnow's mother. Philip, however, for a long time does not perceive life as an orphan in its tragic dimensions, but rather indulges in fantasies of being deprived of parental custody, fantasies which culminate in his actual flight from home. Yet just as ludicrous as these fancies is the outcome of Philip's flight to the Catholic orphanage in the Roth's neighborhood: crossing a feedlot, Philip disturbs grazing horses. This will result in a short loss of consciousness, the loss of his stamp collection and of any further desires to flee to an orphanage. Sobered by this experience, Philip is for the first time able to take stock of his family's situation:

> A father remodeled, a brother restored, a mother recovered, eighteen black silk sutures stitched in my head and my greatest treasure irretrievably lost, and all with a wondrous fairy-tale swiftness. A family both declassed and rerooted overnight, facing neither exile nor expulsion but entrenched still on Summit Avenue, whereas in three short months, Seldon—to whom I was helplessly yoked now that he was going around the neighborhood reveling in having prevented

> me from bleeding to death while disguised in his clothes—Seldon was shipping out. As of September 1, Seldon would be off living with his mother, the only Jewish kid in Danville, Kentucky. (*Plot*, 239)

True sobriety takes hold of him after the frenzy of these developments: on the verge of pogroms, even opportunists like his aunt Evelyn recognize the nature of the Lindbergh Administration, which forces her to seek refuge in the basement of the Roths' house. In his aunt, Philip now discovers a yet even more basic human sentiment, the despair of the one struggling for survival. While he feels helpless in view of her travails, he will discover an inner strength when confronted with innocent suffering.

Thrice transformed: Sanford

During the years between 1940 and 1942, Philip turns from a minor character directed by adult thinking into a contemplative boy who questions authority in general, and finally attempts to take responsibility for another child, Seldon. His development alone deserves our scrutiny, yet even more dramatic changes can be witnessed in his elder brother, Sanford, who is at the outset twelve years of age:

> These were the years when my precocious brother was three different boys in the course of twenty-four months, the years when, for all his unflappability, he could seem to do nothing satisfactory even by excelling. (*Plot*, 358)

Three different boys in two years: first just the elder brother who has "always known everything I [Philip] didn't know" (*Plot*, 93), then a rebellious son who fights for a role outside the ranks of the obedient child, and finally a silenced member of the family, again on the lookout for his voice. His beginnings are equally innocent as Philip's, his merely being a boy capturing his view of America in sketchbooks. He not only portrays family members, but also the one man whose name will soon be treated as a curse among the Roths. Sanford hides his portraits of the great aviator, not out of shame of a sentimental feeling, but because he is fully aware that his admiration for the presidential candidate clashes with his father's conviction. In due time, however, Sanford will publicly display his support and not fear the confrontation with his father. In the course thereof, his gift will turn from a privately applauded talent to an instrument of propaganda.

Thanks to the influence of Aunt Evelyn, Sanford discovers yet another ability, "the uncommon gift to be somebody" (*Plot*, 184) as he is drawn within the ambit of the Office of American Absorption (OAA). Thanks to their immersion program "Just Folks," Sanford can enter the world of the Midwestern Mawhinney family, whose father is

> . . . a Christian, a long-standing member of the great overpowering majority that fought the Revolution and founded the nation and conquered the wilderness and subjugated the Indian and enslaved the Negro and emancipated the Negro and segregated the Negro, . . . one of those unassailable Nordic and Anglo-Saxon

> Protestants who ran America and would always run it—. . . the men who laid down the law and called the shots and read the riot act when they chose to—while my [Philip's] father, of course, was only a Jew. (*Plot*, 93)

As a consequence, Sanford adopts the thinking of his aunt and her fiancé, who also happens to be her boss, Lindbergh supporter Rabbi Bengelsdorf, and is finally allowed to tell the Newark public on behalf of the OAA about his mind-broadening experience among Gentiles, which even earns him an invitation to the White House. Given his insight into the world outside Newark, his daring to taste non-kosher food and his direct involvement with the OAA, Sanford considers his knowledge more profound compared to his father's faith in radio commentator Walter Winchell's every sentence. Sanford does not content himself with assuming his new public role, but he also has to demonstrate his recently developed belief in the new regime, letting him insult his parents as "Ghetto Jews" (*Plot*, 227). His parents' suggestion that Sanford could be manipulated for the sake of political propaganda is in the teenager's eye only a vile suspicion born out of paranoia. All he sees in their precautions are attempts at tying him down and spoiling "his fun," reproaches that are likely to be familiar to most parents of adolescents at the height of puberty. As he calls his father a "dictator *worse* than Hitler" (193), the portrayal of the rebelling youth who constantly struggles with his family receives its last defining touches.

With growing confusion and curiosity, Philip follows not only his brother's mental development, but also his physical coming of age and the subsequent awakening of desires. Yet in spite of the boys' proximity, Sanford never tries to exert his influence on his younger brother and hardly ever explains the events around them to him. Instead, he leaves Philip in the hands of their war-torn cousin Alvin, even though he knows of the latter's spite for him. Sanford becomes even more silent toward the end of the novel, when he is confronted with his erroneous thinking: he sees his aunt fleeing in fright, hears of the pogrom, and even needs to drive out to Kentucky with his father to pick up the now orphaned Seldon—but his voice is hushed. Whatever impression these catastrophic developments have on him, his opinion is lost in the general conundrum. We thus see Sanford as three different boys—the fourth, probably already on the verge of manhood, remains out of our view.

Marcus and George in the mirror

Less than a decade later, another Jewish youth will roam the streets of Newark, and learn "of the terrible, incomprehensible way one's most banal, incidental, even comical choices achieve the most disproportionate result" (*Indignation*, 231): Marcus Messner, recent High School graduate and only son of a kosher butcher and his wife. Comparable to the Roth brothers, Marcus's relationship to his parents, specifically to his father, had been unproblematic and harmonious until the point *Indignation*'s (2008) protagonist and narrator takes up his studies at the local college:

> "almost from the day that I [Marcus] began classes at Robert Treat, my father became frightened that I would die" (2).

Perpetual fear again is the prevailing mood of the story, albeit with an ironic undertone, the constant companion of a father fretting over his son's security, of a mother doubting her husband's common sense—and of a son awaiting his recruitment for the war in Korea. At the prospect of his child's possible draft, the angst of Marcus's father assumes ridiculous shapes when he imagines his son enjoying corruptive pastimes, and thus becomes overly concerned with his son's every step. While Marcus's fears are existential, his father merely fails at coping with his son's coming of age, which renders him

> crazy with worry that his cherished only child was as unprepared for the hazards of life as anyone else entering manhood, crazy with the frightening discovery that a little boy grows up, grows tall, overshadows his parents, and that you can't keep him then, that you have to relinquish him to the world. (*Indignation*, 8)

In his struggle with the fact that his son is already crossing the threshold of adulthood, Marcus's father desperately impedes his son, a far cry from Sophie Portnoy's vileness,[5] from crossing the literal threshold of his own home—which fails to achieve the desired result: instead of binding Marcus to his parents' house, it culminates in the adolescent's decision to no longer expose himself to paternal paranoia and to leave the local college Robert Treat after a single year. He thereby tries not only to flee the daily conflicts, but also to discover an unknown part of America: the non-Jewish, goyish reality of the Midwest.

A Gentile setting reminiscent of the author Philip Roth's own college years at Bucknell University (*Facts*, 48), the small liberal arts college in Winesburg, Ohio, offers a distinct counter-world to Marcus's past environs, a counter-world with twenty fraternities and only two of which admit Jews (*Indignation*, 20). After clashing with his first roommates, all of Jewish descent, Marcus gets to live with an aspiring engineer, whose matter-of-fact demeanor and lack of any sense for pleasures other than his car let Marcus focus on his studies and his trainings for the Reserve Officers' Training Corps (ROTC)—and to pursue his only other college ambition: "I was determined to have intercourse before I died" (*Indignation*, 52). Not only a sexual "novice" (*Indignation*, 63), but also innocent and naïve regarding possible sexual predilections people might have, he finds among his female fellow students the one to initiate him, who even embodies yet another taboo of his times: Olivia Hutton, daughter of a divorced medical doctor.

Just as it is beyond Marcus's imagination that anyone could be either divorced or homosexual, he is completely flabbergasted at Olivia's readiness to gratify his sexual longings without awaiting any affirmative action on his side. His marveling finally permits only one conclusion:

> No, what happened could only be a consequence of something being wrong with her . . . "It's because her parents are divorced," I told myself. (*Indignation*, 58–9)

Mirroring this childish attitude, his behavior likewise lacks insight as he starts to avoid Olivia who even reassures him that her acts had been merely motivated by affection and attraction. But Marcus realizes too late what he risks to lose by his demeanor, since later it is her who withdraws from him and finally states in a letter the reason for her reclusiveness: "a scar across the width of [her] wrist" (*Indignation*, 69). Though on the wrong arm, as a psychiatrically schooled reviewer observed,[6] the scar testifies of a suicide attempt which had brought Olivia first to a sanatorium and then to Winesburg, Ohio. Yes, understanding no one and nothing and only just learning things are indeed central topics of Marcus's second college year (*Indignation*, 74). He hopes, however, that Olivia's revelation and his mannered answer thereto, wherein he pretends to have noticed yet politely ignored her scar, might represent his personal turning point:

> Was this moment to mark the beginning of a lifetime's accumulation of mistakes (had I been given a lifetime in which to make them)? I thought then that it marked, if anything, the beginning of my manhood. . . . The history of drinking, the scar, the sanatorium, the frailty, the fortitude—I was bondage to it all. To the heroism of it all. (*Indignation*, 76–7)

Still, he will only see Olivia again when he himself is confined to a hospital bed due to appendicitis, only to lose her again. When he returns to the campus, she has disappeared without further notice. Marcus's inquiries about her whereabouts set the stage for his second argument with Winesburg's dean. Their first altercation began with the headmaster's casual question as to why Marcus felt forced to change his dorm room three times, ending up in an inhospitable room on his own. This conversation ended with the student's fierce recitation of Bertrand Russell's theses on atheism—and his vomiting on the headmaster's rug, ironically not caused by his disgust with the headmaster's bigotry, but by his appendicitis, the Rothian ailment. While Marcus then still succeeded in reframing his role from accused to accusing, he will this time not escape the unwanted and, in his eyes, undeserved position when he learns of Olivia's breakdown as a reaction to her pregnancy. Olivia's destiny will, to the reader's dismay, be lost out of sight due to a ridiculous series of events which leads the reader to Marcus's deathbed in–yes, Korea. Marcus's expulsion from Winesburg and his premature draft is, however, not a direct effect of his first "fuck you" (*Indignation*, 192) spat into the dean's face, nor does he participate in the snowball fight which degenerates into a raid on the women's dorms. No, his one attempt at outwitting the system proves to be fatal: to circumvent the requirement of attending chapel, he pays a surrogate to register his presence. The surrogate eventually gets caught, and with him Marcus. Who will die in Korea. As his father had always known.

The reader who follows Marcus's paths, his development or lack of it, has to simultaneously register the footsteps of another male youth whose trail reflects the maturation Roth's young protagonist dreamed of.[7] Putting Marcus in front of a distorting mirror, the traces appear of George Willard, whose coming of age is the focal point of Sherwood Anderson's short story cycle *Winesburg, Ohio* (1919). Although Philip Roth explained that the main parallels between his own and Anderson's Winesburg were the grotesque characters,[8] readers of both works will detect similarities in the beginnings of the two protagonists, in their emotional incapacities, and their strained or inexistent relationship with their fathers. Moreover, they both are embedded in a (semi-)formal context of learning. Whereas Marcus's paths are circling around and within the Winesburg campus grounds, George is an aspiring writer who tries to hone his skills at the local newspaper. The latter remark, however, already points out the major difference between the two protagonists: aspiration. While George is discovering an aspiration, possibly a calling, Marcus's aspiration can be summarized in one word–"escape." Thus *Winesburg, Ohio* takes the shape of a more typical *Bildungsroman*, which delineates, quoting James Joyce, *A Portrait of the Artist as a Young Man* (1917).[9]

At the outset, we find in George Willard, son of the local innkeeper, but grown up in the absence of a father, a young man similarly innocent and naïve as Marcus. Yet his longing for a first relationship is not caused by sheer desire; rather he sees therein the only way to write a début love story:

> "I know what I'm going to do. I'm going to fall in love. I've been sitting here and thinking it over and I'm going to do it." (*Winesburg*, 128)

Just like Marcus who decides that he finally wants to become a sexual initiate and tries to steer his development toward manhood, George sees the time ripe for a new experience and wants to force his destiny to take the imagined path. Feelings are not worth any further consideration in George's functionalist view of love; they have to submit to higher ideals. Yet through the stories of the characters populating Winesburg, their loneliness and failure to reach a form of fulfillment in life, the tragic surrendering to principles of those ready with advice for him, or the flights of his coevals,[10] George learns compassion and empathy; he discovers his place in society's infinite chain. As he witnesses the conflict-laden relations between fathers and sons, or between fatherly shadows and sons, he will at the moment of his mother's death be able to forgive his absent father, which transforms the latter to his mere progenitor instead of a silent menace.[11]

The death of his mother not only transforms George's memory of his father, but also marks the actual turning point in his approach to life and his role in society, since he now "for the first time takes the backward view of life. Perhaps this is the moment when he crosses the line into manhood" (*Winesburg*, 238). He becomes aware of his own mortality,[12] a realization which lets him finally recognize the degree to which he is one with his fellow townsmen:[13]

> The sadness of sophistication has come to the boy. With a little gasp he sees himself as merely a leaf blown by the wind through the streets of his village. He knows that in spite of all the stout talk of his fellows he must live and die in uncertainty, a thing blown by the winds, a thing destined like corn to wilt in the sun. . . . Already he hears death calling. (*Winesburg*, 238–9)

Thus matured, George's "Sophistication," simultaneously the title of the climactic story in *Winesburg, Ohio*, lets him reach across the gender divide and establish with the young woman, in whom he once saw only a possible source of inspiration for his love story, a union unachievable for Winesburg's other (failed) couples,[14] or indeed Marcus Messner. George is now emotionally and artistically ripe to follow his calling and to try his luck as a writer in a bigger city, a path that was barred to him as long as he had not crossed the threshold toward manhood.[15]

Another character would step into the void left by Marcus Messner, who was unable to understand Olivia and failed to seek reconciliation with his father, while keeping a wondrous outlook on the world: George Willard, the first literary inhabitant of Winesburg, Ohio, testifies to the transformative power of adolescence, the potential for learning by experience. While Marcus is only ready to look back "under morphine", yet still cannot detect his failures, George has developed a critical view of his own self and thus can search for the artist within him.

3. Of rituals and spaces: Dimensions of change

The changes the three Rothian characters undergo are mirrored in three dimensions: their bodies, changes in space or changes in the relation to space, and the loss of rituals. While these transformations are often only loosely linked to the development of a political consciousness, they are crucial to grasp the development of the characters in their entirety.

The body

Initiation rites often coincide with an individual's major physical development, especially at the end of puberty, and mark the resulting change in social status,[16] which automatically moves the body into the narrator's focus. This can also be observed in the case of the three Rothian youths, who either learn to see their outer shell with fresh eyes or to experience their body in unknown ways. While Sanford and Marcus have long been aware of their otherness amidst the average American population, Philip felt as a part of the masses—he sees himself reflected, so to speak, in society's mirror. He thereby resembles, though not literally, the infant in Jacques Lacan's social development theory which identifies with its specular image and recognizes itself for the first time in its wholeness.[17] Simultaneously, the infant learns to distinguish itself from the "others" around it—yet, as Philip will have to comprehend, time increases the urge to mentally merge with the others and join them in an imaginary community. Although Philip was dimly aware of his father's inability to rise in the ranks of his employers due to his Jewish background, and of his mother's refusal to move to a white Christian neighborhood, it is only in the course of a game with his friend Earl that he learns to see himself with the eyes of the "Other." Earl not only introduces the young boy to the art of lying, another step in Philip's mental development, but also to the art of spotting Jews on the street—and to recognize himself as one of them:

> It was then that I realized—employing all the criteria imparted to me by Earl—that my mother looked Jewish. Her hair, her nose, her eyes—my mother looked *unmistakably* Jewish. But then so must I, who strongly resembled her. I hadn't known. (*Plot*, 134)

When the eyes of the "others" finally betray their dismay at the sight of Jews, Philip will never be able to look into the mirror again and see just another American boy, and society ceases to be his specular image.

While Philip has learned to read his appearance in ethnic and societal terms, he has not yet learned to play with it and to adapt it to his needs. He may steal clothes from Seldon Wishnow for his nightly flight, but he is still not ready to comprehend the rules of disguise and transformation, as they will be tested by other Rothian characters later to be met.[18] Marcus Messner, in contrast, consciously tries to break with his adolescence and the appearance he associates with his life at home, thus striving to "be a new man . . . and to end my being the butcher's son" (*Indignation*, 117). Very much in the manner of classic initiation rites which are accompanied by special clothing, ranging from animalistic masks at tribal rites to the white dress or cowl at the Catholic First Holy Communion, Marcus underlines his intention by purchasing specific college gear which shall bring him closer to the image of the young model students reproduced on Winesburg's brochure. What Marcus fails to see, however, is that a garment alone cannot break inner resistance, and that he cannot merge physically with a community whose rules he otherwise rejects. This oversight dooms his transformation from the outset.

Other than Anderson's George, who will in time recognize how naïve he was, Marcus generally lacks the insight that maturation cannot be initiated artificially, and that maturation is not a project to be constructed and directed by oneself. The underlying emotion of Marcus, spelled out in the novel's title and in the song that set the tune for his encounter with the headmaster, likewise betrays his immaturity: indignation, the snappy reaction of someone unprepared to consider his stance, to think about his position and the possibility that he might not have been treated unjustly. As a consequence, Marcus does not contemplate his actual needs or feelings for a second, but simply pushes ahead "Operation Manhood," which he at least seems to fulfill in its sexual dimension. He enjoys only a "seeming" fulfillment, though, for his puzzlement does betray a certain resemblance to the bewildered Philip who witnesses his elder cousin Alvin masturbate and mistakes the latter's moaning as signs of suffering. In a similar vein, Marcus cannot comprehend sex as an act of mutual pleasure and remains, until the very end, troubled by Olivia's willingness to fulfill his secret wishes:

> Even now (if "now" can be said to mean anything any longer), beyond corporeal existence, alive as I am here (if "here" or "I" means anything) as memory alone (if "memory," strictly speaking, is the all-embracing medium in which I am being sustained as "myself"), I continue to puzzle over Olivia's actions. (*Indignation*, 54–5)

On the surface, Marcus has become a sexual initiate, but his outlook on human relations remains innocent, whether it concerns the complexity of Olivia's mind or the revelation that his first roommate had indeed fancied him; homosexuality, like divorce, had to Marcus so far only been a rumor (*Indignation*, 40). While young Philip is still content to marvel at the brassiere of his friend's mother from a distance and trusts his instincts to know his needs, while Sanford naturally gives in to his desire to flirt, Marcus forces his body into realms he so far cannot understand. He is obviously too preoccupied with his own bodily reality even to see others properly, as his missing of Olivia's scar from her first suicide attempt betrays. Once the scar on her wrist has drawn his attention, he is no longer able to see Olivia as a person, but reduces her to this one wound and can only think about her in bodily terms: either the scar or her sexual daring. Tragically, however, Marcus cannot read the scar as a metonymy and recognize the pain associated with it, but only perceives it in its fleshly reality.

In contrast to their rather halting discovery of their sexuality, all Rothian protagonists learn how their body can turn against them and limit their choices. Marcus's comical outburst in the dean's office leads to his hospitalization due to the classic Rothian ailment, appendicitis (*Facts*, 11). It shows how he still struggles to bring his emotional development in tune with his bodily reality: while the reader thinks that Marcus is vomiting on the dean's carpet to demonstrate how disgusted and enraged he is by the dean's views, it is merely his body demanding relief. Relief is something that Alvin, Philip's elder cousin, will seek in vain: having fled to Canada to join the war against Hitler's Germany, he returns decorated with a medal, but deprived of one of his legs, and walking on a prosthesis. The stump remaining of Alvin's leg and the stench of his fouling teeth are mementos of the war Philip otherwise only knows from the radio news and adult conversations, the one thing making history real. The prosthesis is, so to speak, not simply an aid for Alvin to walk, but likewise for Philip to comprehend. At the same time, his cousin's wound puts Philip for the first time into the position of having to care for another person, of being charged with a duty and a responsibility. He thereby grows from a frightened child that refused to share a room with the war-torn cousin into an eager caretaker who recognizes the needs of others. This change prepares him to attend to another individual beyond the nursing of a concrete, fleshly wound, when the now orphaned Seldon Wishnow moves in with the Roth family:

> There was no stump for me to care for this time. The boy himself was the stump, and until he was taken to live with his mother's married sister in Brooklyn ten months later, I was the prosthesis. (*Plot*, 362)

Rituals

Although certain social or physical transformations in an individual's life are still marked by distinct rituals and symbols, Peter Freese observes that modern youths' socialization is hardly ritualized.[19] Yet this does not mean that those concerned do not long for a ritualistic setting for their initiation or that people nowadays do not perform rituals, consciously or unconsciously.[20] In the case of Roth's protagonists, however, it is at first glance remarkable how they seem relatively unimpressed by typical initiation rites, to a degree that they do not even mention them but let the reader simply close the void. Accordingly, we learn neither how Alvin was received among the ranks of the Canadian army nor whether Marcus was submitted to initiation rituals by the Reserve Officers'

Training Corps (ROTC) at Winesburg, by the Jewish fraternity he finally housed with, or by the American army he was forced to join in the end.

In the course of his story, however, Marcus reveals the importance of rituals in his approach to the world, which eventually shows how their loss or forsaking may induce a maturation. Both Marcus and Philip have to give up rituals during their particular plots, rituals which have shaped their prior lives: while Marcus is no longer involved in the rituals governing the Kosher butchery of his parents, Philip loses his treasured stamp collection. The end of the time as a collector is particularly decisive as it has been observed that this usually accompanies the end of puberty. According to psychoanalytical theory, collections may serve as an erotic substitute which become futile once an individual reaches sexual maturity.[21] Although Philip is still years away from this stage, the lost collection already announces the seizure in his yet young life and the need for him to grow up.[22]

Marcus's experience is contrary to Philip's in that he cannot leave the imagery of the butcher's trade behind, so that when he tries to graphically imagine the combat in Korea, he forcedly recalls his father's knives (*Indignation*, 35), letting resound the possibly metaphoric nature of his surname *Messner*.[23] The associations with the Kosher rituals dominate his imagination to such an extent that he even seeks to explain Olivia's suicide attempt in these terms:

> My point is this: that is what Olivia had tried to do, to kill herself according to kosher specifications by emptying her body of blood. Had she been successful, had she expertly completed the job with a single perfect slice of the blade, she would have rendered herself kosher in accordance with rabbinical law. Olivia's telltale scar came from attempting to perform her own ritual slaughter. (*Indignation*, 160)

The motivation for such a deadly ritual, however, remains beyond Marcus's comprehension. Instead he imagines himself nursing of the wounded girl, which reminds us of Philip's taking care of his cousin's stump. Neither of the two young protagonists can grasp the events leading to the permanent scarring of their protégés, yet they indulge in the idea of overcoming their repulsion and becoming guardians. They forcedly ignore that they have not learned enough about themselves to reach out to others—the pain Philip feels on his flight from home does not indicate the climax of his transition, as pain often does;[24] instead it reminds us of the ridiculousness of many an attempt to grow up.

Even in his intellectual studies, Marcus seems prone to structure things ritually, as his method of studying resembles more the ritualized memorization during a Rothian Bar Mitzvah lesson, than the contemplation of a critical mind.[25] The only quasi-political statement made by Marcus apart from his unwillingness to fight abroad is his opposition to religion, ironically the realm of the last consciously performed rituals, which he expresses in his conversation with Winesburg's headmaster. Instead of explaining his own thoughts on the subject, Marcus proudly explains how he memorized Bertrand Russell's essay "Why I am not a Christian" (1927) and starts, though by leaving out Russell's comments on natural law, to paraphrase and summarize it verbatim (*Indignation*, 111–2). His unequivocal agreement with Russell's theses leaves not only the headmaster with the impression that Marcus has left one step out in his previous approach to the text. Instead of going beyond merely comprehending the arguments of the text and thus starting to base his own arguments or counter-arguments on it, Marcus has become an indoctrinated reader who parrots Russell's every word, accompanied by the beat of the Chinese anthem which he regularly chants in his head.

The void left by the coveted rituals remains for both Philip and Marcus as empty as the place left by their most important guides in life and its rituals, their fathers. Both learn not to blindly trust fatherly judgment and begin to develop their own approach to life, but end up blindly stumbling from one erroneous episode to the other. What they lack is a mentor who would enable them to walk the last steps on their own—much in the way Sanford believes to have found a mentor in the circle of the OAA, albeit a treacherous one. All three stories hence seem to suggest that, whatever age a youth, he will need guidance should he advance further along the path to maturity. The youths' path toward identity and a clear vision of the world is thus interrupted mid-way; they are held in suspense.

Spaces

Sanford leaves his family and Newark to spend time on a farm in Kansas; Alvin flees to Canada, to join the army in the war against Germany; and Marcus takes refuge in Winesburg, Ohio, in order to escape his father's suffocating fears. All three are altered at their transitional point of destination, an intended oxymoron: as van Gennep has already outlined, initiation can be described as a movement, yet at times it literally involves a journey, an initiation journey, as Peter Freese termed it.[26] It is thus of consequence what is happening, but also where it is taking place, and whether this location bears a deeper significance.

In the two novels, both Sanford and Marcus mark the beginning of their transition period by a geographical seizure, as they strive for a spatial separation from their family and the Jewish microcosmos of Newark. Sanford finds a counter-world in the farm life in Kansas, a world where he can breach Jewish taboos running scot-free. Marcus hopes to discover in Winesburg not only a particularly Gentile surrounding, but also a space of personal reinvention. Sanford experiences life in the midst of a Christian farming family, which exposes him to a different class, religion, and lifestyle. This idyllic life indeed represents a transition phase, as described by van Gennep,[27] which is followed by his incorporation into the Organization of American Absorption (OAA), the propaganda machinery of the Lindbergh Administration. The geographic separation is consequently translated into a mental separation from his family, for his allegiance to OAA turns him into an opponent of his parents' beliefs and alienates him from his family's ideas; we can thus speak of a specifically political initiation, taking the shape of indoctrination. What we do not learn, however, is how Sanford will later deal with the insight that he has indeed been manipulated, a conclusion he finally has to reach when the true nature of the Lindbergh Administration can no longer be denied: his second trip to the Midwest together with his father is to take Seldon Wishnow back to Newark. This point would signify a de-initiation, hopefully coupled with the eventual discovery of the limits of his comprehension, which would ultimately denote a true maturation. Roth, though, leaves Sanford's development in limbo, thus demonstrating the reversibility of every initiation.

With a college campus as his point of destination, Marcus's journey to the Midwest is from the beginning a promise of mental growth and maturation, as these developments are the task of such a formal educational setting. Although Marcus will encounter situations that may constitute the climax of an initiation—first sexual experiences, painful surgery, the confrontation with the headmaster—the change of air does not seem to be conducive to his advancement. Repeated spatial changes reflect Marcus's experiences and changes in his attitude, as he appears to be incapable of reuniting new standpoints with an accustomed environment. While his moving out of the first dorm room can still be attributed to the infinite conflict with a particularly obnoxious roommate and Marcus's inability to solve it, leaving the company of an ever strenuous and silent engineer conveys his social incapacity: a derogatory remark about Olivia is enough to provoke a violent outburst and the request for a new room. The new room's remoteness would make it the ideal reflective space, a hermit-like refuge to sort his ideas out and pass the threshold toward adulthood. This potential phase is, however, comically interrupted by Marcus's appendicitis and the necessary hospital visit. Here, Marcus is again tied back to his family, as he is requested to choose between his attachment to his mother and to Olivia. He believes that a return to his college room would simultaneously signify a return to his imagined path of mental progress and to his quasi relationship with Olivia. Yet spaces do not freeze in time, at least only few do, and Marcus has to face his hermitage savaged by a former roommate and Olivia missing. Marcus's subsequent reintroduction into normal housing conditions, namely within the confines of the sole Jewish fraternity, will not only mark the end of his quest for adult independence, but also his last station on the Winesburg campus. For the next room we find him in is a sick bay in Korea. One can thus not shake off the impression that his father's butchery had the most changing effect, as it is the space that inspires all his associations and has shaped his categories of thinking.

In contrast to Sanford and Marcus, Philip is, with the exception of the trip to Washington, confined to the Weequahic section of Newark. While his family's home is the space he sees altered the most, as inner quarrels erupt, it is outside the parental ambit that he learns to grasp the nature of the changes looming ahead. The trip to the U.S. capital, very much in the spirit of what Lauren Berlant mockingly called pilgrimage-to-Washington narratives,[28] has for Philip's father the effect Berlant prophesizes for similar endeavors: although he tries to convince himself and his family of how their ideals of America materialize in Washington, D.C., ugly political realities, such as anti-Semitic resentments, become evident. For Philip, the trip mainly shows how he can no longer rely on his father as an interpretive source of events around him, which lets him seek new explanations.

Whether it is on an excursion with Earl during which Philip learns to see himself as a Jew, or in the cinema where he watches the newsreel, or by messengers who have experienced other places, like Sanford or Alvin, his ideas of society and politics are altered elsewhere. There is, however, one space in the Roths' house where Philip feels the political events and the private world clash, the room he only reluctantly visited anyway: the basement. Associated with irrationality, basic fears, and everything hidden or mysterious,[29] the basement is the place where Philip not only watches the expression of basic human desire, that is his masturbating cousin, but also finds his frightened aunt Evelyn who goes into hiding from possible persecutors. Alvin brought a reminder of history home when he presented his stump, yet with Aunt Evelyn it becomes for the first time palpable, touchable, and comprehensible: he sees for the first time what political persecution in reality means, Philip sees the fear it instills and learns to judge it as a price for a stance previously taken. History indeed is no longer a simple theory for young Philip.

4. Histories and stories—worlds factual and fictitious

"History" versus stories is one of the central *topoi* in *The Plot*. Roth therein succeeds to show the reader the ambiguity of so allegedly clear and simple a term, which is an invitation to delve in the theories on historiography. Moreover and more importantly for this study, Roth also delineates how a child learns to relate "history" to its own world.

Histories, public, and private

> Turned wrong way around, the relentless unforeseen was what we schoolchildren studied as 'History,' harmless history, where everything unexpected in its own time is chronicled on the page as inevitable. The terror of the unforeseen is what the science of history hides, turning a disaster into an epic. (*Plot*, 113–4)

Politics, as history in the making, gains in significance for Philip in that he learns how it can transform his own environment; he becomes aware of the fact that, had it not been for history's incalculable nature, his childhood years might have continued in all innocence. Other than many of his elder contemporaries, he learns that nothing is safe from the tidal wave of history, not even the sacred constitutional order many deemed just as invulnerable as a child believes his parents to be.[30] At the outset, however, Philip clings to the order presented to him by his collection of stamps. Tucking them all neatly away in a book, he cherishes his stamps just as much as he adores the American icons they depict as well as his fellow stamp collector Franklin D. Roosevelt. The order Philip maintains in his stamp collection likewise reflects the pastoral order in the beginning of his tale in 1940, narrated retrospectively by himself as a grown-up, an order that tells Philip who he is and where he belongs.[31]

In the beginning, the stamps are merely Philip's first source of the nation's official history, but then become the screen on which he projects his associations with history and realizes how memory, that is his personal history, and official historiography diverge—and how historiography itself entertains a problematic relationship with memory. The initially innocent adoration for the collected icons is exemplary of the first stage of political consciousness, as Philip relates to political events and themes via outstanding personalities whom he does not question further. He thereby succumbs to the official intention of postal iconography, which aims to speak on behalf of a nation and to perpetuate crucial moments and people in its history.[32] Yet just like his view of Lindbergh, the once admired icon of stewardship and conquest, favored motives of American postal iconography, so does Philip's attitude toward his collection of captured national memories alter. In a nightmare, he sees the national pastoral that is narrated by his stamps challenged:

> ... but instead of a different portrait of Washington on each of the twelve stamps, the portraits were now the same and no longer of Washington but of Hitler. . . . [A]cross everything in America that was the bluest and the greenest and the whitest and to be preserved forever in these pristine reservations, was printed a black swastika. (*Plot*, 43)

Stamps convey the illusion of a perpetual order, which Philip now sees crumbling and clashing with the reality as it evolves around him. When he later permanently loses his collection, he definitely has to seek another means to bring order into his view of the world. The lost collection forces him to recognize that the actual order of the State has been subverted as well and is no longer mirrored by his neat assembly of American hallmarks. Deprived of the icons he once could rely on, he has to start to think of politics independently of single personalities and symbols.

Instead of relying on the stamps as *lieux de mémoire*, a materialized consensus of what is to be remembered and how it shall be viewed,[33] Philip needs to find his own words to describe what he witnesses. Just as stamps incorporate the tense relationship between public memory and actual events, Roth uses the narrative voice in *The Plot* to highlight the difference between the boy's recollections and the political events of which the now grown-up narrator has learned. Briefly put, a rupture can be discerned between the child's narrative voice and the adult narrator's account: while the events within the family and in the neighborhood are mostly recorded from the viewpoint of young Philip, the historical dimension is covered by the adult narrator who looks back at a marking period in his childhood. To a certain extent, it is unclear how much the child truly apprehended at that time and to what extent the adult narrator teaches his past self to interpret the true implications of past episodes: Philip marvels at what he is seeing at the newsreel and mainly comprehends that he sees his aunt Evelyn on the screen, enjoying a presidential reception, whereas the adult voice narrates the events soberly, canceling out personal sentiments and perceptions. This sobriety is accentuated by a strictly chronological and evenly paced narration, which contrasts with the child who tends to rewind the story, so-called analepses, and changes the story's pace frequently, for instance by dedicating longer passages to relatively quick hand movements when he is helping his cousin attend to his stump.

The split voices allow the reader to grasp the moments when "official" history, as primarily narrated by the adult voice, and Philip's life actually clash. In a different vein, *Indignation* relies in its first part on the homodiegetic narrator, Marcus Messner, who relates his memories—as signaled by the first part's title—"Under Morphine," while unconscious on the sickbay in Korea. The second part, "Out from Under," is then forcedly taken over by an extradiegetic narrator who has to inform the reader of Marcus's death, the events leading to it, and its effect on the Messner family. Other than in the case of *The Plot*, the two voices do not contend distinct themes or levels of the story. Instead, the extradiegetic narrator accentuates the absence of thoughts on the Korean War in Marcus's tale. The sudden cut and change of scenes heightens the reader's attention for Marcus's evasiveness, his repression of any consideration of the war's justification, and his future role in it.

The difference between the mature, sober voices which describe the historical context in *The Plot* or the ironic distance of the extradiegetic narrator in the second part of *Indignation* and the youthful voices of Philip and Marcus is also marked when they both revert to elements and tunes reminding the reader of fairy tales, or when they reveal their dependency on rituals. The former does not mean that their stories are based on fairy or folk tales, although Brett Ashley Kaplan recognizes in Sanford's farm experience a variation on the Yiddish short story "The Calf" by Mendele Mokher Sefarim (1836–1917), in which a Yeshiva boy roamed in nature rather than devoted his lifetime to Torah studies.[34] It refers to those aspects of the stories which even Philip describes as fairy tale-like, such as his attempted flight to the orphanage, these results of "fantasies of flight and flight of fancies."[35] Marcus, in contrast, cannot recognize the traits in his father which let him appear to be a character out of a fairy tale or a fable, as Roth himself observed:[36] a character whose warnings are not heeded by his addressees, but who is like Cassandra eventually proven to have been right all along. Nor does Marcus ponder on the grotesqueness of the world surrounding him in Winesburg, Ohio. He stumbles through his reminiscences "under morphine" and accepts certain events with the equanimity usually displayed by fairy tale characters. Although these recollections recur under morphine on his military sick-bed, they do not have a dream-like or foggy quality: they remain the fable of a youth, clear in their shades, but fantastic and ludicrous as adolescence tends to be.

Ironically, the introduction of fairy tale elements on the level of the personal narrations of Philip and Marcus, the level of personal memories so to speak, creates an illusion which is subsequently destroyed in both novels: the marked contrast between the voices of the young protagonists and the sober or ironic-distanced voices of the adult or extradiegetic narrator may insinuate that the personal reminiscences are potentially false and historical accounts superior to private memories. Roth, however, will prove the latter short-sighted.

Fiction and historiography: Balancing on the threshold

"[C]onventional history" may suddenly turn out to be nothing but "a comforting illusion,"[37] a fairy tale which shields our view from the crude reality: hence the impression Philip must have had when the idyllic view offered by his stamp collection was marred in his nightmare by a swastika and in reality by the political changes. The reader who has reached *The Plot*'s end may, however, sigh in relief that actual history has taken another turn, yet he or she might not see therein an "illusion" but truth. For as Nancy Whittier Heer observes, history as it has been related to us as pupils has been fashioned in a way that strengthens us in our loyalty and our role as citizens:

> "[H]istoriography functions in any political system to socialize the coming generation, to legitimate political institutions, to perpetuate established mores and mythology, and to rationalize official policies."[38]

As a consequence, some might tend to return to the view of historiography which dominated in the nineteenth century, namely that there is only one history,[39] which can be transmitted correctly. This approach is not only challenged by modern historiography and historical science, but Roth's novel itself disproves the "comforting illusion" and replaces it with an uneasy aftertaste. The novel shows the alternative turns that history could have taken, thus revealing the actual atmosphere of that time which is preferably hidden in "official" history. *The Plot Against America* is thus more than a typical political scenario novel, or, alternatively put, a "palimpsest"[40] and "an exercise in historical imagination."[41]

Political scenario novels, or counterfactual historical novels,[42] do not only ask "what if?", but also outline the answer to the question and, at times, show that it could have happened here, as did Sinclair Lewis in one of the most famous examples of the genre, the novel *It Can't Happen Here* (1935). Allegories or *romans à clef*, on the other hand, show in an accusatory, yet secretive manner what is happening and where it inevitably has to lead. *The Plot Against America* was repeatedly subsumed under the latter category,[43] which prompted Roth to write the quoted *New York Times* essay wherein he refuted such allegations. One hesitates, though, to add the adverb "unambiguously," for he ended his note mocking the then incumbent President George W. Bush, Jr., as "unfit to run a hardware store let alone a nation like this one."[44] Such utterances explain why certain critics point out the allegoric potential of the novel[45] or even describe it in one case, alluding to one of the key symbols, as a prosthetic screen to read the present.[46] While it would be futile to search the novel for its allegoric qualities once more, *The Plot* can nonetheless be read as a critique: a critique of contemporary historiography whose fictional aspects are often disregarded by the average reader—in other words, it shows how narrow the threshold between fact and fiction tends to be.

Both novelists and historians are, according to Hayden White, basically storytellers:[47] would the historian not use narrative modes, his accounts would be nothing more than chronological lists; hence he resorts to narrative means, well aware of the fact that nothing in history itself forces him to favor one literary mode over another.[48] Put differently, narration is the cognitive link between the contents of history and its form, historiography.[49] When crafting their stories, again both the novelist and the historian are confronted with the same problem, namely the question of what to omit,[50] which forcedly leaves certain stories untold. Once the stories are retrieved and narrated, they can prove to be disruptive to the existing order, since they might contradict treasured myths.[51] White's so-called posthistoricism[52] thus embodies a profound suspicion toward any form of historic metanarrative, which draws it closer to the New Historicism.[53] Although *The Plot* does not confront the (American) reader with an untold story *strictu sensu*, Roth's counterfactual narrative still reveals a blank in the popular history book in that it shows the virulent anti-Semitism which was present in American society of the 1930s:

> "The American triumph is that despite the institutionalized anti-Semitic discrimination of the Protestant hierarchy at that time, despite the virulent Jew hatred of the German-American Bund and the Christian Front, despite the repellent Christian supremacy preached by Henry Ford and Father Coughlin and the Rev. Gerald L. K. Smith, despite the casual distaste for Jews expressed by journalists like Westbrook Pegler and Fulton Lewis, despite the blindly self-loving Aryan anti-Semitism of Lindbergh himself, it didn't happen here."[54]

Gérard Genette sees further parallels between historiographers and novelists in the narrative means at their disposal. In his eyes, factual narrative does not distinguish itself from fiction by temporal order, nor by the speed, frequency, or mode employed; the factual is only limited in the voice it employs, for its author always equals the narrator.[55] For a brief instance, however, Roth lets this barrier between fiction and fact appear blurry, he crosses the threshold between fact and fiction when he lets the reader enter a world resembling the author's factual childhood and introduces the voice of a narrator modeled on himself.

Just like Roth never lets his reader definitely recognize the boundary between the factual and fiction, he cannot draw a clear line between "history" and his "historic imagination": in a comment, Hayden White stated quite the opposite, interpreting the chronology of actual events appended to *The Plot* as a sign of Roth's willingness to accentuate the fictitiousness of his account.[56] Indeed, at a first glance, the appendix serves to reassure the reader that it did not happen here, that is that "[t]he 'what if' in America was somebody else's reality."[57] Yet the selection of the events, the way they are presented and the added speech by Charles Lindbergh, in my eyes, only unsettle the reader once more as it dawns on him or her that fiction could have turned into reality. Moreover, the appendix shows us what Roth actually means by "historical imagining," namely that "what is imagined may in some sense be historical, and that what is historical may in some sense be imagined."[58]

"[T]hat what is historical may in some sense be imagined" is a feeling one heeds while reading *Indignation*: although one knows of the accuracy of the scarce historical information, the facts are too intertwined with the imagined world of Winesburg, Ohio, so that they only seem to be a nightmare rarely haunting the characters at daylight. It thus only seems fitting that the "Historical Note" which closes the novel solely concerns the fictive world of Winesburg College and cannot exert the same confusing and/or edifying effect as the appendix to *The Plot Against America*. Paradoxically, the reader anyway perceives the imagined course of the world in *The Plot* as more realistic than the historical backdrop of *Indignation*, for the simple reason that the former presents the reader with a realistic microcosm, whereas the latter lets us walk through a series of grotesque situations. If the small world on which we focus seems to work in accordance with the laws of plausibility, we seem to be ready to accept the surrounding macrocosm, even against our better knowledge. The rare mentioning of the war in *Indignation* accentuates the reader's feeling that Korea is nothing more than the odd nightmare that every now and then haunts him at daytime, but no longer holds his consciousness in its grip. It is thus hardly surprising that the progenitor of this atmosphere has also conceived history to have a different effect on the awakening of the various protagonists.

5. Conclusion: Seeking identity in times of transition

"History claims everybody, whether they know it or not and whether they like it or not," Philip Roth explained, rather menacingly, in his essay "The Story Behind *The Plot Against America*." For his three youthful protagonists this becomes true as they all have to sacrifice childhood or adolescent illusions to the course of history. Following the paths outlined by van Gennep, they undergo separation and transitional phases, feel incorporated, and thus initiated, only to be ultimately lost and sobered. Their odysseys betray the nonlinearity of any development and maturation, but more importantly, they show how one cannot focus on the development of a political consciousness alone: already Philip's tentative development of political convictions conveys the intricate links between the different spheres of his life, and thus the simultaneity and interconnectedness of his maturation in these ranges. For instance, the recognition of his appearance as "different" from the dominant "Other" is coupled with his growing sense of ethnic and cultural stratification of society—which eventually lets him recognize negative undercurrents and their political implications. While Philip's development mainly illustrates basic assumptions established by political socialization research, its analysis reaches beyond these surveys in that it unravels the significance of innocent hobbies and metaphors, and points toward a question which has not been introduced in political socialization research yet, but is fundamental: a child's understanding of how the public relates to the private sphere. Only if an individual accepts that the public concerns its private life will it deem the political sphere of interest.

All three protagonists struggle with the implications of political changes which did not concern them before. Roth shows how his youngest character slowly comprehends how history enters his home not only as news on the radio, but also as a decisive factor in his family's future. In contrast, Sanford and Marcus see themselves at the verge of becoming, albeit minor, transformative actors in the history of their country, a turning point they both face with opposing strategies: while Sanford embraces the opportunity to become involved in the politics of the Lindbergh Administration, Marcus tries to shut his mind from anything that might distract him from the one way to evade involvement. The way these different characters connect the public, macrolevel so to speak, with their own private microcosm will finally decide their degree of politicization.

3

Guided by the Particularizer: I Married A Communist

1. Introduction

Nathan Zuckerman, Newark-born son of a chiropodist, first appears in *The Ghost Writer* (1979). Already determined to pursue a career as a writer, even against fatherly opposition, he hopes to find a mentor in his literary idol, E. I. Lonoff, who spends his life as a writing hermit in the recluse of the Berkshires. It is only in the later novel *I Married A Communist* (1998) that the reader learns of Zuckerman's earlier quest for a father figure—which he will betray for yet another paternal substitute. The novel which, together with *American Pastoral* (1997) and *The Human Stain* (2000), forms the so-called American Trilogy retraces Zuckerman's early intellectual development, mirroring his political as well as artistic awakenings. While part of the novel's lesson again consists in the recognition of how individual destiny and politics may be (tragically) interwoven, it mainly revolves around the question of how art serves and subverts political thinking and plans.

I Married A Communist can therefore be taken as an invitation to reflect on the idea which lies at the core of this book, an idea received simultaneously with applause and skepticism by literary theory:[1] that political science can learn from fiction. If literature indeed has an effect on an individual's political attitudes and thought, political socialization has to include literature and its impacts in its research agenda. Thus, after a brief reappraisal of the novel's synopsis, Roth will let his readers likewise hear him once applaud, once scold the idea that fiction could transmit actual knowledge to its readers.

2. Little Tom Paine in the company of men: Zuckerman's political initiation

A visit of his former High School teacher in English, Murray Ringold, evokes in Nathan Zuckerman not only memories of his early youth, but also of the man who accompanied his first steps toward independence. Zuckerman will not guide the reader of *I Married A Communist* (1998) alone through his memories, but often steps back as a narrator and lets Murray's voice, the actual dialogue between the two becomes dominant. The episodes Zuckerman remembers thus become contextualized by Murray's tales, which add further layers to Zuckerman's own story.[2]

Young Nathan Zuckerman finds in Ira Ringold, Murray's brother and acclaimed radio actor, the man to allay his hunger for heroic accounts, to suit his "specialty" in "heroic suffering" (*Communist*, 25). The physically strong actor provides the ideal foil for the searching adolescent, since he personifies the

> "self-reliant, independent American who hoboes around the nation taking various manual labour jobs during the depression before serving in the military after America enters the war; yet he also represents the second-generation, working-class, Jewish auto-didact, whose ability brings him fame and wealth as an Abraham Lincoln impersonator and as the popular radio actor Iron Rinn in the post-war years."[3]

Aside from his biography and status, it is Ira's genuine interest in Nathan as a person and conversation partner on equal footing which induces the latter to seek Ira's friendship. A chance encounter on Murray Ringold's lawn lets Ira cast a coincidental glimpse on the book Nathan is carrying around, which leads to a first exchange. Both Ira and Nathan treasure the historical novel *Citizen Tom Paine* (1943) by Howard Fast, a fictional account of the life of the British pamphleteer and revolutionary advocate of American independence—Ira enthuses about it for Howard Fast's, a longtime member of the Communist Party, "guts," and Nathan for his vivid language and the illustration of "heroic suffering."

In the aftermath of their first encounter, the reader sees Zuckerman's political initiation process unfold, which conveys a pattern to become emblematic for Zuckerman's course of life, as has been repeatedly argued:[4] his growing up resembles a succession of betrayals. His friendship to the Ringold brothers will make him betray his father, yet Ira, the new father figure, will again be replaced due to filial tensions, and, as will be seen, even the next substitute cannot rely on his mentee's allegiance. Each father figure, however, accompanies Nathan Zuckerman through different initiatory stages, or, in the case of his father, leads him toward the threshold of adolescence, until Zuckerman finds himself in the one total orphanhood "which is manhood" (*Communist*, 217), an image reminding the reader of "Philip Roth's" fancies in *The Plot Against America* and which will recur in *The Human Stain* (2000) and *Nemesis* (2010).

Zuckerman enters the classical separation phase when his father fails to notice his son's need to assume a new role, his urge "to be someone." As in the case of Sanford Roth in *The Plot*, it is outsiders, namely the Ringold brothers, who grant the youth the chance to prove his intellectual progress:

> The Ringolds were the one-two punch promising to initiate me into the big show, into my beginning to understand what it takes to be a man on the larger scale. The Ringolds compelled me to respond at a level of rigor that felt

> appropriate to who I now was. Be a good boy wasn't the issue with them. The sole issue was my convictions. . . . But once little Tom Paine has been let into the company of men and the father is still educating him as a boy, the father is finished. (*Communist*, 32)

"The sole issue" was his "convictions"—this statement alone shows that Zuckerman's development toward adulthood had a distinctly political dimension. The Ringolds were not to introduce him to the mundane duties of manhood, although the boxing metaphor points to the physical struggles of adolescence. Instead, they initiated him to looming political responsibilities, and the necessity to take a stand on societal issues. Ira equips Nathan with political readings, which the actor himself is urged to study by his own political mentor, the steelworker and adamant adherent to the Communist Party, Johnny O'Day. Ira takes Nathan to political events; Ira lets him read out his first attempts at revolutionary playwriting; Ira, in short, grows as close to Nathan as his father will never be again. Inevitably, Nathan finally has to see what "Philip Roth" in *The Plot* already perceived as an elementary school pupil, namely that a parent is not invulnerable, especially not against injuries inflicted by his own child:

> The moment when you first recognize that your father is vulnerable to others is bad enough, but when you understand that he is vulnerable to *you*, still needs you more than you any longer think you need him, when you realize that you might actually be able to frighten him, even to *quash* him if you wanted to—well, the idea is at such cross-purposes with routine filial inclinations that it does not even begin to make sense. (*Communist*, 106)

This thought crosses Zuckerman's mind as he sets out for what will become the transitory phase of his development, his initiation journey to Ira's shack in a place called Zinc Town, which required paternal permission. In tribal initiation rituals, shacks often serve as places of seclusion that at times symbolize the afterlife, or the somber yet protective womb of the mother, thus being simultaneously the location of ritual death and rebirth.[5] Such a space of concentrated solitude,[6] a "utopia of isolation"[7] indeed turns for Nathan into a place of ideological birth. Thanks to Ira he acquires a definitely shaped ideological framework, just as Ira learned his political lessons from Johnny O'Day in a single boarding room. Yet Ross Posnock rightly points out the irony that the Thoreauvian isolation serves the study of a markedly anti-individualistic ideology, namely Communism.[8]

Although communist thinking will exert a subversive force on Zuckerman's relationship to his father, it will not develop the same power over his mind as it did over Ira's. Traditional initiation rites often entail an element of coercion, be it that the initiand cannot avoid submission to the rite as such or that the transitory teachings allow no contradiction.[9] While Nathan undergoes a voluntary initiation and would indeed be free to question the beliefs he is confronted with, he has been introduced to communist thought by a man who never learned to question the ideology himself. This turns Nathan likewise into a subject of indoctrination: instead of being taught to reflect on Communism, his introduction bears the characteristics of indoctrination, namely nonevidential teaching grounded on pure acceptance of certain truths. Ira repeats what he learned from Johnny O'Day; Nathan repeats what he learns from Ira Ringold. Nathan, however, will eventually realize that the Communist rejection of critical thinking only mirrors McCarthyism and does not offer a true alternative or, as Till Kinzel put it, the needed counter-force.[10] Nathan recognizes how Ira has only been a mind molded into shape by others:

> If you're orphaned as early as Ira was, you fall into the situation that all men must fall into but much, much sooner, which is tricky, because you may either get no education at all or be over susceptible to enthusiasms and beliefs and ripe for indoctrination. (*Communist*, 216)

This reversal already indicates that Zuckerman's transition phase is not followed by being incorporated into the ranks of the Communist party. Instead, he recognizes the naïveté in Ira's ideological convictions with time and with the aid of another mentor. Zuckerman will not only betray Ira in thought, but also in deed as he turns his back to Communism and does not even follow the fate of his mentor and companion when Ira is publicly denounced as a Communist in a book published by his wife.[11] Fittingly, another journey to Zinc Town marks Zuckerman's definite alienation from Ira's views. On this occasion, both Ira and Zuckerman visit an old friend of the radio actor, a taxidermist and erstwhile communist, whose trade becomes emblematic of Zuckerman's relationship with Ira: taxidermy can be read as a metonymy, an "artifice referring to the whole . . . through a part."[12] At the beginning of their friendship, Nathan sees in Ira the idea of something more, an idol able to cast a spell on him, as if he were mistaking the actor for the historic figures he has to impersonate. That Ira, however, soon vanishes in the adolescent's eyes, and only his shell persists.

Neither can the void be filled by Johnny O'Day, although as a college student, Nathan is impressed by the steelworker's stoic dedication to the Communist cause. O'Day's indifference toward his earlier mentee's downfall might irritate Zuckerman, yet he is fascinated by O'Day's readiness to make sacrifices, and he is likewise lured by the prospect of receiving clear guidelines for his future life. Devoting himself to the communist struggle would eventually rid him of all uneasy questions and doubts; it would provide him with a single thread to hold on to. Still, Zuckerman is not ready to follow this path without searching for further counsel and approval from the man who will finally force him to assume the responsibilities of an independent mind. Leo Glucksman, a college teacher and again a man who prefers a solitary over a gregarious life, condemns the youth's aspirations and compels him to read between the lines of the communist story. He induces Zuckerman to recognize that a thinking doubtful and complex being like himself will never be able to fit into the confines of the cut-out simple pawn as conceived by Communist ideology.[13] The "Dubinushka," a recording of the socialistic song given to him by Ira Ringold, fades in Nathan's memory—a sharp contrast to Marcus Messner's being led on by the stomping tune of the Chinese national anthem of the World War II era.

The reader now meets an aged Nathan Zuckerman as a successful writer, and not as an ardent political agitator. Like his former mentor, he has sought the solitude of a small cabin, albeit in his case in the quiet of the Berkshires—a palimpsest of Ira's refuge in Zinc Town, as Ellen Lévy puts it.[14] However, in marked contrast to Ira's retreat, Zuckerman's two-roomed cabin does not serve for political invigoration, instead, it becomes emblematic of his apolitical attitude; Zuckerman becomes guilty, in Murray Ringold's eyes, of withdrawing from any worldly responsibility:

> "If politics requires a morality premised on 'worldly' consciousness, that is, in the first instance, a moral commitment to engagement with the world beyond one's own doorstep, then Zuckerman too seems aware that he may have acquired his own form of 'moral pass.'"[15]

3. Howard Fast et al.: The reader as a political disciple

The first encounter between Nathan and Ira centers on a book; their relationship with Johnny O'Day is maintained by shared readings; and Nathan does not capture his political ideas in tracts or manifestoes, but in plays—in short, literature becomes the means by which Nathan absorbs and expresses political convictions. He apparently tries to imitate the writers of proletarian novels and their successors of the 1950s, the representatives of radical fiction, who were both affiliated with the working class, namely the workers in the heavy industries, and Marxist streams of thought.[16] As a consequence, Zuckerman develops a distinct attitude toward literature, seeing himself simultaneously as literature's political disciple and a literary belligerent:

> I wouldn't care to judge today if something I loved as much as I loved *On a Note of Triumph* was or was not art; it provided me with my first sense of the conjuring power of art and helped strengthen my first ideas as to what I wanted and expected a literary artist's language to do: enshrine the struggles of the embattled. (*Communist*, 38)

Discipleship, however, also entails conflict, and thus it is not surprising that Zuckerman discovers in literature not only a weapon, but also a suitable antagonist to his ideas, for thanks to the Ringolds he

> "... realizes that men can talk about baseball games and prize fights, that their attitude towards books can be as bellicose as the latter exercise. You can box with a book, take it on, wrangle it to the mat."[17]

Although Zuckerman remembers treasuring mainly those books "that affirmed [his] own political sympathies as well as furnishing a venerated source from which [he] could take lines for [his] radio plays" (*Communist*, 153), and thus did not offer much resistance, reading still became his foremost political activity, a dimension of reading which has often been considered by political scientists and literary critics alike.[18]

The way Zuckerman's attitude toward literature evolves lets the reader easily conclude that Roth himself sees literature as a means to grasp more clearly the realities of our unwritten, empirical world.[19] Just like an interlocutor of Socrates, Nathan seems to learn most by consulting the "likely stories"[20] literature offers, since they appeal to his reason by activating his imaginative powers. This idea is also conveyed in earlier novels by Roth, specifically in the first part of the Zuckerman series. In *The Ghost Writer* (1979), Zuckerman imagines young Amy Bellette to be in truth the clandestine Holocaust survivor Anne Frank. Like the real Anne Frank, Amy kept a diary which is published—posthumously, as most believe. The diarist, however, is still alive, but chooses anonymity: only the diary of a killed Anne Frank, thus her conviction, can have a lasting impact on its reader. In crafting the story of his fictitious Anne/Amy, Zuckerman seems to stress once more his belief that reading changes the reader, that literature can at times indeed be a weapon. This idea seemed to have inspired Roth to write *Our Gang (Starring Tricky and His Friends)* (1971), a grotesque closet drama which ridicules the rhetoric and policies of Richard "Tricky Dick" Nixon, the then incumbent President of the United States. Although the play does not convey a specific political conviction, it, in the author's own words, generally aimed at destroying "the protective armor of 'dignity' that shields anyone in an office as high and powerful as the Presidency" (*Reading*, 40) and thus assumedly pursued a political goal.

Political scientists have frequently advocated literary works as sources to understand the individual dimension of politics, that is the effects of political events and ideas on individuals.[21] The idea that literature could have an effect on people's political ideas also explains the curiosity for private libraries, such as the remains of Hitler's book collection,[22] and the constant efforts of political regimes to either suppress or abuse art for propaganda.[23] Martha Nussbaum carries this idea further by claiming that literature not only allows readers to understand others better, but also can have a lasting impact on their own behavior, which cannot be achieved by historiographic or scientific texts. The latter may deliver facts, yet at times some might feel inclined to join Joseph Conrad's *Lord Jim* (1900) in his exclamation, "Facts! They demanded facts from him, as if facts could explain anything!" (18). Literature, in contrast, "summons powerful emotions, it disconcerts and puzzles,"[24] which Nussbaum believes will ultimately lead to understanding and to evoke compassion, or, in Adam Smith's diction, fellow feeling.[25]

Martha Nussbaum develops her theory against the backdrop of the shortcomings she perceives in current social science research, for she observes that

> "[v]ery often in today's political life we lack the capacity to see one another as fully human, as more than 'dreams or dots.' Often, too, those refusals of sympathy are aided and abetted by an excessive reliance on technical ways of modeling human behavior, especially those that derive from economic utilitarianism. These models can be very valuable in their place, but they frequently prove incomplete as a guide to political relations among citizens."[26]

The cure to this mutual indifference lies, according to Nussbaum, in literature which is capable of exerting an emotive power over its readers, of appealing to an innate human capacity she terms—in reference to Charles Dickens—"fancy."[27] While facts as produced by empirical studies satisfy the general need for a seemingly objective source and rationality with regard to public issues, they do not force research to consider their impact from an individual perspective and address their moral impact. Literary works, in contrast, which

> "promote identification and emotional reaction cut through those self-protective stratagems, requiring us to see and to respond to many things that may be difficult to confront—and they make this process palatable by giving us pleasure in the very act of confrontation." [28]

By assuming the position of the "judicious spectator," the reader enables himself to comprehend the inner plight of a person and feelings he never experienced himself. In his *Theory of Moral Sentiments* (1759), Adam Smith envisages the combination of reason and emotion in the "judicious spectator," who shall not only imagine himself—vividly, as Nussbaum stresses—in another person's situation, but also simultaneously judge the situation "with his present reason and judgment."[29] Put in a nutshell, reading shall enable an individual to take at the same time the stand of the rational observer, the spectator, as well as the person concerned, forcing the individual to assume an outside and inside perspective. Literature thus achieves a moral effect, by instilling in its readers compassion or, again in Smith's diction, "fellow-feeling," which eventually turns them into better citizens.

Martha Nussbaum is not the sole adherent to what has been termed a humanist stance on literature,[30] nor was she the first to develop a theory on this topic. She is, however, one of the few scholars in politics and literature who refers to literary works with the same matter of course as to "typical" scientific sources. Her efforts are paralleled by Richard Rorty who argues in a similar vein that citizens can only grasp the nature of current problems by reading novels along with philosophic works.[31] Rorty agrees with Nussbaum that literature gives individuals insight into ways of living otherwise inaccessible, insights which alter one's moral disposition in a way comparable to Nussbaum's theory and which teach compassion.[32] The latter is key to achieve the main goal of liberalism, which consists in, according to Rorty, the reduction of cruelty, as once claimed by the philosopher Judith Shklar.[33] In his eyes, literature heightens our awareness of cruelty on two levels, as Simon Stow summarizes to the point:

> "First, it can teach us about other people, making us more sensitive to cruelty suffered by people to whom we might not normally attend, thereby cultivating the value of *solidarity*. Second, it can teach us about ourselves, making us more sensitive to the cruelty of which we ourselves are capable, thereby cultivating the value of *contingency*."[34]

By dissecting novels of political interest such as Charles Dickens's *Hard Times* (1854), a satiric disclosure as to what effects clinging to cold facts may have, Nussbaum further elaborates the ideas these literary works transport and how they ascertain their impact by appealing to the fancy and emotions of their readers. Young Nathan Zuckerman, avidly devouring Howard Fast's *Citizen Tom Paine* and absorbing, later even advocating the novel's message, seems to be exemplary of Nussbaum's theory just as much as Ira Ringold, who distributes Arthur Miller's *Focus* (1945) to cure anti-Semitism. Roth and Nussbaum—of one mind? For more than half of *I Married A Communist*, everything indeed points to consensus—yet what if Roth lets the literary cure fail?

4. Literature for literature's sake: The freed particularizer

Eve Frame, actress and wife to Ira Ringold, has recreated her life's story in tune with her stage name: the new her exists within a frame which allows no space for a history, an Eve with no mother, and certainly not a Jewish *mame*.[35] Her Jewish self-hatred is only matched by her disdain for people, especially other women with distinctly Jewish features. Yet there is a cure, Ira believes, a cure unfolding its power through the lines of Arthur Miller's début novel, *Focus* (1945), which decries the latent to open anti-Semitism in U.S. society: a simple pair of glasses let Miller's protagonist, an anti-Semite himself, appear remarkably Jewish—an unwanted masquerade which is interpreted as an unmasking by his environs. Miller's protagonist Larry Newman not only loses his job due to his altered appearance and the association it provokes, but he also becomes subject to hostilities in his neighborhood, which change his own attitude toward the Jewish population in his street. Eve submits to the guided reading Ira imposes on her, and pretends to understand the message:

> "She reads this book at Ira's request. She reads what he underlines for her. She listens to his lecture. And what is the subject of the lecture? The subject is the subject of the book—the *subject* is the Jewish face. . . . But a change of heart? . . . [W]hen she found a face inexcusably Jewish . . ., her thoughts weren't Ira's or Arthur Miller's." (*Communist*, 155–6)

Yes, Eve had patiently listened to Ira's elaborations on the novels, yes, she had congratulated Arthur Miller in person for the compelling and gripping read—but no, the message she learned from the book, if any beyond entertainment and aesthetic pleasure, was quite different from the one intended to reach her. "How can we be moved by the fate of Anna Karenina?" an article on the emotional and cognitive impact of fiction once asked[36]—and why should Eve Frame alter her attitude because of the fate of Miller's Larry Newman? Instead of further supplementing Nussbaum's humanist stance with additional storylines annihilating the failed literary discipleship of Eve Frame, *I Married A Communist* edges the former question on and seems to ask, why indeed?

In the course of his maturation, Zuckerman not only finds new mentors, but also, due to them, or rather due to one in particular, finds a new access to literature. His depoliticization, his de-initiation from the political spheres of life are actually launched by his altered view of literature. His college mentor Leo Glucksman confronts him with a valuation of literature diametrically opposed to the view proposed by Ira and O'Day who saw in literature the servant of the political. In Glucksman's eyes, art, and thus literature, is outer-worldly, it "introduces into the world something that wasn't there even at the start" (*Communist*, 224). Submitting art to a political cause deprives art of its nature, thus Glucksman's conviction, for art is only in the service of art:

> "Art is taking the right *stand* on everything? Art as the advocate of good things? Who taught you this? Who taught you art is slogans? Who taught you art is in the service of *'the people'*? Art is in the service of *art*—otherwise there is no art worthy of *anyone's* attention. What *is* the motive for writing serious literature, Mr. Zuckerman? To disarm the enemies of price control? The motive for writing serious literature is *to write serious literature*." (*Communist*, 218)

Glucksman not only sees politicization as a danger to serious art, but also denies the existence of particularly political art, as politics and art must be, in his view, mutually exclusive due to their obverse nature. In this vein he explains:

> "Politics is the great generalizer . . . and literature the great particularizer, and not only are they in an inverse relationship to each other—they are in an *antagonistic* relationship. . . . How can you be an artist and renounce the nuance? But how can you be a politician and *allow* the nuance? . . . To allow for the chaos, to let it in. You *must* let it in. Otherwise you produce propaganda, if not for a political party, a political movement, then stupid propaganda for life itself—for life as it might itself prefer to be publicized. . . . Art also disturbs the organization. Literature disturbs the organization. . . . It disturbs the organization because it is not general. . . . Generalizing suffering: there is Communism. Particularizing suffering: there is literature." (*Communist*, 223)

"Art for art's sake," goes the simple formula that Glucksman's opinion can be boiled down to, which makes him an adherent to the homonymous theory. The phrase first appeared in the diary of Benjamin Constant, who had accompanied Germaine de Staël on her journey to Weimar in winter 1803/1804.[37] In Germany, they were both exposed to and inspired by the writings of Immanuel Kant, particularly by his aesthetic theory from which they concluded that he found art free of purpose, that—to cite Germaine de Staël—"it is not at all in the nature of the fine arts to give lessons."[38] Thus Constant and de Staël paved the way for the *l'art pour l'art* movement, which was, however, based on a misreading, as today's critics believe: in Kant's view, art has indeed both a cognitive and a moral value, yet as it cannot "transmit universal knowledge or universal ethical values", it is reduced to "purposiveness without a purpose."[39]

To a certain extent, the younger Nathan had already internalized the ideas of Glucksman and his spiritual predecessors prior to his political initiation, for he admired Howard Fast more for his voice and rhetoric than for the actual political depiction of *Citizen Tom Paine*. In this light, Glucksman's invective against literature tied to a purpose has only cleared Nathan's mind of the attitude adopted during his initiation process and brings him back to the place from where he set out and from where he will follow the path of the Zuckerman we meet as an ambitious writer in the making in *The Ghost Writer*. Yet while Zuckerman closes *I Married A Communist* in agreement with Glucksman, the reader feels inclined to conclude that he might have heard Roth's voice ringing through. Glucksman becomes indeed audible in his creator's voice, especially in more recent interviews during which Roth declared that he was "not out to make fiction into a political statement."[40] Repeated interpretations of *The Plot Against America* as an allegory on the Administration of George W. Bush, Jr., even induced him to write an article in the New York Times, explaining "The Story Behind *The Plot*," and to stress again in an interview that the novel was "neither an allegory nor a metaphor nor a didactic tract; *The Plot* is about what it is about, which isn't now but then."[41] Philip Roth's denial of any political intention with his works is in unison with his early conviction that, in reference to Sinclair Lewis, "repeating . . . 'It can happen here,' does little to prevent 'it' from happening" (*Reading*, 207).

In Roth's eyes, contrary to the assumption earlier pursued in this chapter and diametrically opposed to O'Day's belief, literature can never be used as a weapon, for reading can have no effect upon the reader except for turning him into a better reader (*Reading*, 147). It would thus testify to a wrong understanding of a writer's role, as Glucksman likewise suggested, to deliver propaganda and support a political cause by writing. Roth clearly says that he does not even see his writing as a crusade against anti-Semitism, since "however much I may loathe anti-Semitism . . . my job in a work of fiction is not to offer consolation to Jewish sufferers or to mount an attack upon their persecutors" (*Reading*, 109). He seems to agree with "Philip" in *Deception* (1990), who views literature as outside of the political sphere and thus immune to political charges:

> "You are out of order! It is not for you to interrogate the court but to answer the questions of the court. You are charged with sexism, misogyny, woman abuse, slander of women, denigration of women, defamation of women, and ruthless seduction, crimes all carrying the most severe penalties. People like you are not treated kindly if found guilty, and for good reason. . . . Why did you publish books that cause women suffering? Didn't you think that those writings could be used against us by our enemies?"
>
> ["Philip":] "I can only reply that this self-styled equal-rights democracy has aims and objectives that are not mine as a writer." (*Deception*, 109–110)

Read jointly, both Philip Roth's personal statements and the closure of *I Married A Communist* are antithetical to Martha Nussbaum's theory, which only seconds ago seemed to be supported by the same author and novel. Similarly ambiguous as Roth's attitude turns out to be after a closer reading is the scholarly reception of Nussbaum's idea. While Rorty has developed a theory which shows certain parallels to her thought, empirical studies offer mixed results: the main claim that reading enhances compassion and empathy has been tackled by psychologists and literary scholars alike, with diverging results. While some have found no correlation between empathy and exposure to fiction, or even suggested a negative relation,[42] other studies reached quite a contrary conclusion.[43]

Although reviewers of Nussbaum's main publication on politics and literature, *Poetic Justice* (1995), have criticized the simplified view on emotions and the neglect of neuropsychological findings,[44] they mainly focus on the literary methodology applied by Nussbaum, namely her interpretations and her application of literary findings to empirical reality. Simon Stow has extensively criticized Nussbaum's approach on the grounds of these two aspects, suggesting that she has on the one hand fallen prey to receptive fallacy, and on the other hand become an overreader in the Rothian sense. Already the pioneers in the field of politics and literature had been charged with *affective* fallacy, when early political readings of Shakespeare's works were scrutinized by literary scholars with the conclusion that these political scientists

> "have a worthy aim: to give a great poet a voice in the great concerns of practical life. But they have not yet learned to distinguish between the poet's voice and their own—so that, though I greet the aim, I must withhold the applause."[45]

Thus, they have not only confused their own opinion with Shakespeare's, but were also allegedly unable to distinguish between the text as such and its effect on them, on which they built their interpretation. In short, they reached an affective fallacy in the terms of W. K. Wimsatt and Monroe Beardsley.[46] This concept is sustained by the idea that a text already bears meaning in itself, leading to a divide between the text and the reader as such. Yet this idea has been surpassed by the so-called reader-response criticism which sees the reader "both as producer and comprehender":[47]

> ". . . the reader's response is not *to* the meaning; it *is* the meaning . . . ."[48]

Reader-response theorists argue that representatives of New Criticism like Wimsatt and Beardsley may believe that their interpretation of a text is based exclusively on the text's meaning; they develop their idea of its intrinsic meaning, however, from their own response to the text.[49] It is thus the reader's reaction to a text which becomes crucial, for it gives the text its meaning, claim theorists like Stanley Fish. If one follows their reasoning, Nussbaum can no longer be charged with affective, but with *receptive* fallacy: she aims at discerning "the message that a text transmits to its audience by examining the *text* rather than the *audience*."[50]

Although Nussbaum seems to adhere to New Criticism's view of literature, namely that the text itself has a meaning independent of its reader, she still tries to unravel this meaning on her own, not contemplating that her reading might differ from someone else's. Stow therefore sardonically concludes that Nussbaum is pursuing a "'supply side' theory of the novel,"[51] which completely disregards its impact on the demand side. As a consequence, it is hardly surprising that humanist theorists on literature's impact on politics may favor similar novels for their studies, but hardly agree on their substance, as one critic observes.[52] Had Ira Ringold been acquainted with reader-response theory, he would have realized why Eve would never read *Focus* the same way as he had. Accordingly, the interpretations suggested by humanist theorists on politics and literature could be accused by some of gaining too much of a lecturing tone in that they disregard every single reader's role in the construction of meaning to a text and seem to impose an allegedly correct reading on him, prescribing even the effect the text should have on the reader.

"Art as the advocate of good things?" (*Communist*, 218)—Stow nearly echoes Glucksman, albeit not in the tone of the outraged advocate of art's purity. It is instead in the name of political science and its methodology that Stow attacks the alleged weaknesses in Nussbaum's argument. In addition to questioning the possibility of anyone assuming the role of a judicious spectator,[53] it is mainly the way Nussbaum—and with her other political scientists—treat exemplary readings as evidence. Stow therein not only sees a case of receptive fallacy, but also of "overreading," of importing ideas into a text not signified within it.[54] Stow believes to find support against overreading in Philip Roth's works, for in both *American Pastoral* (1997) and *I Married A Communist* Roth lets characters suffer for their clinging to texts:

> "Those readers, such as Merry Levov of *Pastoral*, and Ira Ringold of *Communist*, who seem incapable of separating their reading from their politics, seem to perish in part *because* of this inability to separate them. Both read to confirm what they already know or believe to be true, and as such they perhaps serve as a warning to those of us who might seek to do the same: to use the *written* world as evidence for claims about the *unwritten* world."[55]

Stow detects the same mistake in Nussbaum's reasoning, namely the lack of a clear distinction between the written and the unwritten world, that is the story world or the world as created in a novel and our empirical "reality." In his eyes, the instances when literary works are forwarded to support a claim, they only exert the power of illustration, instead of serving as evidence, which they are intended to do. Maybe because they are, after all, "only" works of art? Thus seems to be Stow's conviction:

> "[Literature] can show us how little we know and, indeed, how little we know about *how* we know. . . . Most obviously, literature cannot—as a general rule—serve as empirical evidence for claims about the *unwritten* world, because the standards of justification demanded by literary analysis are lower than those required for analysis of the *written* world. . . . Literature can, that is to say, lead us to consider alternative possibilities, but it is not—for the most part—itself evidence for the existence of these possibilities."[56]

In Stow's eyes, texts, stories, and novels alone will not transform their readers into more empathetic, understanding, and less self-centered beings; however, discussions about one's readings may, as he suggests. Since a text itself has no meaning independent from the reader, he adds, readers should embrace the opportunity and exchange their opinions and reactions, so that reading will no longer remain a solipsistic act, but a chance for dialogue—and maybe even for the effects desired by Nussbaum and other humanist theorists.

5. Conclusion, or attempt at a closure: Why I keep overreading

The Great Particularizer as an opener for the Great Generalizer—Simon Stow used Roth's voice to drown others, to back his criticism (illustratively, certainly not as evidence, he might interject), whereby he finally drowned Roth's voice in this chapter, or rather, my comprehension of it. If we decided now what to keep for the records, what to take down as Roth's final word on the matter, the space foreseen for the notes would remain either remarkably empty, bear the word "ambiguous," or it would be halved for a table, reserving one column for his arguments pro-Martha Nussbaum and the other one pro-Stow. While the latter would reduce Roth's works again to illustrative purposes, the former would hardly warrant the papers filled with the above observations and arguments. So—what?

Roth loves playing games with his readers. As we have already learned in the previous chapter, neither can the reader trust paratexts which are declared to be factual and not to be an example of textual manipulation which renders facts into fiction nor can we expect hypothetical scenarios not to bear a kernel of truth. It is therefore hardly surprising that Roth has not treated the relationship between literature and politics, and the question whether literature can change its readers in a straightforward manner. Yet whether it is in this case part of another Rothian hide-and-seek game is also anything but clear, for it could very well be that Roth has never resolved the puzzle for himself—or found another answer each time he tried. The only idea he always adamantly adhered to was that art indeed should not serve a political cause, that it should not let itself be tamed or restrained by politics or anything else seeking to influence its contents and forms, be they religious institutions, the media, or family voices. It would thus not be permissible to bend his works in such a way as to make out one single political message and declare him its adherent. We shall, however, not let our reading be hindered by any other source: if reading makes us better readers if the meaning of a text is only to be derived in an internal conversation with the reader himself, it is futile to ask whether Roth or anyone would approve of this endeavor to derive from his texts lessons for political socialization research. So—what!

As a consequence, reading itself has to become a part of the research agenda in political socialization: reading has an effect on the reader, and on the younger reader even more so. In the case of Nathan Zuckerman, fiction could only sustain a political influence on him as long as he coveted the idea of literature's political duty, but with a changed view of the relationship between art and politics this influence evaporated. Yet his example shows—or illustrates, if you prefer so—that our perception of how certain areas of life relate to each other also defines from where we derive ideas. Research on the development of political ideas thus has to ask what sources people perceive as legitimate, how they relate to fiction, and what effects it has on us personally. Books have been, still are, or have been threatened to be censored, including Roth's work—had they not an impact on our emotions, thought, and actions, politics would hardly have attributed them so much attention in the past. It is therefore inadmissible to leave them out of the picture if researchers want to understand the way our political thinking evolves.

4

Political Odysseys: Prague, Israel, and Elsewhere

1. Introduction: Movements, oscillatory and otherwise

Crossing borders, stepping over thresholds, overcoming obstacles: initiation is routinely compared to spatial movement and consequently has been likened to a journey. Not only do journey and initiations share a tripartite structure,[1] but traveling itself can also be a means to reach the objectives of an initiation process, namely self-recognition and the assumption of a new role, or a new outlook on the world.[2] Both are liminal experiences, for the traveler is likewise held in limbo, between origin and destination, whereas the initiand remains held in suspense between his former and his new self.[3] It is thus hardly surprising that the reader would have already in the previously discussed novels come across instances of a journey as a major step toward self-recognition or the key to a fundamental change in a protagonist. From Portnoy's disastrous trip to Israel, where his manliness fails him, to Sanford Roth's exploration of Gentile farming life in the Midwest, to Marcus Messner's struggles for manhood in Ohio, and finally to Ira's and Zuckerman's withdrawal from society to the confines of an isolated shack, Roth submits his protagonists often to what Peter Freese has termed "initiation journeys," as goes the title of his treatise.[4] The following subchapters will analyze to what degree Roth's novels testify an initiatory effect of traveling, and how space influences the creation of political identity, as in the case of journeys to socialist Prague in *The Prague Orgy* (1985) and the land of Israel in *The Counterlife* (1986) and *Operation Shylock* (1993). Given the Jewish background of the writer and the protagonists, the relationship between identity and space will forcedly be tenuous,[5] as it is tied to the question whether a collective identity can be developed without a common space.

From the perspective of literary theory, this analysis will automatically be confronted with the different motifs which structure tales of initiation journeys, as they have been explored by Peter Freese, and the way these images are interlinked with travel writing beyond the mere fact that they both focus on an individual's movement through different spaces. Freese distinguishes between three motifs of initiation journeys, namely a *regressus ad uterum*, a *descensus ad infernos*, and the *Nachtmeerfahrt*:[6] the first describes the return to the mythological origins of life, for example Mother Earth, which leads to one's rebirth as a changed and transformed individual. Similarly, the *descensus ad infernos* narrates an individual's descent to the underworld, from where he might return heroically and purified. The *Nachtmeerfahrt*, as experienced by the Greek lunar goddess Danaë during her existential voyage in a chest across the sea, depicts the devouring of the self and thus self-destruction as a precondition for rebirth. While readers of Roth will encounter only the first motif in its most abstract form, I suggest that the spatial movements they all ascribe will be retrieved and can be compared to the typology of hermeneutical movements Ottmar Ette identified in travel literature:[7] circular, pendular, linear, star-shaped, and erratic or jumpy.

Both the *regressus ad uterum* and the *descensus ad infernos* entail the initiate's return to the point of departure, which lets him or her inscribe a *circular* motion. The *Nachtmeerfahrt*, in contrast, usually leads away from one's origins and does not foresee a return. It is therefore closest to a *linear* movement which, according to Ette, is often followed in pursuit of a transcendental experience, a desired oneness with the destination. While these two types of movement are guided by a clear destination, the idea of a destination as such vanishes in the other three types identified by Ette: as its name indicates, the *pendular* movement is characterized by the oscillation between two places which leaves the traveler in constant limbo—beginning and endpoint become indistinguishable. Although a *stellar* movement knows its starting point, it is hard to define its actual destination: taking one point as the origin of various shorter or longer trips which always lead back, such stellar excursions can be likened to the movement of a child who starts to explore its environs, but always returns to its mother. *Jumpy or erratic* travelers are finally an example of definitely aimless moving, where motion becomes the sole *raison d'être*.

As will become evident during the identification of such movements in the novels of Philip Roth, talking of the relation between individual and space always entails the question of the relation between space and time: spaces comprise not only the present and coexistent, but also encompass social and timely spheres, thus evoking the presence of things past and coming.[8] When the reader follows the Rothian protagonists on their journeys to Prague and Israel, he or she is likewise exploring an historical component of their identity. Specifically, we will explore the tensions between collective and individual identity, as well as collective and individual memory, as the subsequent journeys likewise follow the path of Roth's Jewish ancestors and fellows: their roots in Eastern Europe; their vision of a sovereign nation in Israel; and their present life in the United States.

2. Roots, literary and otherwise: Prague

Prague already fascinated David Kepesh, Roth's *Professor of Desire* (1977), who visited the city in search of traces of his literary idol, Franz Kafka.[9] In contrast, Nathan Zuckerman's excursion to the then Czechoslovakian capital in 1976 is less driven by a personal desire to reach for the roots of Yiddish culture, but rather by a mission: *The Prague Orgy* (1985) is opened by the Czech writer-in-exile Zdenek Sisovsky who confides in Zuckerman the tragic end of his father's life. During the first years of the war, the elder Sisovsky could benefit from a Gestapo officer's passion for chess, since the latter protected Sisovsky for his brilliant chess skills. This peculiar union, however, ended lethally on grounds of a quarrel between his protector and another officer:

> "One Sunday, a Sunday probably much like today, the two Gestapo officers went out drinking together and they got drunk, much the way, thanks to your hospitality, we are getting nicely drunk here. They had an argument. They were good friends, so it must have been a terrible argument, because the one who played chess with my father was so angry that he walked over to the dentist's house and got the dentist out of bed and shot him. This enraged the other Nazi so much that the next morning he came to our house and he shot my father, and my brother also, who was eight. When he was taken before the German commandant, my father's murderer explained, 'He shot my Jew, so I shot his.' 'But why did you shoot the child?' 'That's how God-damn angry I was, sir.'" (*Prague*, 19–20)

Yet Zdenek Sisovsky's father left him a valuable legacy, a collection of his own Yiddish stories the son and now famous writer deems worthy of being preserved and published. Unfortunately, though, Sisovsky left the manuscript in the custody of his wife, whom he had deserted, which renders it almost impossible for him to retrieve the stories. With Zuckerman's aid, however, the prospect of saving the manuscript and finally publishing it becomes within reach—and with Zuckerman's assent to search for the texts in Prague begins the *Orgy* concluding the series *Zuckerman Bound*. It thus happens that Zuckerman drifts through the nightlife of the Prague élite and tries to understand the rules of an artist's life under a socialist regime, to which the struggling writer Bolotka offers his insights. While coping with the political reality and the obstacles it presents, Zuckerman likewise explores Prague as a cradle and former center of Jewish culture—until he is expelled from the country under a shady pretext, naturally losing Sisovsky's manuscript in the process.

Zuckerman's trip to Prague constitutes a political education, an initiation journey to socialism, so to speak, displaying all the elements required for such a characterization: a naïve departure, an erudite and sobering arrival and sojourn, and a return with a changed and broadened mind. The circular movement thus inscribed accentuates the value this journey will have for Zuckerman's future work and his attitude on socialism. His development is reminiscent of Roth's own experiences in Eastern Europe, although no equalization of author and protagonist will be proposed. Yet it would be wrong to suppress any reference to Roth's own formative journeys, for they testify to the impact a confrontation with a regime alien by name and nature may have on an individual. Roth himself speaks of his frequent stays in Prague as "a little crash course in political repression" (*Reading*, 140) where he not only noticed a politicization in the sense of

> a daily awareness of government *as a coercive force*, its continuous presence in one's thoughts as far more than just an institutionalized, imperfect system of necessary controls (*Reading*, 10),

but also a growing awareness of the effect of politics on culture:

> In a totalitarian state, however, all culture is dictated by the regime; fortunately we Americans live in Reagan's and not Plato's Republic, and aside from their stupid medal, culture is almost entirely ignored. . . . When I was first in Czechoslovakia, it occurred to me that I work in a society where as a writer everything goes and nothing matters, while for the Czech writers I met in Prague, nothing goes and everything matters. (*Reading*, 145)

Zuckerman mainly caricatures the at-times ridiculous outcomes of a totalitarian cultural policy. Consequently, he learns during his nightly encounters, why a writer should be a good spy, but why a good writer will not necessarily receive any merits from the state, wherefore the latter has to put up with award winning writers who, however, make bad spies. Yet while the regime only provokes his mockery, Zuckerman develops an even greater admiration for Prague's writers, as he recognizes the escape their work offers and the rebellious potential it bears:

> Here where the literary culture is held hostage, the art of narration flourishes by mouth. In Prague, stories aren't simply stories; it's what they have instead of life. Here they have become their stories, in lieu of being permitted to be anything else. Storytelling is the form their resistance has taken against the coercion of the powers-that-be. (*Prague*, 64)

As hinted at before, Zuckerman does not remain stuck in Prague's present, but rather perceives the place in its historical dimension, specifically in its significance to him as a Jew and to Jews in general. He explores the city simultaneously with the eyes of a regime critic and of someone trying to recognize his home town after a long absence:

> On foot, and with the help of a Prague map, I proceed to lose my way but also to shake my escort. . . . This is the city I imagined the Jews would buy when they had accumulated enough money for a homeland. I knew about Palestine and the hearty Jewish teenagers there reclaiming the desert and draining the swamps, but I also recalled, from our vague family chronicle, shadowy, cramped streets where the innkeepers and distillery workers who were our Old World forebears had dwelled apart, as strangers, from the notorious Poles—and so, what I privately pictured the Jews able to afford with the nickels and dimes I collected was a used city, a broken city, a city so worn and grim that nobody else would even put in a bid. (*Prague*, 62)

Obviously, Zuckerman's journey not only depicts a circle in a spatial sense; Prague also means a visit to the past for him, a visit recalling Kafka's settings and, more importantly, the images evoked by the stories of Zuckerman's childhood. Salman Rushdie had described in *Imaginary Homelands* (1992) that those in exile would "not be capable of reclaiming precisely the thing that was lost" and that they would "create fictions, not actual cities or villages, but invisible ones, imaginary homelands" (10)—a process Zuckerman's family likewise undergoes. He thus visits the imaginary homeland of his ancestors, and for the first time strides through the space which unites his family's past with the histories he invented as a child. Prague is shaped by stories, past and present, actual and imagined, lost and found.

Ironically, this subchapter can likewise finish with a circular loop, referring once again to the synopsis, in particular the tale of Sisovsky's father: Prague is shaped by stories, as the human memory is; Zuckerman's journey was motivated by stories, namely the retrieval of a manuscript. This twist in the plot reunites all the attributes previously listed—stories past and present, actual and imagined—for Roth's imagined story on found (and later lost) stories is inspired by the actual story of a past writer whose one manuscript is presumably lost: Bruno Schulz (1892–1942). In Sisovsky's quoted tale, his father could easily be substituted by Bruno Schulz, who, in the Polish town of Drohobycz during the first years of occupation, enjoyed the protection of a Gestapo officer who admired his drawings and paintings.[10] Only shortly before his planned escape, Schulz was shot publicly on the street by another officer. In spite of contradictory evidence, it is widely believed that the second officer shot Schulz in revenge for the execution of "his" Jew, who is indeed thought to have been a dentist, as in Sisovsky's account. In contrast to the latter's father, though, Schulz's work had in parts already been published prior to his murder, and, as the fictionalization testifies, has received broad attention. Yet a seed of fact even lies in the idea of the lost manuscript, for in the mid-1980s, rumors were spread that the lost manuscript of Schulz's *The Messiah* had been found in Stockholm. This incident inspired Cynthia Ozick in *The Messiah of Stockholm* (1987) to tell the story of Lars Andemening who believes himself to be the orphaned son of Bruno Schulz and discovers, much to his agitation, possible proof of the manuscript's existence. Interestingly, Lars is aware of his own predilection for impersonation, much in the manner of Rothian characters:

> Who was there to prevent it? He had an orphan's terrifying freedom to choose. He could become whatever he wished; no one could prohibit it, he could choose his own history. He could choose and he could relinquish. He was horribly, horribly free. (*Messiah*, 102)

Similarly Zuckerman, with his status as a fictional character, plays with the possibility that his account might be read as either the "factual" notes of the same fictional character or perhaps a fictitious creation within fiction. When his papers are inspected by a soldier, Zuckerman accordingly comments on the scene with irony:

> He reads over the biographical details—to determine, you see, if I am fiction or fact . . . (*Prague*, 85)

Yet the similarities between the tales of Lars and Zuckerman do not stop with their common taste for self-invention, nor with the parallels in the synopsis and the shadow of Schulz looming over both stories. Ozick even dedicated her *Messiah* to Philip Roth, who, prior to the publication of her variation on Schulz's aftermaths, had presented her with two original drawings by the same author, to show his appreciation of her review of *The Street of Crocodiles*.[11] Consequently, we can speak of a veritable literary dialogue between Ozick and Roth on the works and impact of Bruno Schulz.

Though intriguing on a literary and historical level, the intertextual linkage of Ozick and Roth does not shed more light on the relation between identity and territory, but it does speak of what Edward Said once described as a "generalized condition of homelessness"[12] of the Jewish Diaspora. For Lars Andemening, the imaginary Jew, territorial belonging is of no importance, as he has no clear idea of where he should be rooted at all. He thus seeks home in the lecture of Eastern European writers, hoping to develop a sense of belonging, the elements of his narrative identity. Thereby, he alienates himself from his Swedish colleagues who find his predilection singular, if not strange. Imaginary homelands also play a role in the development of Zuckerman's perception of himself as a Jew, or more precisely of his perception of what should constitute part of the Jewish collective identity. Although he does not see himself as a Jew in the sense of a member of a religious community, he is aware of a distinct Jewish culture which he clearly links to Eastern Europe. During his visit, however, he is not able to develop an affinity with Prague beyond the ancestral ties and the images shaping his idea of a regime hostile to what he holds dear as an artist. Moreover, it unwittingly subverts his relationship to the "other" Jewish homeland, which seems even more fictitious to Zuckerman than the lands of the abandoned *shtetls* of Eastern Europe:

> "The final irony of the book is that having been accused of disregarding the legacy of Jewish history and having accused himself of betraying the bonds of the Jewish family throughout *Zuckerman Bound*, Zuckerman ends by being accused of acting on behalf of the Jewish State and by accusing himself of sentimentally attempting to restore a piece of Jewish family history and to rewrite Jewish literary history."[13]

3. Home, biblical: Israel

Already in the novel following his trip to Prague, Zuckerman travels to the Jewish homeland for which he was accused of acting as a spy: *The Counterlife* (1986) leads Nathan Zuckerman to Israeli lands, where he is forced to question his Jewish identity. Similarly, a narrator-protagonist named after the author himself embarks, in *Operation Shylock* (1993), on a mission to retrieve pieces of his identity as well as images of his supposed homeland. Both novels have as one of their central themes the question of Israel's significance for a secular American Jew, for any Jew who lives outside Israel's borders in the Diaspora. Roth is forced to face the assumption that American Jews increasingly set their identity against the background of Israel which allegedly offers a clearer vision of Jewish life and values,[14] just like assumed or "imaginary" communities tend "to be attached to imagined places."[15]

In order to enhance the identification with Judaism and Israel among young members of the Jewish Diaspora, various organizations, among them "Israel Experience," offer trips for Jewish teenagers to explore the country.[16] As several evaluations from today and back to the 1970s show, these journeys have a significant impact on the young travelers, who, in a majority of cases, develop a positive attitude toward Israel, and express a firmer identification with Jewish religion and culture.[17] Consequently, the goal is to let the journey across the country have an initiatory effect, in other words to let the youths experience an initiation journey. We can see the participants follow a circular travel pattern, following their *regressus ad uterum*: they eventually return to their nominal home countries, yet enriched and altered by their discovery of their ancestral territories, and the unique situation of a Jewish state, be it culturally or politically. Both *The Counterlife* and *Operation Shylock*, however, will offer a narrative that counters these experiences, for they will neither show the travelers to be reinforced in their Jewish identity nor redefine Israel as their point of reference to determine where they belong and who they actually are.

Basel—Judea—Aloft—Gloucestershire—Christendom: space structures *The Counterlife*, as each section of the novel is located in a different region or (in the case of "Aloft": in-between) place indicated in the chapter headings. Rather than simply signaling a change of location, each chapter also announces a new perspective, a variation, or a counter-story, so to speak, of the original setting.[18] "Basel" describes how Nathan Zuckerman's brother Henry, the usually reasonable, conservative dentist and family man, begins an affair with his office assistant. This evokes the images of his past passion for a married Swiss woman from Basel. In order to fully consummate the relationship, Henry even decides to undergo surgery to regain his virility, yet with a lethal end, thus making Nathan his brother's eulogist. From Basel, the birthplace of the Zionist movement, the reader is catapulted to "Judea" and to the fulfillment of Herzl's ambitions, Israel, where the previous story is reset. Henry has survived the surgery and embarks on a convalescence journey to Israel. This lets him undergo a change of mind that is disturbing to his brother and family:

> Until his trip to Israel eight months after the bypass surgery, my brother, Henry, had never shown any interest at all in the country's existence or in its possible meaning for him as a Jewish homeland, and even that visit arose from neither awakening of Jewish consciousness nor out of curiosity about the archaeological traces of Jewish history but strictly as a therapeutic measure. (*Counterlife*, 61)

With his arrival in Israel, however, Henry discovers the Jew in himself and devotes himself to his newly discovered identity, which is solidified by his involvement in a group of fundamentalist Jews and their charismatic leader. For Henry, coming to Israel unexpectedly develops a linear travel pattern, as the country gains for him a mystical dimension and leads him to his roots—a distorted and slightly satirical *regressus ad uterum*: Henry, in other words, becomes a politico-religious initiate, albeit in all too swift a manner. His brother Nathan and narrator, in contrast, eyes this transformation with a mixture of disbelief, skepticism, and mockery. Instead of becoming a religious disciple himself or at least discovering a previously unknown attachment to Israel and Judaism, Nathan Zuckerman has never felt as alienated from his supposed fellow Jews as in Israel, a feeling which becomes palpable at the Wailing Wall:

> I think that I would have felt less detached from seventeen Jews who openly admitted that they were talking to rock than from these seventeen who imagined themselves telexing the Creator directly; had I known for sure it was rock and rock alone that they knew they were addressing, I might even have joined in. (*Counterlife*, 90)

The reality of Israeli life, bluntly commented by Zuckerman's former university friend Shuki Elchanan, strips the narrator bare from any remaining illusions, as he witnesses the way Israelis, especially recent immigrants, struggle to reunite their vision of a homeland with the smoldering conflict with the Palestinian neighbors, and the Arabs in the midst of Israeli society. Differently from the time in Prague, Zuckerman does not develop any interest in at least grasping the territorial reality of the country, but he rather drifts through unreal and shapeless zones, whose surreal quality he does not want to disturb by consulting a demystifying map.

The chapter "Aloft," set on a plane back to London, assumes a transitional position not only physically, but also in content and tone: in a burlesque side-plot, the reader is for once not confronted with yet another variation, yet another counter-story, but is instead meditating on the trip to "Judea" with Zuckerman who sees how the Israeli territories are less shaped by borders or topographic characteristics than by the stories spread and the intentions of its residents and others:

> I hadn't seen anything really of what Israel was, but I had at least begun to get an idea of what it could be made *into* in the minds of a small number of its residents. (*Counterlife*, 160)

This view also resounds in Edward Said's contemplation of Jerusalem, the most contested and coveted territory in the region:

> "Jerusalem, a city, an idea, an entire history, and of course a specifiable geographical locale often typified by a photograph of the Dome of the Rock, the city walls, and the surrounding houses seen from the Mount of Olives; it too is overdetermined when it comes to memory, as well as all sorts of invented histories and traditions, all of them emanating from it, but most of them in conflict with each other. This conflict is intensified by Jerusalem's mythological—as opposed to actual geographical—location, in which landscape, buildings, streets, and the like are overlain and, I would say, even covered entirely with symbolic associations totally obscuring the existential reality of what as a city and real place Jerusalem is."[19]

Space in its purely geometrical and geographical sense is negligible when it becomes a projection screen for divergent visions of the past and future, the screen upon which people project their ideas of collective selves and transcendental identities. The view of the territory itself, of the topography as such, becomes diverted by the contesting visions enforced upon an individual, who will therefore either adopt one of these viewpoints, as Zuckerman's brother Henry did, or try to filter the cacophony of voices, yet remain deaf to their message like Nathan. While Zuckerman can close his minds to the different urges though, he has to realize that, being a Jew, he cannot entirely escape them. Even high above the clouds and on his way back he is haunted by Israeli madness, as he is seated next to an aspiring Jewish suicide bomber.

Traces of this interlude only dimly appear in the chapter "Gloucestershire," which reverses the situation described in "Basel": now it is Nathan who dies after cardiac surgery and Henry is forced to settle his brother's affairs. The episode turns into one of Roth's favored hide-and-seek situations for his readers, since he plays with the indistinct edges of fact and fiction, the omnipresent suspicion that fiction is only dimly concealed fact, and authors confined to their own experience. In this metafictional vein, Henry discovers Nathan's manuscript for the book the reader is holding in his hands, making the reader and the central figure conspirators in the latter's literary games. The reader is, so to speak, witnessing a metalepsis within the book itself. A more serious tone soon has to be adopted as Nathan enters "Christendom," which is a relationship with a British woman, naturally called Maria, and pursues life with her in England. While in New York and Chicago Zuckerman never felt expressly Jewish nor felt the need to justify his roots, England and its people make him oddly aware of his distinct cultural identity. Although Maria scolds him for an exaggerated sensitivity and a tendency to read anti-Semitism—perhaps unwarrantedly—into people's actions and utterances, Zuckerman feels singled out as a Jew, and, for the first time, meditates on the birth rite which marked him permanently as such:

> Circumcision confirms that there is an us, and an us that isn't solely him and me. England's made a Jew of me in only eight weeks, which, on reflection, might be the least painful method. A Jew without Jews, without Judaism, without Zionism, without Jewishness, without a temple or an army or even a pistol, a Jew clearly without a home, just the object itself, like a glass or an apple. (*Counterlife*, 328)

The Counterlife follows a stellar motion, weaving a cobweb, with Zuckerman constantly rewinding and resetting plots, returning to his point of departure and exploring new varieties of his narrative quest for his Jewish identity. Other than the typical stellar movement of a child, however, Zuckerman spins threads between his excursions and lets his different virtual selves interconnect. He is not aimlessly hopping from one location to the other, but rather visits places which bear a symbolic relevance for Jews and are meant to shape his self-understanding as a Jew. He deliberately imagines a scene caught between air and ground, thus held in suspense, and he seeks a supposedly neutral ground to finally realize the inescapability of his Jewishness.

Roth's second literary trip to Israel, in contrast, follows a circular movement leading from American to Israeli lunacy and back to U.S. normalcy, with the narrator's ontological security constantly threatened: in *Operation Shylock*, Roth's homonymous protagonist has to fly to Israel because an impostor is pronouncing his political opinions in "Roth's" name and abuses the author-narrator's name to advocate a vision of "Diasporism": the return of all Jews to the countries they had fled from, to embrace existence in the Diaspora, since Israel would only represent a threat to Jewish integrity and stifle the Jews' creative and intellectual forces. Still weakened by the side-effects of the sedative Halcion, "Philip Roth" initially believes that the figure is unreal or at best a hallucination, but he soon has to accept the "other" Philip Roth as a fact:

> In other words, if it's not Halcion and it's no dream, then it's got to be literature—as though there cannot be a life-without ten thousand times more unimaginable than the life-within. (*Shylock*, 34)

The game between fact and fiction is thus launched:[20] A protagonist bearing the name of his author; a protagonist conducting an interview with Aharon Appelfeld in Israel which the writer Philip Roth had indeed recorded (*Shop*, 18–39); a protagonist who follows the trial of John Demjanjuk in 1988, accused as "Ivan the Terrible" of crimes committed at the Nazi concentration camp Treblinka;[21] a double pronouncing political ideas many readers suspect Philip Roth of; and a final note to the reader at the end of the text, a metatextual means of confusion, which states that the book is a work of fiction, yet "[t]his confession is false" (*Shylock*, 399). Roth is thus moving along the brinks of the written and the unwritten world, whereby he also tackles the question of personal identity: as Maureen Whitebrook explains in detail, it becomes clear how one's identity is also dependent on the perceptions of others, and may even become conditional on recognition by others.[22] This plight is paralleled by the insecure situation of Israel as a nation, whose statehood and identity are likewise contested, not least by the second "Philip Roth" moving through the novel.

These hide-and-seek games at the thresholds to the core text already divert the mind so that the reader shall no longer be able to focus on the true "Roth," who struggles to differentiate himself from his living copy.[23] He at least succeeds in re-baptizing the person parading as himself, whereby he gives his double a name underlying the liminality of the game he is playing—and the doubts as to whether the "other" is indeed not just Roth himself: Moishe Pipik—Moses Bellybutton,

> . . . the little guy who wants to be a big shot, the kid who pisses in his pants, the someone who is a bit ridiculous, a bit funny, a bit childish, the comical shadow alongside whom we had all grown up, that little folkloric fall guy whose surname designated the *thing* that for most children was neither here nor there, neither a part nor an orifice . . . . (*Shylock*, 116)

"Roth" starts losing the grip on his self, although he tries to reverse the game by intruding into the life of his opponent via the latter's companion, tellingly called Jinx Possesski. The plot seems to be jinxed itself, and shows "Roth" increasingly derailed by the presence of his double. Elaine B. Safer points out that the strength of the double may stem from the fact that doubles offer a "projection of a person's own unacceptable desires,"[24] which can lead the "original" to a mental descent when it acts out the latter's (un)conscious desires. Is Pipik speaking "Roth's" mind or is Pipik just a "Rothian" hallucination? In any case, Pipik is a challenge to the narrator's ontological security, which is accentuated by a mortal illness threatening the double:[25]

> "While Philip's sense of self is breaking down, Pipik is in the process of constructing his, and the one he constructs is Philip's. He is the writer's true counterself, the one who not only appropriates the other's identity as his own, but constructs Philip's as well."[26]

In this game of Pipikism versus Rothism,[27] other -isms quickly vanish in the reader's perception and turn into a barely audible background noise, which is eventually suffocated by newly absurd turns in the plot which finally present us "Roth" in the role of a Mossad aide. From the few things the reader manages to comprehend, however, an echo from *The Counterlife* reaches him: Pipik's vision of Diasporism resonates with Shuki's observation that it is in Israel that Jewish abnormality culminates, whereas Jewish culture still manages to prosper in the Diaspora. From their point of view, life in a sovereign state has only disrupted Jewish culture and brought out the worst in its members. To some extent, the voices of Daniel and Jonathan Boyarin resonate. They

> "propose a privileging of Diaspora, a dissociation of ethnicities and political hegemonies as the only social structure that even begins to make possible a maintenance of cultural identity in a world grown thoroughly and inextricably interdependent. . . . Assimilating the lesson of Diaspora, namely that peoples and lands are not naturally and organically connected, could help prevent bloodshed such as that occurring in Eastern Europe today. . . . Diaspora can teach us that it is possible for a people to maintain its distinctive culture, its difference, without controlling land, a fortiori without controlling other people or developing a need to dispossess them of their lands. . . . Yet the renunciation of sovereignty (justified by discourses of autochthony, indigenousness, and territorial self-determination), combined with a fierce tenacity in holding onto cultural identity, might well have something to offer to a world in which these two forces, together, kill thousands daily."[28]

Although Roth/"Roth"/Zuckerman agrees that a Jewish identity can be preserved outside a specifically Jewish territorial context, and even decries the tendency of American Jews to see Israel as a point of reference, he does not present Diasporism as a possible solution, worth being taken seriously. Instead of taking *Operation Shylock* as a chance for a political initiation journey and an opportunity to develop his own vision for Israel, "Roth" only manages to provide us with a burlesque on ideology.

Not even the encounter of Nathan Zuckerman's former friend from student days, George Ziad, motivates him to take a more serious stance. While *The Counterlife* provided the reader with moderate Israeli views as forwarded by Shuki and their extremist antipode represented by Lippman, finally an Arabic voice is granted more room, albeit at subdued volume. Ziad does not continue the exaggeratedly balanced monologue by Shuki; he instead tries to open "Roth's" mind to see things from the Palestinian angle, beyond stereotyped justification for violence:

> "What do you do here, Zee?"
> Smiling at me benignly, he answered, "Hate."
> . . .
> "I am a word-throwing Arab." (*Shylock*, 121)

Ziad is portrayed as an embittered intellectual who does not even shy from accusing Israel of using the Shoa as a blanket for its misdeeds. He sees it as his moral duty and as a form of resistance to keep his family within "the oppressor's natural habitat" (*Shylock*, 120), thus dragging himself and the ones closest to him deeper into the frustrations of the conflict—and leaving him with no illusion as to the possibilities of peace:

> "Woody Allen believes that Jews aren't capable of violence. Woody Allen doesn't believe that he is reading the papers correctly—he just can't believe that Jews break bones. Tell us another one, Woody. The first bone they break in defense – to put it charitably; the second in winning; the third gives them pleasure: and the fourth is already a reflex." (*Shylock*, 155)

Ziad's hatred is the only form of politicization witnessed in the novel that becomes palpable and comprehensible, yet credible, to the reader. The suffering of Ziad, a U.S. educated man who prospered in the environs of his university, sees the barriers maintained not only against himself, but also against the future of his son. Although he keeps in touch with the thoughts and writings of the Jewish "Other" he once valued, he recognizes their self-denial and demands a fair trial, so to speak. Briefly put, Ziad's arrival in Israel indeed constituted a political initiation, for his experiences on allegedly occupied grounds transformed his attitude toward and outlook on politics and life as such forever.

While Demjanjuk has to stand trial for the atrocities he allegedly committed against Jews, atrocities which set the stage for the rise of Israel, and an Israeli military court in Ramallah investigates charges against Palestinians, Pipik and Zee open a trial against Israel on the grounds of its illegitimate actions and the atrocities allegedly committed against its neighbors. The recurring trope of the trial finally lets "Philip Roth" ponder on the one trial in world literature which, in his eyes, banned Jews forever to the stalls of the accused: Shakespeare's *Merchant of Venice* (1596–1598).

> And in the very first line, the opening line of the third scene of the very first act, I came with a shock upon the three words with which Shylock introduced himself onto the world stage nearly four hundred years ago. Yes, for four hundred years now, Jewish people have lived in the shadow of this Shylock. In the modern

> world, the Jew has been perpetually on trial; still *today* the Jew is on trial, in the person of the Israeli—and this modern trial of the Jew, this trial which never ends, begins with the trial of Shylock. (*Shylock*, 274)

Court rooms thus become the dominating space within which individuals and states refigure their identity in *Operation Shylock*. Besides hotel rooms, habitable metaphors of transition, court rooms are the only places to receive a conclusive description, while the topography of Israel and specifically the transitional zones of the occupied territories remain blurry and roughly cut. Again, Israel was not a place of awakening for "Philip Roth." Instead, his journey to the alleged homestead and with this to its past takes a circular shape, leading him back to what is to him truly home.

In both novels, however, Roth lets his protagonists struggle with spurts of guilt for their feelings toward Israel. They approach the country aware that they are expected to feel a special attachment to its lands, and as such "Roth" cannot applaud his double's cocky suggestion of a "Diasporism", nor can Zuckerman chime in with anti-Israel tunes. Their reluctance stems from the omnipresent question of authenticity, the question as to what constitutes an authentic Jew, an authentic Jewish life, and whether such an existence can be thought of outside the borders of a Jewish state.[29] In *Imaginary Jews*, Alain Finkielkraut tackled this problem by ridiculing the distinction between "true" and "false" Jews—"there are no phony Jews, there are only authentic inquisitors."[30] He claims that the Judaism of his generation, the children of the survivors, had been emptied of all substance as their parents simultaneously tried to assimilate and to live in the shadow of the dead,[31] further complicating their children's coming of age:

> "Yet the Jewish child grows up in a state of increasing confusion. . . . Apart from the family, the Jewish community is a fiction that exists only in the rhetoric of its promoters. . . . Growing up for this young Jew means losing his bearings. He who was solemnly ready to choose between faith and rejecting his people confronts the absolute vanity these alternatives imply. Assimilation is not the rite of passage he had come to expect. No odyssey of initiation will take place. There's nothing to boast about, for he's had to do away with any such voyage. Both his point of embarkation and the land of his homecoming – his community's Jewishness, and France as one nation indivisible—have disappeared from the map. If they can be found, it's only as remnants. The heir to a divided world acclimatizes himself slowly to a new social geography."[32]

The only basis for a Jewish collective identity is, according to Finkielkraut, to be found in the idea of "loss and the prescription not to lose."[33] This situation has led to a reversal of past assimilationist strategies, for while in the past one was a member of the crowd in the street and a Jew at home, his generation now took up Jewishness as a public role, yet their private lives bore no traces of Jewishness.[34] As a consequence, Finkielkraut denies Israel the role ascribed to it by essentialists, who regard it as the only country where Jews can lead an "authentic" Jewish life and thus make it the one point of reference for post-Holocaust Jewish identity.

Zuckerman's friend Shuki, while he may not agree with Finkielkraut on the inexistence of "authentic" Jews, does not find in *The Counterlife* the Promised Land of authenticity, as he openly admits to Zuckerman:

> "Yes? You think in the *Diaspora* it's abnormal? Come live here. This is the *homeland* of Jewish abnormality. . . . we are the excitable, ghettoized, jittery little Jews of the Diaspora, and you are the Jews with all the confidence and cultivation that comes of feeling at home where you are." (*Counterlife*, 77–8)
>
> . . .
>
> "This, you understand, was supposed to be the place where to become a normal Jew was the *goal*. Instead we have become the Jewish obsessional prison par excellence! Instead it has become the breeding ground of every brand of madness that Jewish genius can devise!" (*Counterlife*, 81)

Ghetto, prison—Shuki's spatial associations with his homeland are all confinements unable to capture either Zuckerman or "Roth." Although both experience an introduction to the plural realities of Israel, they do not undergo any transformation. Instead they are assured in their belief to have found the one space, the one place to which they belong:

> To be the Jew that I was, I told Shuki's father, which was neither more nor less than the Jew I wished to be, I didn't need to live in a Jewish nation any more than he, from what I understood, felt obliged to pray in a synagogue three times a day. My landscape wasn't the Negev wilderness, or the Galilean hills, or the coastal plain of ancient Philistia; it was industrial, immigrant America—Newark where I'd been raised, Chicago where I'd been educated, and New York where I was living in a basement apartment on a Lower East Side street among poor Ukrainians and Puerto Ricans. My sacred text wasn't the Bible but novels . . . (*Counterlife*, 57)

4. Home, actual: America and spaces within

Home is where journeys begin and where they eventually end, if they do not follow a linear or an erratic pattern; in Roth's case, his protagonists rely on America as home, as their point of reference, and thus see therein the base on which they construct their identities.[35] Instead of leading to a fundamental change, journeys abroad serve rather as a temporary alienation from themselves which culminates in the affirmation of their sense of belonging to the United States. In spite of past currents of anti-Semitism within U.S. society, the country seems to the protagonists to be the one place where they do not have to justify themselves for their background and are free to (re)create their identity according to their own devices, for it is "America, a country that did not have at its center the idea of exclusion" (*Counterlife*, 58).

This does not mean that Roth views America naïvely, blind for stratifications that are entrenched in the country's social geography, but rather that he sees the country as the space where his protagonists can test the performativity of their identity. His characters are aware of divergences that can also be perceived in the characters' geographic location. In this vein, Roth often tackles the dichotomies: city—suburb, East Coast—Midwest; also geographic opposites which traditionally furnish initiation and coming of age stories, such as parents' home—college, or home in a town or suburb—remote shack. At times, these differences are only indicative of the different social strata to which characters belong. For instance, in *Letting Go* (1962) Roth portrays two young Jewish men who are both based in New York, yet the two boroughs Bronx and Brooklyn to which they belong already mark the distance between their experiences: the two neighborhoods become emblematic for different social classes, different approaches to life, and the different conceptions of responsibility and sense.[36] Chicago, or more specifically the campus of the University of Chicago, is where these two representatives meet, on neutral ground so to speak, but also in a setting that is designed and intended to transform personalities. In the case of these two young men the spatial spell fails, as they remain tied to the selves once developed in their home boroughs of New York.

While using city parts as a denominator of social backgrounds might be an obvious and commonplace approach, it is, in my opinion, symptomatic of Roth's much more detailed view of America compared to the descriptions and observations rendered on Europe or Israel. The American landscape gains shape and color, it admits different shadings, depths, and heights, its edifices create microcosms which let us connect more intimately with the protagonists. Be it in the remote shack, the classical symbol of rebirth,[37] or in the depth of the basement, which allows peeks under skirts as views of desire, the spatial intimacy also lets the reader move closer. Moreover, the means by which the protagonists gain their impressions of the American landscape are more diverse than in other cases. While Israel and England are mainly understood through personal encounters, at times also through their history or their literature, albeit with no interest in the physical space of the country, the characters recreate the vastness of the American landscape by different means in their minds. They also do this from an early age, initially by symbols and icons as did Philip Roth himself as a child:

> Just as I first learned the names of the great institutions of higher learning by trafficking in football pools for a neighborhood bookmaker rather than from our high school's college adviser, so my feel for the American landscape came less from what I learned in the classroom about Lewis and Clark than from following the major league clubs on their road trips and reading about the minor leagues in the back pages of The Sporting News. (*Reading*, 221)

Similarly, "Philip" learns in *The Plot* to identify landmarks and symbols of American history with the aid of his stamp collection, which manifests according to Jeffrey Severs the child's "icon-based view of history and citizenship."[38] The loss of his stamps thus also stands for the end of this pastoral view of American politics and history, which is gradually exchanged for a more abstract and sober view of the situation. Accordingly, young Philip is no longer referring to his stamps when he needs to understand a situation, but—at the command of his mother—learns to visualize it by consulting maps. The pictorial displays of the stamps are replaced by the lines, dots, shades, and the flatness of cartography, which helps Philip locate the Jewish families who were forced to move under the Lindbergh government as well as to understand the impact of the political changes under way. His "cartographic maturation," as Severs puts it, furthermore lets Philip realize how personal space actually is: while the individual narrative is practically confined to the Roth family's home and the streets of Weequahic Newark, the radio, cousin Alvin, and even Philip's brother Sanford report from places beyond Philip's imagination. At times, he can relate these tales to some of his stamps and the icons represented thereon, but now, with the map as a point of reference, he also develops a sense of his world's limitations.

Compared to a traveler who draws his own map and thus learns to transmit his experiences,[39] the pre-adolescent Philip learns to understand the geographic implications of historic events for his fellows by registering them on the map. Thereby, he gains a more intimate knowledge of the country's dimensions and learns to think spatially, in the sense of learning to place events and to establish to what extent they can touch him in Newark, and what it would take to influence them from his current position. The map, this web of lines and dots to which we refer when we tread on unknown terrain, thus can also become a means to learn other facets of the place which we regard as home, adding a new perspective to it, as in the case of Philip, a macro view.

In a sense, the map also symbolizes simultaneity in that it forces the individual who stands at a defined spot to picture himself or herself at another place, to take a perspective, a birds-eye view not achievable by other means, or to take a walk, before his or her inner eye, through streets and along paths present on the map, yet so far never actually seen. Therefore, whether a map is consulted indicates not only how well an individual already knows a place, but also to what extent he or she is ready to analyze its surroundings. In this vein, it is noteworthy how Roth's travelers in Israel and Great Britain never consulted a map which would have helped them to gain a more abstract view of things present. Only Prague, the city whose paths had already existed in Zuckerman's mind since childhood and had gained additional shape due to his interest in Eastern European literature, specifically his predilection for Kafka, only this city with which he already felt he had a bond will also be viewed via a map.

The other territories to which Roth's characters travel remain hazy impressions, a convolution of vague ideas and visions, but not with any staying power. In the case of Israel, this invites one to draw on a comparison made by Liisa Malkki, who likened maps to art:

> "Look now instead at the ethnographic and political map of an area of the modern world. It resembles not Kokoschka, but, say, Modigliani. There is very little shading; neat flat surfaces are clearly separated from each other, it is generally plain where one begins and another ends, and there is little if any ambiguity or overlap."[40]

As for Israel the idea that "[o]ne country cannot at the same time be another country"[41] is only applicable with reservations. In fact, Israel resembles more Malkki's view of paintings by Kokoshka with bleeding boundaries, and resists being captured adequately by maps. Its bleary boundaries therefore invite literary games with identity; the territory perceived as insecure and indefinite serves as a testing ground for various creations of the self, which would be less vigorously pursued on home territory, for it would question the ontological security any subject enjoys there. Roth underlines the significance of his home territory when he says that:

> America allows me the greatest possible freedom to practice my vocation. America has the only audience that I can ever imagine taking any sustained pleasure in my fiction. America is the place I know best in the world. It's the *only* place I know in the world. My consciousness and my language were shaped by America. I'm an American writer in ways that a plumber isn't an American plumber or a miner an American miner or a cardiologist an American cardiologist. Rather, what the heart is to the cardiologist, the coal to the miner, the kitchen sink to the plumber, America is to me. (*Reading*, 110)

Yet Roth is aware that America, the territory spurring his creative work, the territory against whose backdrop one has developed an identity, is also bound to change, and the place once intimately known could suddenly turn alien, even inimical. This awareness might, together with his Jewish background, explain why one does not find metaphors in Roth's works which prominently underline the natural connection between a people and a soil, an idea Malkki usually sees captured by botanical, dominantly arborescent images.

Not only displacement or emigration can render oneself homeless, as Zuckerman had to notice in *The Anatomy Lesson*:

> Zuckerman had lost his subject. His health, his hair, and his subject. Just as well he couldn't find a posture for writing. What he'd made his fiction from was gone—his birthplace the burnt-out landscape of a racial war and the people who'd been giants to him dead. The great Jewish struggle was with the Arab states; here it was over, the Jersey side of the Hudson, his West Bank, occupied now by an alien tribe. No new Newark was going to spring up again for Zuckerman, not like the first one: no fathers like those pioneering Jewish fathers bursting with taboos, no sons like their sons boiling with temptations, no loyalties, no ambitions, no rebellions, no capitulations, no clashes quite so convulsive again. (39–40)

In his following appearances, Zuckerman will find a remedy against this feeling of alienation: he travels—to Prague and Israel, where from afar he can call the United States his home again so that, once returned, he can dedicate his writing again to his home territory, as Roth will let him see in the "American Trilogy."

5. Conclusion: Home, at last

> That such things can happen—there's the moral of the stories—that such things happen to me, to him, to her, to you, to us. That is the national anthem of the Jewish homeland. By all rights, when you hear someone there begin telling a story—when you see the Jewish faces mastering anxiety and feigning innocence and registering astonishment at their own fortitude—you ought to stand and put your hand to your heart. (*Prague*, 64)

Home is a feeling—home is a story: in congruence with the opinion of political scientists, Roth's characters demonstrate the importance of a definite home for the creation of a stable identity. Beyond the scientific argument, however, they also show us what role the actual territory of home can play. As the quote suggests, home is, a banal yet often disregarded truth, only an idea, a story we tell ourselves which is different for those who, on the face of it, share the same home. Shared stories can thus evoke the feeling of being at home, even if the actual home is either far away or no longer existent in the form memory preserves. Yet to recognize the importance of "home" for one's identity, we sometimes need to dissociate ourselves from the places we are used to, whereby we can learn to appreciate "home" afresh and actually learn to grasp its significance. The consequences thereof are persuasively visualized in Roth's *Prague Orgy*, but even more so in *The Counterlife* and *Operation Shylock*, which further illustrate the role of illusionary homelands and the inner conflicts they provoke in individuals supposed to feel connected with these territories. Exploring one's relation to different spaces becomes especially important for members of migrant or Diaspora communities, which are literally held in a liminal, in-between situation. In the case of Roth's protagonists, the reader can explore the way in which third generation members of such Diaspora communities may cope with this situation, thus how they deal with the question as to what extent they still perceive their situation as "abnormal," and how what to their ancestors represented a foreign country has become home to them, albeit a home they keep questioning becomes visible.

Roth's protagonists particularly show that the construction of their narrative identity is complicated by the various territorial ties and that these ties render it more difficult for characters such as Zuckerman to become the titular *Zuckerman Unbound*. He finds himself caught in a cobweb of stories that link him to different territories, whether it is due to his ancestry or to a collective claim. Naturally enough, he and "Roth" can only identify with the one country that (at first sight) does not impose a particular identity on him, that gives him space for constant reinvention, free of any religious or historical restrictions. As a consequence, Roth's main characters never truly leave the United States, but always pursue a circular or stellar travel pattern which will lead them back to their point of origin, their home. Only Henry Zuckerman in *The Counterlife* saw himself as a "linear" traveler, whereas Moishe Pipik in *Operation Shylock* erratically crossed borders, creating an incomplete map of his journey, as befits the homeless doppelganger, who has no identity independent from his model. Just like young Philip in *The Plot*, Roth's characters approach these alleged homes with an icon-based view, letting themselves be guided by vague ideas and stories which they have never sought to verify.

Home is a feeling, home is a story—and "home" is the standard of comparison for "elsewhere" and "away." Roth's fictional travel accounts not only demonstrate how journeys can help an individual to fortify his or her "home identity" and gain different insights into "home" by means of comparison, but also show how "elsewhere" is defined in our minds by the stories of others as well as our own.

Part Three

Initiation as Radical Self-Invention

5

Passing and Other Escapes from the Hereditary Predicament

1. Introduction: Identity as a palimpsest

"How can you be Jewish? Chinese people don't do such things."

. . .

"Jewish is American," Mona says. "American means being whatever you want, and I happened to pick being Jewish."

(Gish Jen, *Mona*, 45 and 49)

Mona Chang, the eponymous heroine portrayed by her creator Gish Jen *in the Promised Land* (1996), pursues the idea of self-creation beyond the general meaning associated with the American self-made man and truly assumes the self of her choice: Mona, the Chinese-born Jew. If being American indeed presupposes "an act of self-fashioning and the assumption of a mask,"[1] as Julia Faisst suggests, the label forced upon an American by birth and education can be torn away and be exchanged for any other description he or she prefers to go by. Especially in the case of immigrant or ethnically mixed backgrounds, American identity becomes, with reference to Homi K. Bhaba,[2] the formula to define an individual's "in-between" identity, to construct his or her self-story outside the confines of origins and beginnings. Protagonists like Mona not only thematize the liminality of their identity, being torn between their Chinese roots and the multicultural reality of their new home-country; they moreover ridicule the idea of a fixed ethnic identity, defined by birth and unchallenged by its bearer. Instead, Mona proves her "self" to be just as much a palimpsest as it has been claimed of the Jewish identity,[3] a story to be scratched out, rewritten, and replaced by new plotlines and ideas. She defies the notion of the "hyphenated American," as a "Chinese-American" would have been called at the turn of the twentieth century.[4] Rather, she explores the space in between, gliding along the hyphen, and makes herself a potential candidate for any identity category—with one exception.

Confronted with her daughter's struggle for an identity of her own choice, Mrs. Chang exasperatedly proclaims that Mona might, in a next identity fad, turn into an African-American. At this point, however, Mona stops her short:

"How can I turn black? That's a race, not a religion." (*Mona*, 49)

Mona reduces the "Others" to one dimension: Judaism is only a religion, the term African-American refers only to a race. While the former thus seems accessible to her, the reality of her body precludes her becoming African-American. Mona specifically conveys a general American attitude pursuant to which, while identity boundaries may be blurring in the hybrid everyday play, one Other is definite, namely the African-American.[5] In her case, this binary ethnical divide is upheld, according to which ethnically mixed people are assigned the status of the socially weaker group.[6] Yet both Mona and the society, which devised the described attribution scheme, underestimate the performativity of identity which introduced a novel form of tricksters and their preferred act in society and literature: passing.

"Passing" describes an individual's crossing of those perceived boundaries which delimitate different social or ethnic groups, usually in order to avoid discrimination and therewith social disadvantages.[7] The most prominent example of "passing" individuals, and the one deemed impossible by Mona, is the colored person who passes as white. Passing renders an individual's identity unrecognizable as a palimpsest; the original text is suppressed and, depending on the passer's goals and skills, might be irretrievably lost. Such self-recreation not only challenges society's clear-cut conception of belonging, but also allows the opportunity to witness identity in the making: as external forces and the individual's desires clash and the story of the self visibly evolves, the formative elements of identity are laid bare.

Although Mona herself definitely is an exemplary case of identity-construction, her story is nourished by Philip Roth's works, which not only teach one of Gish Jen's protagonists to pronounce "diaphragm" correctly (*Mona*, 39), but also offer her a first view of the perils of Jewish identity construction in *Goodbye, Columbus* (1959). While "passing" as the most extreme case of voluntary identity creation will be discussed toward the end of this chapter in light of *The Human Stain* (2000), the previous paragraphs are dedicated to less radical steps of self-creation. Before reaching racial redefinition, a subchapter will discuss the socioeconomic aspects of identity and the attempt to cross the boundaries between cultures and ethnicities by rising economically and, as a consequence, affording to blend in physically. The next subchapter takes a step further, and shows the price of assimilation and the forsaking of all religious ties, which is a consequence of the oscillatory nature of identity as such. The crossing of ethno-racial boundaries is then the most extreme movement across the hyphen.

2. Assimilation as transformation: Of noses and kafkaesque nightmares

In *Goodbye, Columbus* the changing situation of American Jews during the 1950s becomes palpable with the encounter between the Newark youth Neil Klugman and a Jewish college girl living in suburbia, Brenda Patimkin. Their summer break lets two distinct economic groups within the Jewish population touch, reconnecting the protagonists with the recent past of their immigrant ancestors. Both adolescents struggle with their role as young Jews in a dominantly Gentile society, yet develop different strategies to cope with it. These strategies also determine their approach to the world and, ultimately, to politics. While Neil seeks a path independently of conventions and conformism, always aware of the attitudes held by his parents' generation, Brenda stands for a group striving to blend into the dominant Gentile society.[8]

Already the Patimkin family's choice of residence conveys the desire to loosen their ties with the Jewish community, and shows how the hyphen with which they have been living is also reflected geographically and economically: affluent as they have become, they flee Newark for the suburbs of Short Hills, crossing the socioeconomic demarcation line between the wealthy and the rest.[9] Simultaneously, their move marks a divide between an emerging group of economically successful Jews and the generation of Neil's Aunt Gladys who is still fretting about waste and the feared emptiness of the refrigerator. In her perception, America's Jews are still part of the less affluent city population, which causes her to doubt the Patimkins' claim to a shared identity:

> "Since when do Jewish people live in Short Hills? They couldn't be real Jews believe me." (*Goodbye*, 49)

The Patimkin's fridge, for Barry Gross a core metaphor for the generational shift from subsistence to affluence,[10] is moved from the city to the suburb where it always stands nicely filled, and its proprietors never scared of it being empty one day—alas: sometimes the Patimkins relapse into their old mode and bemoan how Neil helps himself to their fresh fruit. Such backslides betray their subconscious anxiety that they might, eventually, fall back to their former socioeconomic status.[11] Meanwhile, however, they zealously strive to blend into their new environment, even physically.

When confronted with the idea that she could opt for an African-American identity, Gish Jen's Mona points out the inescapability of her body. Thereby, she not only underestimated the blurriness of ethnic boundaries, she also misjudged the changeability of our physiognomy. Once viewed as an important racial index and abused accordingly in caricature and anti-Semitic propaganda, the nose becomes to the Patimkins what color is to members of other ethnic groups: a visible marker of their difference. As long as a convex nasal bone exposes their face as Semitic, the Patimkins will always stand out as new arrivals to suburbia, as the ones who actually belong to the despised city. Brenda, in the midst of her college years at Radcliffe and thus in a liminal phase of her life, counters this perceived defect with aesthetic surgery. To her, entering adulthood is linked with a physical incorporation into Gentile society, at the expense of being separated from her origins. In more theoretical terms, Brenda's decision can be explained with reference to George H. Mead's concept of symbolic interaction, whereby he explained the development of the self with reference to social processes.[12] To this end, he distinguishes between the "I" and the "me,"[13] the latter being, in Mead's diction, the "censor" of the "I." This restricting relationship stems from the fact that "me" represents a group of attitudes an individual assumes others to have, to which the "I" reacts. In the case of Brenda, it can be deduced that she assumes her environment to take more to her new Gentile appearance—the "me," however, is not a given, and can inspire the "I" to take other steps at a later point in time.

Brenda's strategy of physical transformation is notably mirrored in Jen's *Mona in the Promised Land* by the slightly younger Barbara Gugelstein; in whose case, however, it is still a sign of parental control and not of an initiation or dawning independence. Barbara succumbs to her mother's wish and desire for assimilation, her mother's "me," by having her nose "fixed."[14] Although one can hardly compare plastic surgery to mutilation, both cases are reminiscent of tribal initiatory rites which include mutilation as an act of collective differentiation.[15] In comparison to the masks used in tribal initiation rites Brenda's facial change does not call for human imagination to make the illusion work; it has lost all the ambiguity inherent in a mask.[16] Moreover, while masks often represent ancestors, and at times are even believed to bear an ancestor's spirit, Brenda's "mask" will suppress all ancestral traits.

Wealth and the desire to rise on the social scale both culminate in the nose surgery of these two Jewish adolescents who turn the desire no longer to stick out into—physical—reality. Yet every operation leaves scars: while Barbara feels humiliated by the mere fact that her mother forced her to straighten her nose, Brenda's demonstrative indifference to all references to her transformation leaves Neil constantly nagging her as to whether she needs something else fixed.[17] He thereby betrays his incomprehension at the Patimkins' transformation, which becomes noticeable not only in their new residence or Brenda's new nose, but also in their son studying in Ohio, a Jewish *terra incognita* as Marcus Messner's tale illustrated. Redefining one's identity as if it truly were a blank canvas is, to Neil, a doomed project and impossible to accomplish. Such endeavors reduce people to their surface, Neil seems to conclude when meeting Brenda's future sister-in-law:

> All was surfaces, and she seemed a perfect match for Ron, and too for the Patimkins. (*Goodbye*, 67)

However, the Newark youth misjudges Brenda's attitude to submitting to this transformation process, for in contrast to Barbara Gugelstein she is not only content with the decision for plastic surgery, but she is also ready for her physical integration into the Gentile environment.

This will, however, not remain the last instance for Neil to underestimate Brenda's grip on her own story and the pace of her development: it is he who forces her to acquire an erstwhile symbol of sexual self-determination, a diaphragm; but ultimately he becomes the victim of her newly gained confidence and independence.[18] Quicker than Neil had anticipated Brenda recognizes her sexual power over him and thus is fully aware of the effect it would have on him if they were found out. She thereby manages to turn the object previously perceived as a sign of her submission and humiliation into a symbol of her independence. The way she contrives her mother's discovery of the diaphragm testifies to her talent for stealth and disguise: innocently left at home, at a spot easily reached—on purpose or just a stupid coincidence? In Neil's eyes, Brenda may be far from a person conscious of her heritage and her belonging, but in actuality, Brenda has already developed the role she wants to play, and developed her own identity, which happens not to center on her Jewish origins. She has seized her feminine power and embraced the opportunity to "pass" as a Gentile, which might, at some point, come in handy. Given her relative unpopularity with her parents, she knows that she has to find her own way and, under a veil of naïveté, is ready and able to do so. She has thus solved the dilemma between culture and economic success in favor of the latter.[19]

While Eve Frame, Ira Ringold's wife in *I Married A Communist*, disguises her Jewish heritage simply by a new name and a false identity carried around in, as the name says, a frame, Brenda has pushed the game of hide-and-seek further by changing her appearance. Both women play with the fact that one has only to change the official label, comparable to the genre information added by the publisher of a book as a paratext,[20] in order to alter the way they are approached. Although the following quotation refers to paratexts, those thresholds to a text which also serve as its frame, it simultaneously describes the effect Eve desires to achieve with her telling stage name, and Brenda with her straightened nose:

> "The frame may act as a means of leading the eye into the picture, and the reader into the text, thus presenting itself as the key to a solipsistic world; or it may deliberately lead the eye out, and encourage the reader to concentrate on the context rather than the text. Sometimes indeed the frame defines the text, by appropriateness or complementarity; at others it defines the context like an elaborately carved art nouveau setting to a simple mirror."[21]

A small alteration of their personal para- and metatext, an emancipation from the identity label attached to them by society—and they both redefine the frame which holds the portrait others perceive. They demonstrate on an individual level the power of the right setting, as we know it from the para- and metatextual games Philip Roth loves to play with his readers, or the framing strategies pursued by journalists, politicians, and anyone else trying to convey a certain image to the public.[22] In the same manner as Roth does in his paratexts, Brenda, Eve, and others "passing" try to steer the perception of their counterparts in order to inspire the desired idea in their minds.

Brenda's nose moreover becomes the symbol not only of assimilation, but also of her maturation: with her coming of age, she turns her back on her ancestors. Yet it is questionable whether she can truly escape them. She has willingly reduced the complexity of her identity quest which liberates her for future endeavors—while Neil keeps contending with his heritage and the surrounding struggles he witnesses. "Are you a Negro?" (*Goodbye*, 14) Brenda asked, not devoid of irony, when she first received a call from Neil. She had only caught a glimpse of him at the Country Club where they first met, and thus was in need of a physical description. Dark, dark as many Jews, answered Neil, unaware that for the Patimkins being Jewish no longer bore an ethnic dimension, which reduces the world to black and white.[23] Sander Gilman sees in the Patimkins "versions of Kafka's tales of failed metamorphosis,"[24] spotting their failure in the denial of their roots as well as in their exaggerated efforts at integration, which turns them sometimes into mere parodies of over-adapted Jews. They succeed, however, in economic and social terms, because they still refer to an "Other" that helps them define themselves. As integrated Jews, their "Other" is no longer the Gentile majority, but the African-American minority. Their transformation is thus only a failed one, if one compares it with the true Kafkaesque nightmare Roth has enacted in *The Breast* (1972): Prof Kepesh, turned into a gigantic mammal gland, loses according to Debra Shostak any sense of "me" and "other", which deprives him of any identity.[25]

Neil, however, has so far not reduced society to a binary divide and still places himself in a third category within which he is seeking his place, torn between the Jewishness of his parents and something still undefined. In his part-time job at a public library he will finally be confronted with the binary ethnic reasoning and question the concept as a whole—as it is an African-American boy with whom he develops the strongest bond, but who provokes hostile reactions by the library staff. The encounter with the young boy who asks for the "heart"—art—section of the library becomes the pivotal point in Neil's coming of age,[26] making the shy kid, who gets lost in Gauguin's paintings, his unlikely—and unwitting—mentor. For it is this young representative of the stereotypical U.S. "Other" whose mere presence makes Neil comprehend the "Othering" reflex exerted by the majority of society against African-Americans, whereas he feels a mental rapprochement. Indeed, he detects similarities in the social position formally held by American Jews and African-Americans when he passes the boundaries between the suburbs and the city:

> Now, in fact, the Negroes were making the same migration, following the steps of the Jews, and those who remained in the Third Ward lived the most squalid of lives and dreamed in the fetid mattresses of the piny smell of Georgia nights. . . . Who would come after the Negroes? Who was left? (*Goodbye,* 72)

In contrast to the Patimkins and his own surroundings, Neil recognizes the flexibility of ethnic boundaries, in the sense that they can be reinterpreted as social boundaries. He expects the same upward mobility of Newark's urban African-American population, their turning goy. As a consequence thereof, Neil cannot define himself against a stereotypical "Other," but he is forced to develop his identity against a more complex background than the Patimkins.

How their contrasting maturation process will influence their political attitudes remains obscure in the novella, yet we can already speak of a political initiation: the mental development of Neil and Brenda gains a specifically political dimension in that they both determine with which social group they want to align themselves—they are indeed in the rare position of an actual choice, for they are both brought up in a time of change for the U.S. Jewish community. While Neil's quest remains ongoing, but indicates a decision against the Conservative bliss of suburbia, Brenda adapts to her Gentile environment and desires to submit to her parents' values, as her decision to repent for her diaphragm finally proves. It might be, however, that she will recognize what sacrifices the Patimkins' suburban future demands—as is the case with another Rothian protagonist whom we encounter in the same volume as *Goodbye, Columbus*: "Eli, the Fanatic."

3. Assimilation as disguise: Eli, the believer

In the suburb of Woodenton, Roth lets his readers of "Eli, the Fanatic" (1959) meet a community of assimilated Jews who have left behind the superstitions and allegedly odd ways of the past—a community of Patimkins, so to speak. Little do they suspect that leaving the ghetto has actually turned them into ghettoized, ever self-conscious beings, who constantly dread the loss of their routine.[27] It becomes obvious, however, when their recreated identities are challenged by the presence of an institution reminding them of their "otherness," of their past as the "Others" as opposed to the Gentile suburban population: a yeshiva, a religious school, in the midst of their coveted community.

Eli Peck, spokesman of the community and soon to-be father, is supposed to persuade the director of the yeshiva to abandon the public display of Jewishness, particularly by dressing an elderly resident in secular garments rather than in his black, visibly Orthodox outfit. But in the course of their encounter, it is Eli who is confronted, namely with his roots and his lost identity.[28] While Eli's friends and neighbors see in the Orthodox Jews a reminder of their (as they believe) past difference,[29] he sees in them a reflection of his renounced heritage and, consequently, of himself. Thus, the carefully constructed identity of the secular lawyer Eli, of the integrated, enlightened Jewish member of a suburban haven forcibly starts to crumble. Eli realizes that the strategy of the suburban Jewish community to block out their past ways and to strip themselves bare of anything tied to it left them all living with, and as part of, a fictitious account, which at some point had to be disrupted by reality, reality as laid down in their past. Eli's punishment is a reversal of his own identity narrative, a process running counter to the Patimkins' story.

While Eli's friends egg him on to defend their secular peace, reciting at length how they have left their ancestors' way behind them and have become part of modernity, Eli often falls silent and finds it difficult to join them in complaining. Instead, he seeks the yeshiva's proximity, even gives one of his suits to the old Orthodox Jew whose former garments had disturbed the community. The exchange of clothing leads to Eli's awakening, reminding the reader of the ancestral imagery of tribal masks. But while in these rites the altered appearance shall thematize the initiand's change in social status and projects toward his or her future, it reminds Eli of a lost past: it dawns on the lawyer that he has forsaken his heritage and replaced it with nothing but an inner void. Putting on the Orthodox clothing may help him realize the alienation from his roots, may separate him from his carefully created secular self;[30] yet it eventually only accentuates his loss of a secure, stable identity. This truth becomes inescapable when he wants to greet his son's birth dressed in this foreign, however related way, but is sedated and treated like a mentally ill person by the hospital staff. The judgment of the Woodenton community is exemplified by the medical personnel who, as Thomas Frank argues, assume the role of cultural supervisors, punishing Eli's violation of the norms of social conformity.[31]

Like the Patimkins, Eli tries to narrate his life as the story of a secular, well adapted, assimilated Jew who is perfectly integrated into the suburban Gentile community. Yet he fails to realize that his narrative is that of an annihilated identity, of a denial which ultimately had to lead to a reversal. His encounter with the yeshiva's headmaster and the old Orthodox Jew, who both literally display Eli's European origins, triggers a looming initiation: Eli's masquerade as an Orthodox separated him from the community to which he once belonged. Yet for the lack of an alternative group to join, he is stuck in the limbo of the misunderstood and lost. He thus becomes an example of the limits of our capacity to narrate our identity according to our own terms and wishes, which shines as a warning to the Patimkins—and even more extreme forms of recreated identities.

4. Assimilation as renunciation: Passing the color-line

"How can I turn black?" Mona exclaims: she could see herself crossing religious and cultural lines, just like Eli Peck tried and the Patimkins for the moment accomplished, to cross socioeconomic boundaries—but what W. E. B. DuBois refers to as the "color-line"[32] looks impenetrable to her. African-Americans thus seem to be predestined as the ideal "Others," the one clear point of reference to differentiate oneself as a Jewish Asian, a Jew or an assimilated Jew. Yet this at-first-sight distinct boundary becomes increasingly misty if we already take into account how quickly ethnic distinctions can be redrawn: as mentioned before, while "Jew" first was considered to be an ethnic or racial category, it became reduced to a religious, nowadays even only a cultural, category.[33] Although Mona is unconsciously aware of the ambiguity of the terms "ethnicity" or "race" when she remembers class-mates imitating their African-American counterparts' dress, demeanor, and speech, the category still remains valid in her perception.

As we have seen, Mona is not the only one who upholds the artificial binary black/white in her mind, given that it has for a long time been part of the American perception of racial belonging: pursuant to a hypodescent approach, people of mixed descent were automatically attributed to the minority group in postbellum America, however small the percentage of that heritage.[34] One literary result of this policy appeared in the figure of the "tragic mulatto,"[35] a character of mixed racial background whose in-between identity condemns him to be an outcast in both the white and the black world. An example of this is James Weldon Johnson's *The Autobiography of an Ex-Colored Man* (1912), which captures the fictional coming of age of a biracial young man, who, during the first years of his life, did not even notice his mixed background and considered himself to be white. Finding out about his heritage, and realizing that society would not let him choose on which side of the racial binary he belongs, his whole perception of the world around him is drastically altered. This may give the reader a faint idea how an individual's assumed identity steers his or her thinking:[36]

> And so I have often lived through that hour, that day, that week in which was wrought the miracle of my transition from one world into another; for I did indeed pass into another world. From that time I looked out through other eyes, my thoughts were colored, my words dictated, my actions limited by one dominating, all-pervading idea which constantly increased in force and weight until I finally realized in it a great, tangible fact. (*Autobiography*, 13)

But although the unnamed *Ex-Colored Man* at first seeks to become part of the African-American community, even speaks of an "entrance to the race" and an "initiation into the . . . freemasonry of the race" (46–7), he eventually pursues an exit strategy copied by other inventive and ambitious individuals who are trapped in this twilight situation: "passing," that is crossing the color-line and impersonating a white—a transgressive act, if we accept the binary assumption.[37] Examples of "passing" mulattos or very fair skinned African-Americans are also documented in U.S. legal cases of the first half of the twentieth century,[38] yet the inner struggles of those who pass as whites and African-Americans confronted with passing members of their community become only comprehensible in stories and novels such as the *Ex-Colored Man* or Nella Larsen's *Passing* (1929).

In *Passing*, Larsen confronts Irene Redfield, a light-skinned African-American woman, who nevertheless married an African-American, with her childhood friend Clare Kendry, who uses her own fair complexion to rise socioeconomically through a marriage to a white man, a racist at that. Their encounter lets Irene think about the inventiveness passing entails, how much it requires her friend to create a new self and spin a proper narrative identity:

> The truth was, she was curious. There were things that she wanted to ask Clare Kendry. She wished to find out about this hazardous business of "passing," this breaking away from all that was familiar and friendly to take one's chance in another environment, not entirely strange, perhaps, but certainly not entirely friendly. What, for example, one did about background, how one accounted for oneself. And how one felt when one came into contact with other Negroes. (*Passing*, 24)

Irene stresses in her reflections that passing signifies not only forsaking one's own identity in exchange for a construction, but also leaving behind one's ancestry and thus a collective identity,[39] very similar to Eli's and the Patimkins' secularization and realization of their suburban dreams. Passing thus involves the choice "between group identity and the freedom of individuals to define their own identity,"[40] as Françoise Kral puts it. Yet it is less a negotiation "between the 'given' and the 'chosen,'" as she further suggests, for the "given" is thereby reduced to appearances, whereby it is neglected that the "white identity" can already be part of the given, the individual's heritage. As a consequence, it is more precise to speak of a decision against the inherited, socially constructed identity, which is scratched off and overwritten with a new narrative—evoking again the idea of our identity as a palimpsest. It also reinforces the idea of unavoidable frictions as alluded to in the title of Kral's essay, which are caused by the corrosion between the chosen and the given. Although it cannot be established whether she was inspired by him, the chosen image points toward Ottmar Ette who termed travel literature as "frictional literature," since it constantly oscillates between fiction and fact, eroding the boundaries between these two counterparts.[41]

In this vein, passing individuals blur the contours of their given and their chosen identities, as Roth lets his protagonist test in *The Human Stain* (2000) when he penetrates the color-line and scratches the black color off his skin and his story. The distinguished literary critic Anatole Broyard publicly remained silent about his Creole background, thereby reminding many critics of Coleman Silk,[42] the self-"made" man/protagonist who disturbs Zuckerman's loneliness and quiet in the Berkshires. A former professor of Classics at the neighboring, tellingly named Athena College, he urges Zuckerman to write his story, *Spooks*, in order ultimately to punish the alleged murderers of his wife. As the writing hermit gradually finds out, Silk became the victim of the purifying zest reigning during the summer of 1996, the summer when Bill Clinton's adulterous affairs where dragged to the global light.[43] Silk's own crime consisted in the ill use of a simple word at the beginning of one of his classes:

> "Does anyone know these people? Do they exist or are they spooks?" (*Stain*, 6)

Spooks. Ghosts, specters he meant, but the two absent students were "spooks" in the pejorative sense—African-Americans. Words sometimes also reside on a threshold, are held in liminal suspense, so that their sense can fall to the wrong side. Coleman Silk, the white Jewish professor, is forced to resign, a backlash followed by another personal tragedy, the death of his wife. So now he seeks revenge against those who misjudged his words by instrumentalizing the power of the word and gets his story written down. Zuckerman, however, will write a different story, for he gets to know the most powerful spook in Silk's life: his African-American self.

Nella Larsen's heroines talked of a friend passing as a Jew (*Passing*, 37)—and here we find him again in Coleman Silk. His physical "givens," his light skin, and the circumcised penis, in the U.S. at the time of his birth a marker of the middle class[44] and until today widely practiced for nonreligious reasons,[45] permitted him to choose a new identity, to rewrite his life as a Jew. Initially, however, it was not his own idea to pass, he was instead encouraged to do so by his boxing coach, a reminder of the boxing language used to describe Nathan's coming of age in *I Married A Communist*, who described Silk's complexion as Jewish. The ease with which Coleman Silk manages to pass and the increasing awareness of the toll his heritage takes on his life will animate Silk to finally cross the color-line. Similarly to the *Ex-Colored Man*, he grasps only as an adult the true burden of his ethnicity, when he is, during his college years in the South, insulted as a "nigger." While his race has previously never been an issue for him, he starts viewing it as an undesired and unmerited marker.

After the death of his father he enlists in the army as a Jew, and when he loses his first true love because of her inability to live with African-American in-laws, he cuts all ties to his family: at the eve of his marriage to a Jewish woman, he denies his mother's existence and tells her that, from now on, he shall be orphaned, that she shall never see her grandchildren. In other words, he commits a virtual matricide.[46] Alas, it is not the concealed mother who sees herself as the victim—instead, she declares him a prisoner of his own binary thinking: "You're white as snow and you think like a slave" (*Stain*, 139). His mother unmasks him as a captive of the socially constructed race patterns, unable to define himself independently of the given terms of identity and thus submitting himself to the stereotypical ideal. Thereby, however, she underestimates Silk's desire to define his identity free of social constrictions, especially of any prejudices, so that he does not have to develop a narrative of struggle and can follow a smoother path instead. It is only as a prisoner of Mead's "me," so to speak, that Silk's "I" can act freely. In this vein, Silk's sister Ernestine assumes that for him, passing means to finally become a man (*Stain*, 327), alluding to the idea already heeded by other Rothian characters that manhood is nothing but orphanhood—whereas his brother, Walt, therein sees the contrary, a perpetuation of racial innocence.

To a certain extent, "passing" can indeed be compared to an initiation process, for it not only follows three stages, but also has a similar aim: passing individuals separate themselves from their known community; they then develop their new life story and thus recreate their identity, until they are finally incorporated into a new social group. In this case they become part of another race. Thereby, Julia Faisst suggests,[47] they likewise subvert the existing order. I would relativize this view and liken the attitude of passing individuals toward societal order to the one of initiands in general: they may test its limits, yet they do not undermine it. Passing individuals may inwardly reject the binary approach to race, or the oppression of one ethnicity in general. Their crossing of the color-line, if not detected, upholds the existing order, even reinforces it as they favor the stronger side and employ their strengths accordingly. Coleman Silk would have had the chance to let the line, or seemingly solid wall, crumble a bit, had he taken off his white mask after the "spooks incident." Thereby he would not only have succeeded in ridiculing the perverted results of a misunderstood political correctness, he would even have proved wrong the prejudice of the Jew teaching classics, allegedly the whitest subject. By clutching to his constructed self the elaborate narrative of his identity, he only fell into another racial trap: "Thrown out of a Norfolk whorehouse for being black, thrown out of Athena College for being white" (*Stain*, 16).

Coleman Silk has invested too much in the fiction of his self to succumb, has achieved too much to forsake only one pleasure of his whiteness. Not even the possibility that his offspring might take away his white veil hindered him in continuing his tale, although each pregnancy of his wife made him suffer and fear just as much as Nella Larsen's passing protagonist. With the birth of a colored child, both their secrets would have been exposed—and they could no longer move around as spooks: spooks, because nobody seems to recognize their true nature; spooks, not only because their roots are invisible, but also their remaining unseen aligns them with Ralph Ellison's *Invisible Man* (1952).[48] At the outset, the unnamed *Invisible Man* says, "I am invisible, understand, simply because people refuse to see me" (3). The same feature that lets people ignore the latter remains unseen in Coleman Silk:

> This man constructed along the most convincing emotional lines, the force with a history as a force, this benignly wily, smoothly charming, seeming totality of a manly man nonetheless has a gigantic secret. (*Stain*, 212–3)

Silk can guard his secret until the very last second of his life—but he is punished for it like all the other Rothian figures who created an identity beyond ethnic, religious, or cultural constraints: the Patimkins become a parody of Gentile reality, Eli loses all security of selfhood, the Swede in *American Pastoral* suffers under the self-destruction of his daughter;[49] Silk is left defenseless when he is confronted with the allegation of racism. Roth thus lets an individual's roots appear as a predicament, and all attempts to escape will be punished—radical self-recreation comes at a dear prize.

Due to his recreation, Silk to a certain extent lost his ability to view behind people's façade as he reduced his own biography to the superficial. Neither does he comprehend the double meaning of the fatal word "spooks," nor does he recognize that his young lover Faunia Farley only pretends to be illiterate while his hostile former colleague Delphine Roux is fighting against the overpowering image of her mother. Paradoxically, he scorns political correctness, constantly aiming at the destruction of the virtuous appearance—while, simultaneously, he cannot allow his actual surface to receive any cracks. For the same reason, his passing had to entail a de-initiation from anything political, since such an involvement might attack surfaces he trusted to shield him. Moreover, his constructed identity would not have permitted him to define a clear standpoint: his ideas would have lacked the fundamental of a stable identity.

The intricacy of Coleman Silk's self-narration is mirrored in the way Zuckerman relates the story to his readers: on the one hand, Nathan Zuckerman illustrates the pitfalls, the doubts, and the manifold lies and fictions a passing individual such as Coleman Silk has to avoid, face, and develop. On the other hand, Zuckerman confronts the reader with a cobweb of perceived and imagined identities that are impossible to disentangle. The space he leaves for Silk's monologues, in which he introduces himself as the Jewish Professor, the façade he wants the reader to be content with, is paralleled by the narrative of Silk's hidden self, as retold by his sister Ernestine. Her account is the basis for Zuckerman to weave the story of passing into Silk's official narrative identity, without letting the reader learn to what extent Zuckerman's own imagination provided the missing pieces to the puzzle. The cobweb is thus a suitable metaphor, for it reflects the artistic not only in Silks self-narration, but also in Zuckerman's account. At the same time, it also accentuates the fragility of such stories, which in the end are only as hindering as cobwebs in the attic where one stores memories.

5. Conclusion: Assimilation and identity-creation revoked

The interest of the three texts for literary studies is quickly detected, whereas the political scientist is rather confined to the role of the listener. Yet both disciplines gain from a joint reading: all of the stories contain elements of an initiation, *Goodbye, Columbus* being the most typical case, as it captures indeed the protagonist's coming of age. They are, however, special in that they do not simply describe transitions between different statuses in their characters' lives, but focalize on transitions into a different social group. The different motifs and symbols used in each of the texts—the dichotomy between suburbs and cities, or the omnipresent image of the fridge, the role of clothing, the boxing world as a metaphor for life's battles, or again the color white—underline the dimensions in which these transitions are considered: socioeconomic, religious, or racial. Thus they become a valuable document of a society allegedly open to self-invention, but which still struggles with hybrid identities, turning the identity choices taken by the protagonists into political acts.

Yet all three stories would not be captured by research in political socialization as it is. The shell of the protagonists—white, suburban, Jewish—would be taken into consideration, thus leaving out the determining process of their development: the creation of their new identity, the weaving of their narrative political identity. Certain political convictions and desires already shine through in the reasons for changing signs, for choosing assimilation as self-annihilation. In the cases of our suburban group, we recognize the opportunistic upward-moving conservatives, who, paradoxically, change the existing order by entering a group which previously excluded them, but at the same time become this order's fiercest protectors. While Eli's neighbors want to spare their Gentile environment the view of a yeshiva, the Patimkins even transform themselves physically so as not to disturb the visual appearance of their neighborhood and to fit in smoothly. Passing, in contrast, can be interpreted as a political act in itself, as the passing individual thereby claims rights and freedoms to which any citizen should be entitled. An individual's disregard for the traditional ethnic order and the person's allotted position in that order amount to a silent protest against the system.

With *The Human Stain*, the intricacy of Coleman Silk's self-creation is already mirrored in the narrative strategies used by Zuckerman. His usage of proleptic and analeptic jumps, the missing revelation that all details had been covered by Silk's sister Ernestine, transports the reader to a metalevel and let him ponder the frictionality of everyday stories. Silk takes his ambiguous appearance, which permits people to identify him as a member of different ethnic groups, and gives it a determinate interpretation by developing the matching story. Like all "passing" individuals, he is in a liminal situation *par excellence*: if he withholds the definite label white/black, society will not be able to put him in the correct category, which leaves him on the racial threshold. He has, however, chosen to step onto one side, and thus to develop the story of Silk, the Jew. In contrast, Eli and the Patimkins have to fashion themselves to actualize their transformation: they already have their ideal self-story outlined, but now need to adapt to it. The Patimkins successfully do so by moving to a wealthy suburb, assuming a lifestyle in accordance with their neighborhood or changing their appearance, whereas Eli is initially settled in his life's story, and now starts questioning it. The Orthodox garments offer him the opportunity to test an alternative self, they mark the beginning of a liminal, transitory phase in his life that might decide what self—the assimilated or the observant—Eli definitely wants to assume in light of his fatherhood.

While Eli has lost any coherence in his self-narration and thus in his narrative political identity, Silk and the Patimkins exemplify how individuals attempt to guarantee a fitting tale which covers their self in its entirety.

6

The Religious Void, or Terrorist Art: Fanaticism as a Quest for Identity

1. Introduction

> I am an American, Chicago born . . .
>
> Saul Bellow, *The Adventures of Augie March* (1949), 3

> My name is Karim Amir, and I am an Englishman born and bred, almost. I am often considered to be a funny kind of Englishman, a new breed as it were, having emerged from two old histories. But I don't care – Englishman I am (though not proud of it), from the South London suburbs and going somewhere. Perhaps it is the odd mixture of continents and blood, of here and there, of belonging and not, that makes me restless and easily bored.
>
> Hanif Kureishi, *The Buddha of Suburbia* (1990), 3

"An Englishman . . . almost." While Roth (*Reading*, 104) sees his own attitude mirrored in Bellow's assertive declaration which leaves no room for hyphenated identities, Hanif Kureishi's opening of his début novel *The Buddha of Suburbia* (1990) already captures the problem of his protagonists. They are born second generation in Britain, originating from the Indian subcontinent, in Karim's case even of mixed background, and Muslim by denomination. They move through a country seen by their fathers as a land of opportunity, but by themselves as an in-between space in that it provides them only with an in-between identity, a sense of half belonging, half being separated from their coeval purely British peers. Although Kureishi's protagonists eventually succeed in embracing their hybrid identities and explore the limits of the hyphen squeezed between their national allegiance, their struggles reveal the challenges of multicultural identity, for the individual as well as for the society as a whole. For, in light of political turmoil, one is tempted to ask how much it takes for a hybrid to turn out to be a chimera.

According to Greek mythology, Chimera, the daughter of Typhon and Echidna, was a fire-breathing monster who possessed the body of a lioness, the head of a goat, and a tail ending in a snake's head:[1] a foolish fantasy of a creature, as her name literally suggests. A parody of such a creature Nathan Zuckerman discovered in his brother Henry who, during his trip to Israel in *The Counterlife* (1986), dropped the hyphen and the word behind it, turning from a Jewish-American into a Jew "*as deep as those Jews*"

(*Counterlife*, 65; emphasis in the original).[2] The hyphen was replaced by religion, yet mixed with political motives. At times indistinguishably interlinked, interwoven and mixed, political extremism, understood as behavior strongly controlled by ideology and beyond the influence of other potentially mitigating forces,[3] and fundamentalism, in its most narrow sense the belief in the inerrancy of scriptures[4]—these are the catchwords to describe Henry Zuckerman's attitude. Both –isms become, however, hardly distinguishable from each other. Fundamentalist reasoning often gains shades of fanaticism, or a "misplaced simplicity":[5] just like political extremists who will not allow any arguments formulated outside their ideological spheres of thought, fanatics only perceive the world through one particular lens, for instance a religious one, independent of the categories better suited to the nature of a problem.

Thus shaped, fundamentalism and political extremism become the fire ignited by modern chimeras, as they are depicted in the media. While the dangers represented by them are well described and feared, political science still lacks an explanation for the reasons behind their transformation. Although researchers in political psychology have tried to make out the roots of political extremism, of terrorism in particular, they are far from a consensus.[6] Writers have likewise ventured into the field, often in the wake of actual events, yet, interestingly, they mainly render comprehensible why true understanding is hard to establish. Roth's Israel novels are therein paired with exemplary writings by John Updike's *Terrorist* (2006) and by Hanif Kureishi's *Black Album* (1995). This group of novels is brutally contrasted by yet another Roth novel, *American Pastoral* (1997), and the—in a sense—even more radical *Leviathan* (1992) by Paul Auster. The latter two abandon attempts at explanation and thereby promise a truly different angle on the issue.

2. Apprentice fanatics in limbo

The further back in time one looks, the more diffused the image becomes: such conventional wisdom does not hold in the case of fundamentalist initiations as they are described by John Updike, Hanif Kureishi, and Philip Roth. With *Terrorist*, John Updike depicts a post-9/11 world, whose transformation he witnessed himself and whose fears and internal struggles he tries to capture relatively soon after the actual event. While he offers a picture of his youthful protagonist's introduction to fundamentalist circles, which is clear in its coloring and rather too sure of its accuracy, Hanif Kureishi's *Black Album* is more nuanced and has already gained appropriate distance from the actual events serving as its background, namely the Muslim protests in Great Britain against the distribution of Salman Rushdie's *Satanic Verses* (1988). Philip Roth's two Israel novels, *The Counterlife* and *Operation Shylock*, are yet again of a different nature in that they tell of a timeless political radicalism or fundamentalism whose force does not show itself in a culmination of events, but is rather a monotonous background noise in the Israeli landscape. All three authors, however, share common explanatory and narrative patterns, which also move them close to the few settled opinions in political psychology on extremism—and all three seem to tell tales of development and initiation. In the following sections, these stories will be summarized, in order to pinpoint in a second stage how they are illustrative of the current findings of political psychology. It will then be shown, however, that they are even more illustrative case studies of terrorist biographies as they are shared by the media and of the actual incomprehension of the terrorist phenomenon.

Religious voids: Initiations to spiritual/violent spheres

Ahmad in post-9/11 New Jersey; Shahid in the London of the late 1980s; and Henry Zuckerman in the Judea unbound by time: three encounters with fundamentalism, all three less likely than they might appear at first glance. The likeliest case of a potential terrorist certainly is Ahmad Ashmad Mallowy, the titular disciple *Terrorist* created by John Updike. As the name already suggests, Ahmad is of mixed background, with his absent father coming originally from Egypt and his mother of Irish descent. While she makes no attempt to introduce her son to any religion, the father's belief interests Ahmad already at an early age, so that his mosque and the Imam teaching him become his second home. Ahmad indeed discovers religion at an age when most children content themselves to oblige their parents' religious desires, yet not more, as High School counselor Jack Levy observes in his first conversation with Ahmad:

> Levy pursues it: "How old were you when you . . . when you found your faith?"
> "Age eleven, sir."
> "Funny – that's the age when I announced I was giving up the violin. . . ."
> . . . Ahmad's clasped hand is so limp and damp Jack is startled: still a shy kid, not yet a man. (*Terrorist*, 40)

This brief passage already encapsulates the essence of Ahmad's calling, for we learn that his presumably firm belief is probably only a support during a time when the young long for guidance. The lack of assertiveness in his handshake conveys to Levy how unsettled Ahmad's position in life remains, and that he has not yet reached the secure stage of an initiate. Indeed, he is still in the midst of his initiation process, facing a transition which is marked by frequent sessions with his Imam. With every teaching Ahmad absorbs, he further loses touch with the world of his peers at school and with his mother, whose free spiritedness only meets with Ahmad's disapproval. To follow his religious mentor, Ahmad even forsakes worldly teachings and does not apply for college, but rather starts practicing and studying for a truck driver's license in order to work for a Lebanese shopkeeper and his son. In the latter, Ahmad finds a brotherly figure who initially succeeds in dispelling any doubts, but then reveals his own double morality by arranging his mentee's sexual initiation.

Ahmad's coming of age, his emancipation from his mother, and his growing involvement with fundamentalist circles are paralleled by High School counselor Jack Levy's "midlife crisis narrative":[7] both characters, observed by an extradiegetic narrator who finds easier access to Levy's mind, have reached a turning point in their lives, which eventually connects them. As Levy starts an extramarital affair with Ahmad's mother, he becomes aware of the danger looming for the adolescent and it is he who prevents Ahmad's attempt to commit a suicidal attack on a highway tunnel. The way toward the tunnel and the abrupt halt before its entrance is thus rather straightforward, although it remains unclear to the reader how an individual can at one point be determined to die for a cause, and then abandon it without much ado.

In contrast, Hanif Kureishi's protagonists follow less straight paths, but, paradoxically, the less clear their direction the more comprehensible their struggles appear to the reader. Kureishi's protagonists are similar to Updike's Ahmad in that they live as Muslims in a predominantly Christian society, and two of them encounter fundamentalist movements. But Kureishi provides us with two distinct perspectives on an individual's immersion in such groups, as he covers both the external and the internal views, which simultaneously show a generational cleavage:[8] in his film script "My Son the Fanatic" (1997), based on a short story of the same title, the focal person is the father, the person exterior to the fundamentalist movement, while in *The Black Album* (1995) the extradiegetic narrator concentrates on the thoughts and actions of Shahid, a young man getting involved with a fundamentalist group.

Parvez, father to the title-giving "Fanatic" Farid (or Ali in the short story), observes how his son gets rid of belongings that he had once treasured. This leads the father to suspect him of needing money to purchase drugs. He is, however, scarcely relieved when he finds out that his son is not desperately hoarding cash for drugs, but instead gives his ungodly clothing away without anything in return and devotes himself to his five daily prayers. It is incomprehensible to Parvez that his secularly raised son should feverishly turn to religion and long for the father's home country Pakistan, on which Farid has never set foot. Parvez, in contrast, resembles the elder Lebanese shopkeeper in Updike's *Terrorist*, in that he embraces the values of Great Britain and proclaims that his son might one day enjoy the benefits of the British middle class to which he himself will never belong.[9] Although Parvez has to suffer in the same way from racism and other demeaning attacks as his son does, he mainly perceives the advantages of his British life and indulges in the freedoms it offers to him. As a consequence, Parvez is unable to enter a constructive dialogue with his son and merely tries to force his worldview on him. This is doomed to failure as he loses any claim to authority in the eyes of his son: disgusted by his father's alcohol abuse and his friendly relationship with a prostitute, Farid can only meet his father's attacks with spite and his own resistance. In his mother Farid finds an ally, for she has not become accustomed to Great Britain as her husband did, nor can she find fault in her son's hosting a *maulvi*, a Sunni scholar, who incites Muslim youths to attack prostitutes and drug-addicts. Consequently, in the climactic scene of the plot, she sides with her son Farid.

The "other" side of the story, the son's tale so to speak, is found in an earlier work by Hanif Kureishi, his novel *The Black Album*, which is set in London at the end of the 1980s. The central figure, Shahid, could be viewed as an unwitting counterpart to Karim, the protagonist and narrator of *The Buddha of Suburbia* quoted in the introduction, for they both embody hybridity, and initially have to play with it before they feel comfortable in their skin. Karim, bearing the nickname "Creamy" due to his fair complexion, literally learns to play with his background as an actor who has to exaggerate, virtually reconstruct his background by once covering himself in a brownish cream to play the part of Mowgli with a heavy Bengali accent,[10] and finally even utilizes a migrant friend's struggles as an inspiration for another role. Shahid's games with hybridity and identity, on the other hand, are less obvious, for he recounts his story at the outset as an initiatory tale, contributing the necessary ingredients of a separation from his home, a mentor, a new community, and, eventually, a calling, though the wrong one from his later mentor's perspective: having moved to London for his studies, Shahid is quickly drawn to Riaz, his charismatic neighbor at the students' residence. Riaz not only introduces him to the local Muslim community, but also seems to awaken the believer in the freshman, albeit a doubting one—a process which unfolds with a surprising swiftness, demanding only a few pages for its development.

At the same time as his introduction to Riaz's realm, Shahid develops an attachment of a quite different nature, namely an affair with his lecturer Deedee Osgood. Thus, we witness Shahid struggling in the triangle of sex, religion, and art, as he is once transcribing Riaz's religious poetry and attending the exhibition of an eggplant allegedly depicting the Prophet, while only hours earlier or later he experiments with drugs and sex—and his gender identity: the title *Black Album* not only stands in opposition to the *White Album* recorded by The Beatles,[11] the essence of British pop culture, but also quotes the homonymous album by Prince whom Deedee calls "half black and half white, half man, half woman, half size, feminine but macho too." (*Album*, 25). This paratextual reference is a play on Shahid's ethnic background, and it also indicates the limits of sexual identity and how they can be dissolved, for instance when Shahid cross-dresses to Deedee's delight and enjoys the domination of his older and more experienced companion.

What seems at first a paradoxical situation, the taboo-breaking relationship paralleled by meetings with Riaz's group and visits to the mosque, can be read as Shahid's transitional phase: he is experimenting with two possible stories of his self, two potential narrative identities, a circumstance that forces him to follow two different plot lines. Having left his familiar environs, Shahid is stumbling through London in search for his calling, as Bradley Buchanan confirms,[12] masquerading in the different identities proposed to him: once from the liberal university lecturer, another time by his fundamentalist friends, ever attempting to escape his family's plans. By exploring and testing various modes of being, he also has to listen to different narratives of the world and of British society in particular, through which he learns that he is not capable of trusting one narrative alone as his religious friends would demand of him.[13] Thus he cannot join in the burning of an allegedly offensive novel, which remains untitled but reminds the reader of the height of the so-called Rushdie affair in 1989.[14] The latter was marked by the publication of Salman Rushdie's novel *The Satanic Verses* in 1988, which was followed by Iran's Ayatollah Rhuollah Khomeini pronouncing a fatwa on the grounds of blasphemy or apostasy.[15] Kureishi does not cite the incident by name, yet the scenario is undoubtedly an allusion to the events in Great Britain during that period—artistically exaggerated, however, for like the narrator who could not truly believe in a decent boy turning to terrorism, the reader struggles to visualize a mob of Muslim students beleaguering the apartment of Deedee, a lecturer.

In the case of Updike's Ahmad, the reader is surprised how little persuasion the young man needed to abandon his fundamentalist path. In the case of Shahid, one wonders why he could become interested in fundamentalism in the first place, yet one also sees how it can offer a second home even to a free spirit like him. The difficulty to grasp an individual mind's radicalization becomes even more palpable in Philip Roth's Israel novels, which, in contrast to Kureishi's and Updike's stories, were not written in the wake of a major event. Nathan Zuckerman gets to know Israel in *The Counterlife* as the territory of his brother Henry's spiritual rebirth; as the territory of fundamentalist and ultranationalist Mordecai Lippman and his entourage; as the country of reasonable but rare voices like Shuki's; in a nutshell and in Shuki's words, Zuckerman sees the "*homeland* of Jewish abnormality" (*Counterlife*, 77). In a similar vein, in *Operation Shylock* "Philip Roth" travels through a country that turns his erstwhile friend from university days, George "Zee" Ziad, into an ardent opponent of Israeli statehood; through a country his doppelganger wants to see abandoned by Jews in order to embrace life in the Diaspora again; and in his doppelganger's words, "Roth" moves through a country which is "the greatest threat to Jewish survival since the end of World War Two" (*Shylock*, 34).

"All the madness of the human race is in the sanctification of that book[,]" thus Zuckerman's friend and guide through Israeli madness, Shuki, disqualifies the Bible. Yet Zuckerman's brother, who in the section of *The Counterlife* entitled "Judea" and thus in the second possible version of both their destinies discovers his religious self,[16] seems less steered by the Torah than by an obscure sense of belonging:

> "And that's when I began to realize that of all that I am, I am nothing, I have never been *anything*, the way that I am this Jew. I didn't know this, had no idea of it, all of my life I was swimming against it – then sitting and listening to those kids outside that cheder window, suddenly it *belonged* to me. Everything else was superficial, everything else *was* burned away. . . . I am not *just* a Jew, I'm not *also* a Jew – *I'm a Jew as deep as those Jews.* Everything else is nothing. And it's that, *that*, that all these months has been staring me right in the face. The fact that that is the root of my life." (*Counterlife*, 65)

But why? Or to join in Nathan's exclamation: "Henry, when are you going to stop being an apprentice fanatic and start practicing dentistry again?" (*Counterlife*, 142). Yet I would have exchanged the verb "being" for "playing" or "impersonating," for an impersonation of an apprentice fanatic is all Henry delivers. His alleged initiation story does not provide the depth and the insight to make his transformation believable, nor can his mechanical repetition of fundamental platitudes convince us of his arrival in the midst of Lippman's circle. Both Lippman and his disciples move in front of our eyes like satirical interpretations of themselves. Not even the feared Arab "Other" gains shape so as to render its threatening potential credible, since Roth reduces the visible Arabs to harmless restaurant owners,[17] as Andrew Furman convincingly argues, whereas the opponents referred to by Lippman remain spooks.

Among believers: Manichean worlds and charismatic leaders

Rational choice, social learning, frustration-aggression hypothesis, relative deprivation theory, oppression theory, national cultural theory, identity theories, narcissism, paranoia, cognitive theory, novelty-seeking, humiliation-revenge, theories of group process: Jeff Victoroff has compiled an extensive list of theoretical approaches to terrorism, and frameworks to explain the terrorist's personality, many of which he rejects due to the lack of valid proof. Yet he could make out four characteristic traits which a majority of researchers have identified as specific to terrorists: firstly, a "high affective valence regarding an ideological issue" which is, secondly, accentuated by a personal stake; thirdly, a low tolerance for ambiguity; and, lastly, a "capacity to suppress both instinctive and learned moral constraints against harming innocents."[18] The tales of Ahmad, Shahid, and Henry Zuckerman serve, in a cursory manner, as an instructive illustration of these findings, in that they particularly point out how a lack of one of those traits can easily cause a person's retreat from extremist circles.

To begin with, Ahmad, Shahid, and Henry are exemplary in their apparent normalcy: in rejection of identity theory, scholars agree that terrorists show no signs of psychopathy.[19] That means that terrorists cannot be demarcated from non-terrorists on the grounds of innate personality traits or socialization history, as Arie W. Kruglanski and Shira Fishman explain; in other words, terrorism is not a syndrome, but a tool.[20] The focus of the question has thus to shift from the terrorist's personality to the circumstances that motivate a person to become a terrorist, ultimately to become a tool. A first clue is to be found in the cause they serve, the ideology or religion which offers a stable frame of reference. Stability, though, may be represented as simplicity, which invites overgeneralization, dichotomous thinking, and, eventually, a tunnel vision of the world.[21] This is the case not only with Ahmad or Shahid's fellow disciples, who can no longer judge the world other than through an Islamist lens, but also with Henry Zuckerman, who has likewise turned to a guide who conveniently divides the world into black and white. Yet Henry's suddenly discovered faith is not grounded on a textual source. Instead, his only reference is the leader of a notorious radical Orthodox community, a fact which pinpoints two other factors widely believed to be constitutive for terrorism: a group and a (manipulative) leader.

In the course of a personality's development, as Robins and Post explain, it is common that elements of national identity are incorporated into a person's identity, thus solidifying a feeling of national belonging.[22] It is likewise normal to develop negative feelings toward the "Other" or to project inner conflicts onto external objects. However, it becomes problematic when a person with an insecure personal identity seeks the protection of a possibly paranoid group, and develops a sense of unity between his or her selfhood and the group, practically eradicating his or her own needs and feelings. Any threats against the group are then perceived as a sign of the "Other's" badness, for the individual identifies himself or herself and thus his or her group as good.[23] Fundamentalist groups indeed lure individuals with their promise of ontological security,[24] as the reader can see in the cases under scrutiny: Henry no longer fears that something sets him apart from society, but feels suddenly whole as part of a Jewish community, and even alters his name to highlight his changed loyalty; Ahmad desperately seeks to be initiated into a group, which would offer him a purpose worth pursuing, while his mother's tolerance and relative indifference provide him with no ideological or religious frame of reference. While some might remember their adolescence as a struggle for the "I," to be viewed as an individual and no longer an extension of their parents, Ahmad strives for a "we". He no longer wants to think of himself as a singularized pronoun, rather he aspires to rewrite his story as a synecdoche, a part standing for a larger entity,[25] rendering his story exemplary for the Muslim community.

Shahid first follows the same direction, but then reverses his decision and again strives for individuality. However, his decision against the group is not a condemnation of Islam as such. Moreover, violence is not the means propagated by the Muslim community in which he becomes involved. Even the fundamentalist inner circle held together by Riaz first enters the scene as the defender of community members against racist attacks. Violence is thus not portrayed as a constituent characteristic of Islam, but rather, the community serves as a protection against it. The group not only provides Shahid with a space where he does not have to justify his presence, it moreover shields him against external abuse. Still he is not willing to stifle his creative side for this security. As a consequence, he abandons the communitarian plotline and seeks to further develop the narrative of Shahid, the writer, a Shahid who embraces his hybrid reality and continues to experiment with his cultural backgrounds and other "givens."

It is doubtful whether Shahid would ever have been forced to choose between an "I" and a "we," had he not come across his charismatic room neighbor, Riaz, who served as the moral and tactical center of the group. In the same vein, it is Mordechai Lippman who wins Henry's dedication; it is the Imam who inspires in Ahmad the wish to sacrifice his life. In light of these examples, it is not surprising that Jerrold M. Post underlines the role of the terrorist group leaders themselves. Post compares these characters to "malevolent group therapist[s]"[26] who can direct the group members' discontent toward a third party as they

> "provide[] a 'sense-making' explanation for what has gone wrong in their lives, identifying the external enemy as the cause, as well as drawing together into a collective identity otherwise disparate individuals who may be discontented and aggrieved, but who, without the powerful presence of the leader, will remain isolated and individually aggrieved."[27]

Lippman, for instance, is not so much motivated by the religiously founded claim to Israel, but instead advocates a Machiavellian view of the relationship between the country and its neighbors.[28] He propagates violence against the "Other," the enemy beyond the disputed border and beyond the settlements; he distills a sense of paranoia and decries the secularization of American Jews such as Nathan, and all this in a manner letting Nathan Zuckerman, the writer, feel like a rhetorical dilettante. A strong orator, a charismatic leader with an already established fellowship, a man with a message and a mission—hence, an ideal mentor and group leader, he fulfills the criteria stipulated by Post.

It is qualities such as these which give terrorist group leaders the persuasive power to motivate young men such as Ahmad to make the ultimate sacrifice, to become a suicide bomber. Motivated by the illusion of gaining status as a martyr, to perpetuate their life beyond death and to give it meaning,[29] they are willing to become tools in the strictest sense—if other circumstances are likewise conducive to taking this ultimate step. As we have seen in the case of Ahmad, he was not adamant in his decision and could thus easily be convinced to refrain from his plan. Like Shahid, he had not yet reached the point where he could close his mind to ambiguity and develop a tunnel vision that would shield his view from considerations hostile to his allegedly religious mission. Their introduction to terrorist circles thus illustrates not only the plausibility of the hypotheses made by political psychology; they also show a point of return, the conditions under which an individual can be persuaded to back out of this vicious circle: a mind still open to counter-arguments and a world to return to.

Who is the fanatic now?—Through the distorting mirror

Illustrate, depict, demonstrate, show: as the verbs used convey, the novels and the screenplay have so far been discussed only as mere case studies to serve as confirmation of the findings in political psychology. However realistic fictional portrayals of terrorism may be, though, their value goes beyond the solely illustrative, as psychologists Alice LoCicero and Samuel J. Sinclair argue. From their point of view, fictional accounts of terrorism are particularly interesting as the basis of general discussions, since, in contrast to actual terrorist attacks, they do not instill people with allegedly justified fear and thus permit a discussion detached from immediate desires for survival.[30] I would slightly alter this argument by suggesting that the works under scrutiny specifically invite readers to reflect the ways they tend to think of the terrorist as "the Other" and as a stereotyped Other at that. Both Kureishi and Updike, the latter probably without intention, reveal how the occidental reader is the one to adapt a tunnel vision and shield his perception from any information contradicting firm beliefs.

"My Son the Fanatic" climaxes when Parvez no longer has the force to confront his son verbally, and instead attacks him physically. Farid counters his father's violent outburst by asking sardonically, "You call me fanatic, dirty man, but who is the fanatic now?" ("Fanatic," 146) Farid's utterance heightens the reader's as well as the viewer's awareness of how much he or she was drawn into Parvez' perspective: from the father's point of view, all the reader witnessed was a youth's seemingly sudden conversion to Islam and an equally quick readiness to use violent means in defense of his faith and the values he associates with it. Such little information hardly helps the readers construct a compelling initiation story. It rather lets them question the father's approach to the problematic situation, for in all his clichéd Western tolerance he fails to even once ask his son about his motives.[31] Kureishi's "My Son the Fanatic" thus also suits the pattern of stories which depict the helpless parent confronted with this allegedly errant offspring. In contrast to Updike, Kureishi's story is more compelling in that the form of a film script and drama makes the father's incomprehension more palpable, and sharpens the recipient's mind for the biased perspective offered. With the last word spoken by Farid, it becomes clear that we are lacking the other side of the story, that the stereotypical elements of the setting were perceived in that way due to their particular presentation. The reader may not learn anything about Farid's initiation to fundamentalism, if that be the true nature of his belief, yet he or she becomes once more alert to the way prejudices are constructed and his or her ways of thinking (mis)led by narrative techniques, in this case the focus on the father and the scant room left for Farid's views.

In contrast, *The Black Album*, which has been criticized as a moralistic novel[32] and which earned Kureishi a reputation of being a denigrator of his community,[33] cannot be accused of delivering a stereotyped and simplified view of Islam as the rather roughly cut image provided in "My Son the Fanatic."[34] Indeed Shahid's account teaches the reader how a modern youth such as he can be drawn to religion, for he shows us in the mosque a hybrid community, involving members of various nations and ethnicities, which defies the view of a united block.[35]

Quite the opposite can be said of Updike's depiction of Ahmad's world, which gives the reader the core ingredients of what he or she might take as a typical coming of age story of a future terrorist: a youth experiencing a sense of loss and lacking fatherly guidance, as well as a clear sense of belonging; a religious community filling that void yet at the expense of freedom, in that it alienates him from his environs and constrains him in his job choices; a substitute brother who does not only guide him through the world of manly responsibilities, but also arranges his sexual initiation; truck driving lessons which remind us of the plane flying lessons taken by a group of Muslim terrorists prior to 9/11; and the stereotypical Imam preaching hatred. As predicted by the textbook, the Muslim community aids Ahmad to build a self which rests on a group identity vilifying outsiders.[36] He even adopts a stereotypical language which resembles more a "cartoon-like mock-martyr language,"[37] or, quoting *New York Times* critic Michiko Kakutani's even harsher verdict:

> ". . . Ahmad talks not like a teenager who was born and grew up in New Jersey but like an Islamic terrorist in a bad action-adventure movie, or someone who has been brainwashed and programmed to spout jihadist clichés. Much of the time he sounds like someone who has learned English as a second language."[38]

The stereotypical Muslim extremist in the making is mirrored by the kind-hearted, yet easily misled High School counselor Jack Levy who, in his degree of quasi-fatherly concern for Ahmad, resembles the idolized teacher figures in coming of age movies set against the backdrop of High School or College life such as *Dead Poets Society* (1989), directed by Peter Weir. Levy is the one who recognizes in the quoted passage Ahmad's inner weakness and insecurity, which will give him the certainty that he can prevent the catastrophe from taking place. For, of course, an initiation novel like *Terrorist* demands a climactic initiation ritual which, to stick with the clichés, amounts in Ahmad's case to a suicide bombing: as suspected, his truck driving skills were not intended solely to serve the Lebanese business, but are destined to fulfill a higher purpose.

Yet why was it so easy for Levy to dissuade Ahmad from his plan? It seems especially unlikely in light of our knowledge that Ahmad believes with the conviction of the textbook-like convert for he

> feels his pride of isolation and willed identity to be threatened by the masses of ordinary, hard-pressed men and plain, practical women who are enrolled in Islam as a lazy matter of ethnic identity. (*Terrorist*, 174)

Why, then, should his adulterous Jewish High School counselor be in any position to bring Ahmad around? Because Ahmad is not the fundamentalist his stanzas sell him for. From a certain angle, Ahmad is unripe in his religious ardency:

> "There is no political-theological commitment, little thought, no great wish to damage the Great Satan, America, no dedication to Osama bin Laden, only a pliancy that belongs to the truly naïve. He knows the Koranic suras that attack unbelievers as deserving of death of course verbatim, and mouths the proposition that blowing up the Lincoln tunnel would be a triumph for Islam. But not a fundamentalist."[39]

Yet Levy's heroic intervention not only results from Ahmad's insecurity and readiness to be guided in another direction, it likewise gives a familiar sounding case study of fundamentalist violence a fairy tale-like twist, which might be due to its being set in the midst of U.S. society. An American raised boy to turn fundamentalist and violent? Updike conveys his incredulity already in the way he lets Ahmad talk, thus setting him apart from his environs and, so to speak, normalcy. The author thereby fails to tell us an insightful story of fundamentalist initiation, but he succeeds in pulling up a mirror in front of his readers' eyes, as one could argue with slight deviation from Mita Banerjee's standpoint:[40] Ahmad's story affirms common prejudices, yet lets them parade in an unwittingly comic manner that exposes the embarrassing simplicity of some folk explanations of the terrorist mind. The stereotyped "Other" first appears in the shape which has gained overbearing presence in the public imagination, but its failure to gain credibility and thus convince the reader unveils the shortcomings of the idea. As a consequence, the depiction of Ahmad and his environs unfold an instructive effect, as it forces the reader to seek further for a convincing argument.

In my eyes, Ahmad's portrayal suggests that Updike could not overcome the incredulity he already felt when he followed the tumbling of the World Trade Center on television:

> "It seemed, at that first glance, more curious than horrendous: smoke speckled with bits of paper curled into the cloudless sky, and strange inky rivulets ran down the giant structure's vertically corrugated surface. . . . As we watched the second tower burst into ballooning flame (an intervening building had hidden the approach of the second airplane), there persisted the notion that, as on television, this was not quite real; it could be fixed; the technocracy the towers symbolized would find a way to put out the fire and reverse the damage."[41]

It is with the same amazement that he follows his own protagonist's development into an apprentice terrorist—yet he is not alone with his incredulity. Kureishi may offer a more nuanced view of the Muslim community as such, but he can likewise not decipher the mechanisms that lure Shahid and Farid into fundamentalist groups. In this way they resemble Nathan Zuckerman, who expresses his lack of understanding for fanaticism and does not even attempt to understand the changes in his brother. Political psychology may offer explanations, some of which we find reflected in the works discussed, but the key to all the questions raised is yet to be found.

3. Rebels without a cause or the art of terror

Roth's accounts have been forced to the background in the preceding considerations, as his protagonists' positions on fanaticism, political, or religious, only culminated in incomprehension. Although some of his observations could indeed illustrate findings in political psychology and serve the purpose suggested by LoCicero and Sinclair, his main answer to terrorism's "why" remains a silence. Years after the Israel novels, however, Roth provided, with *American Pastoral* (1997), attempts at an answer which no longer fit into the categories of political psychology, yet are therefore all the more intriguing. In stuttering Meredith Levov, raised in an all too secular, prosperous household in which Americana is coveted like nowhere else, he presents the unlikeliest bomber, who can only be topped by Benjamin Sachs, the writer turned bomber created by Paul Auster in *Leviathan* (1992). Both authors offer an answer transcending the reasoning of political science, and might thus help us move on: terrorism becomes an act of art and self-creation.

Merry, Audrey, and the bomb

While Nathan Zuckerman in *The Counterlife* deals with the constant reinvention and recreation of identities, lives, and alternative selves, in short with everything held in limbo, in *American Pastoral* (1997) Roth lets him meet his former High School hero who is too sure of what he is, what he wants to be, and for what he stands: Seymour "the Swede" Levov embodies not only a Jewish High School boy's dream identity, but he also lives the clichéd all American dream by physically standing out, becoming a High School sports legend, and ending up marrying Miss New Jersey, who raises cattle and complements her successful husband and entrepreneur. The Swede seems to top the assimilatory dreams pursued by the Patimkins and Eli Peck, and even decades after their High School years Nathan Zuckerman sees the same self-assured man who, in spite of a divergent announcement, has no shadow episodes to disclose. He appears to be the same goyish Jew—a smooth surface, repelling all attempts to scratch it and reach for the raw underneath, as Zuckerman exasperatedly observes:

> The Jewishness that he wore so lightly as one of the tall, blond athletic winners must have spoken to us too – in our idolizing the Swede and his unconscious

> oneness with America, I suppose there was a tinge of shame and self-rejection. Conflicting Jewish desires awakened by the sight of him were simultaneously becalmed by him; the contradiction in Jews who want to fit in and want to stand out, who insist they are different and insist they are no different, resolved itself in the triumphant spectacle of this Swede who was actually only another of our neighborhood Seymours whose forebears had been Solomons and Sauls and who would themselves beget Stephens who would in turn beget Shawns. Where was the Jew in him? . . .Where was the irrationality in him? (*Pastoral*, 20)

Yet another acquaintance from his High School years, this time at a class reunion, reveals to Zuckerman that the man he dismissed as "the embodiment of nothing" (*Pastoral*, 39) indeed got to know suffering—and even lost the conviction and assuredness of a definite identity. The Swede's younger brother and erstwhile friend of Zuckerman, Jerry, exposes the actual narrative of a disrupted paradise which the all American dreamer tries to cloth anew, the story of a literal bomb that exploded in the midst of his pastoral and tore away all illusionary dreams:[42] the bomb laid by his own daughter during the years of the Vietnam war, his daughter Meredith.

> "Meredith Levov. Seymour's daughter. The 'Rimrock Bomber' was Seymour's daughter. The high school kid who blew up the post office and killed the doctor. The kid who stopped the war in Vietnam by blowing up somebody out mailing a letter at five A.M. . . . Seymour was into quaint Americana. But the kid wasn't." (*Pastoral*, 68)

The smooth surface cracks and lays bare the shambles of what should have been a life turned into a fairy tale, but which instead ended in an endless nightmare. Based on the few pieces to the puzzle that the Swede constitutes for Zuckerman and that the younger Levov brother shares with him, Roth's author-protagonist tries to assemble the whole picture lying behind the façade with which he was supposed to be contented. This is simultaneously an attempt to grasp the mystery of the man he looked up to and believed as a teenager and saw through as an adult, and to understand the dynamics behind the actions of the Swede's daughter who refused to fit into her parents' pastoral vision of life.

Meredith Levov moves into the center of the novel, actually into the "anarchic center of the novel,"[43] when Zuckerman imagines how she, in her early teens, starts pulling at the staging of her parents' private arcadia. Even before reaching puberty, "Merry," as her parents with unwitting irony call the constantly angered girl, disturbs the peace of the perfect home by a slight malfunction, her seemingly incurable stutter. She further smudges the shining surface of the life of the erstwhile sports hero and his cattle raising Miss New Jersey by unscrupulously stuffing herself with fast food, thus setting her audibly and visibly apart from her parents. Merry cannot accept boundaries, neither to her appetite nor to her anger[44]—disproving the Swede's starry-eyed vision of her on the swings in front of their home, the swings Ottmar Ette reads as a picture of adolescence as the time of testing limits and shifting between the innocence of childhood and the freedom of adulthood:[45]

> In the fall—just as he had always planned it—he'd be sure to get home from work before the sun went down, and there she would be—just as he had planned it—swinging high up over the fallen leaves encircling the maple by the front door, their largest tree, from which he'd first suspended that swing for her when she was only two. Up she would swing, nearly into the leaves of the branches that spread just beyond the panes of their bedroom windows . . . and, though to him those precious moments at the end of each day had symbolized the realization of his every hope, to her they had meant not a goddamn thing. She turned out to love the trees no more than Dawn had loved the house. (*Pastoral*, 326)

Merry could not leave her view focused on her home; she had to look beyond the confinements of Old Rimrock, her hometown:

> What *she* worried about was Algeria. *She* loved Algeria. The kid in that swing, the kid in that tree. (*Pastoral*, 326)

The swings Merry was forced to sit on by her parents could not lift her to the heights she intended to reach, wherefore she never even tried to test the ambit of the swings—from the very beginning, she tried to tear the constitutive ropes apart. Her coming of age coincides with the war against the Vietcong, letting her grow up with pictures in her mind of monks setting themselves on fire. The indifference conveyed by her parents and the sense of powerlessness effused by her grandfather's protest letters to the President further alienate her from her upbringing. Much in the manner of any rebellious adolescent, she claims her growing independence by leaving her parents in the dark as to her whereabouts during her frequent visits to New York City. Every "Conversation #X about New York" resembles more the kind of interrogations all parents swore never to submit their child to, since they want to show him or her the trust their own parents were never able to give them, yet they end up with unwittingly doing so. With every "conversation" the Swede loses his daughter more, understands her less, increasingly feels deprived of the certitude on which he had started building his aspirations of a life as Seymour "Appleseed"—until the conversations stop and the bomb finally explodes.

Meredith "Merry" Levov becomes a "Weathergirl" and places an explosive in the local post office of Old Rimrock, and thus she disappears from the Levov home, yet keeps her parents locked in her presence. Her stutter and her obesity had already presented a constant questioning of everything the Swede longed for and believed in, but the bomb finally destroyed the story of his self, leaving a narrative void impenetrable for Zuckerman and others trying to dig beneath the surface. The dynamite not only blew up the post office, but also no longer permitted the Swede's innocent view:

> And then the loss of the daughter, the fourth American generation, a daughter on the run who was to have been the perfected image of himself as he had been the perfected image of his father, and his father the perfected image of his father's

> father . . . the angry, rebarbative spitting-out daughter with no interest whatever in being the next successful Levov, flushing him out of hiding as if he were a fugitive—initiating the Swede into the displacement of another America entirely, the daughter and the decade blasting to smithereens his particular form of utopian thinking, the America infiltrating the Swede's castle and there infecting everyone. The daughter who transports him out of the longed-for American pastoral and into everything that is its antithesis and its enemy, into the fury, the violence, and the desperation of the counterpastoral—into the indigenous American berserk. (*Pastoral*, 85–6)

What would have potentially been the inferno announcing the Swede's awakening, remains, however, only the starting point of an extensive search, with the abandoned and betrayed father longing to know what really led his daughter to plant the bomb. In this vein, his daughter's crime does not induce his own initiation to crude reality. Rather, it lets his mind repeatedly race around possible initiatory instances that might have led to Merry's fall. Interestingly, he indeed does not seriously reflect on her upbringing or her environs as possible sources, but focuses on single moments, potential turning points. The kiss he pressed on her mouth when she begged to be kissed like "umumumother" (*Pastoral*, 89). The Buddhist monks, "these gentle p-p-people" (*Pastoral*, 154), she watched going up in flames. Yet all his ruminations on *the* event, the one event leading her to place the dynamite, lock the Swede in mental impasses and impede his serious consideration of the ideas his daughter had actually embraced.

The Swede's attempts to find the key event opening the door to Merry's madness are futile, and his appraisals of his daughter's political world appear ridiculous, as Ross Posnock argues:[46] he never truly evaluates socialist thinking; instead, he loses himself in sentimental broodings and engages in imagined conversations with Angela Davis, a Black Panther activist. Even an invitation for an all too literal *regressus ad uterum*, an initiation journey to the metaphoric maternal womb,[47] does not tempt him to probe things further. Granted, the opened labia of Rita Cohen's, alleged companion of Merry, vulva are a ridiculously visual motif for the Swede's reluctance to fathom anything deeper. Yet their exposure is not coincidental: "The aim? Sure. To introduce you to reality. That's the aim[,]" (*Pastoral*, 143) Cohen answers matter-of-factly when the Swede mumbles why he should sleep with or touch the messenger of his lost daughter intimately. The untouched private parts of the figure from the underground remain a witness, though a ludicrously expressive one, to Levov's reluctance to face truth.

To be able to grasp the true reasons for Merry's violent descent, the Swede would have had to face himself, which would not simply have disrupted his life's narrative, but erased it and proved it to be nothing more than a tale of passing. It is Jerry, the Swede's younger brother, who already at the beginning of the novel points to the roots of Merry's anger when he describes his brother and his wife Dawn as a

> "[k]nockout couple. The two of them all smiles on their outward trip into the USA. She's post-Catholic, he's post-Jewish, together they're going to go out there to Old Rimrock to raise little post-toasties." (*Pastoral*, 73)

Post-everything: her father's choice to raise her in a cultural void, deprived of any roots, in contrast to Eli Peck or the Patimkins, with not even a notion left of where she might belong, lets Merry seek feverishly for directions from an early age.[48] She, the clandestinely baptized daughter of a Jew, first turns into an ardent Catholic who adorns her room with all the religious kitsch available, before turning into an equally observant and fervent admirer, imitator, and worshipper of Audrey Hepburn, the—ironically—anorectic movie icon. The counterselves with which Nathan Zuckerman loves to experiment and play are for Merry the expression of an ungrounded self: whereas Zuckerman breaks taboos, tries to run counter to his heritage and reinvent his life in order to return to the core of his self which he maintains throughout his transformations, Merry has nothing to cling to except the façade her parents erected, which cannot support the slightest shake. No narrative of a self and an "us" in contrast to "Others" was related to her. Instead, her parents only preached independence in the creation of the self and, at the same time, total conformity, submission to the shiny surface: no ancestral and cultural strings attached which might reduce the swings' ambit, yet the dominant rules of the Gentile U.S. society are to be observed. This *prima facie* indifference lets the Levovs remain bystanders to Merry's zealous devotion to changing subjects, until she finally undergoes her transformation to "Ho Chi Levov" (*Pastoral*, 100). The same "perfectionist fanaticism", as Kinzel coined it,[49] which led Merry to place the literal bomb, had already guided her through her childhood identities as a devout Catholic and a Hepburn aficionada. Therefore, it would have thus been detectable as a characteristic trait. Yet the latter counter-identities did not run counter to the post-post order of things; instead, they were accepted as stages in Merry's coming of age and not interpreted as the struggles of a girl deprived of any referential identity.

Ironically, Merry's quest for a self ends by forsaking all selfhood:[50] at their re-encounter five years after her disappearance, the Swede finds his daughter having turned to Jainism, a religion which forbids her to hurt any organism, and, as the ultimate consequence, renounce all her needs, including her identity. After idolizing the immaculateness of the Virgin Mary and the harmless romantic characters impersonated by Audrey Hepburn, Merry believes to have found the way to innocence and purity in Jainism, echoing the Swede's eternal aspiration. Yet her father sees in her striving only another form of descent and of her fading humanity, as he sees proven when he takes in her odor:

> But what he smelled now, while pulling open her mouth, was a human being and not a building, a mad human being who grubs about for pleasure in its own shit. Her foulness had reached him. She is disgusting. His daughter is a human mess stinking of human waste. Her smell is the smell of everything organic breaking down. It is the smell of no coherence. It is the smell of all she's become. She could do it, and she did do it and this reverence for life is the final obscenity. (*Pastoral*, 265)

The Swede rejects his daughter, while indeed her smell betrays her continuing humanity,[51] and thus the possibility to reach out for her and pull her out of the mess she constitutes. Merry thus reaches none of her ambitions: neither can she develop a stable sense of selfhood, nor does she achieve the total dissolution of her humanity. Her call for an initiation into any realm remains unheeded and her identity lost in limbo. The story of an initiation into political extremism only thinly veils the underlying dominant narrative of a quest for selfhood which followed any referential frame available, political or religious, whatever promised certitude and stability instead of her parents' relativism.

As a consequence, it is only mildly surprising that Merry the Marxist leaves only the impression of a "cartoon insurrectionist" or a "cartoon of adolescent rebellion,"[52] just like Ahmad sounds like a mock-jihadist, for she clings to ideas with the same vehemence as the over-assimilated suburban Jews in Roth's earliest fiction strive to blend in with the rest. Merry cannot undergo a credible transformation as long as she lacks an original canvas to cover with a new painting, and instead has to fight a vacuum. Yet the lack of logic in her turning to violence is also due to the narrator, who is portraying her development and who has created the Swede, the man trying to make sense of his daughter's dramatic change: although Nathan Zuckerman tricks the reader into following Merry's story as if it matched the "facts," he is indeed only building his account on the basis of a few words exchanged with Jerry Levov. He makes his readers aware of this toward the end of the novel when he relates two alternative ends to a garden party at the Swede's, one bringing Merry back to the Old Rimrock scenery and the other reminding us of Zuckerman's burlesque predilections.

In this light, it becomes evident that the Swede as written by Zuckerman could never be able to comprehend what led Merry to resort to terrorism, just like Merry, as written by Zuckerman, could not become a credible terrorist: the narrator of *American Pastoral* already proved in *The Counterlife* how alien to him is any personal transformation that is not grounded in an aesthetic or artistic motivation, and how alien are varieties of fanaticism which focus on ideas, religious or political, rather than art. Instead of exploring the dynamics behind Merry's sudden willingness to plant a bomb, the mechanisms of ideological persuasiveness, Zuckerman/Roth merely wants to explain the violent eruption as part of a project of ceaseless self-invention. The political thus becomes a marginal issue in Zuckerman's account, whereas the inability to comprehend moves into focus, highlighted by the ridiculous twists in the story. While such an endeavor might compel Zuckerman to write, it cannot, however, satisfactorily account for the readiness of a Middle Class teenager to throw bombs.

Sachs, Sophie, and the phantom of liberty

Merry Levov finds her equal in Paul Auster's *Leviathan* (1992), in which the writer Peter Aaron, probably modeled on Paul Auster himself,[53] tries to comprehend how a friend of his could plant bombs. Again an artist tries to understand a presumably political act, and again he will not be able to understand the reasons which drive an individual to terrorist means. In this approach free of theoretical background, however, Peter Aaron will present a new view of terrorism that is not on the map of political psychology. This distinctly artistic view, born out of the same incomprehension,[54] is also conveyed by Art

Spiegelman in his post-9/11 comic *In the Shadow of No Towers* (2004), when he lets a figure comment on the destruction of the Twin Towers: "If not for all the tragedy and death, I could think of the attack as some sort of radical architectural criticism" (2). The likening of 9/11 to art was pushed even further by the modernist composer Karlheinz Stockhausen who called the event "the greatest work of art of all time,"[55] thus provoking a public outrage. The idea of terrorist acts as a performance, a spectacle created for a specific audience that had to obey a certain dramaturgy to impress, is, however, only a side-aspect here. Aaron/Auster rather shows how a terrorist act can in fact be viewed as a work of art, even as an artistic act of self-creation.

In the course of the novel, Peter Aaron's narrative gains similarity with Nathan Zuckerman's as he can only weave a straight storyline from those threads of which he has actually been part. In contrast with Zuckerman, however, Peter Aaron constantly reminds the reader that his story is only the truth as he imagines it, that he may err in every point, and that all things related to him might have been lies. According to Aliki Varvogli, it is Peter Aaron's consciousness of his tale's constructed nature which links it to the title, *Leviathan*: those who expect an allegory on Thomas Hobbes's treatise of *Leviathan* (1651) will be disappointed to discover that the writer-protagonist purportedly chose the title only as a homage to his friend's last literary project, a second novel to be titled thus. As no reference is made to the manuscript's content, it is impossible to see a bridge between the story, the biblical monster in the Book of Job and the Hobbesian world. Yet Varvogli points out how Hobbes's introduction delivers a powerful metaphor to Auster/Aaron:

> "In his introduction, he writes: 'For by Art is created that great LEVIATHAN called a COMMON-WEALTH, or STATE, (in latine CIVITAS), which is but an Artificiall Man.' Auster borrows Hobbes's main conceit, the image of the artificial man, a construct which has parts corresponding to nature but which is 'of greater a stature and strength,' but he uses it not so much for its political implications as for the way in which it can be seen as a metaphor for the act of writing, and what that writing reflects of people's lives. Writing thus becomes an attempt to find a pattern, to put together the fragments. The novel is an artificial body whose parts correspond metaphorically to real life . . ."[56]

In this manner, Peter Aaron tries to decipher the pattern of his friend's, fellow writer Benjamin Sachs's, actions: after an unlucky accident and a long struggle to shake off his lethargy, Sachs retreats to his wife's and his own house in Vermont, reminding us of Thoreau's and Zuckerman's hermitage, to work on his second novel, *Leviathan*. After months of feverish work, however, he suddenly disappears from the scene and Aaron meets him only once more by sheer chance. This last encounter provides Aaron with the information needed to make sense of what the FBI men calling at his home relate to him. He learns that a person had been impersonating him and signing books on his behalf, the person being the same one who became notorious as "the Phantom of Liberty": for blowing up replicas of the Statue of Liberty across the country. In light of his final conversation with his friend, Aaron realizes that Sachs must have been the

Phantom of Liberty, the Phantom that now blew itself up. Before the FBI will figure out the link between Sachs and the Phantom, Aaron sits down to write the story of his friend—to the extent he knows it, to the extent he can make it out.

Very much in the manner of Swede Levov in Zuckerman's imagination; Aaron tries to find the turning point in Sachs's life which led him astray. The actual incident paving Sachs's way to terrorism was the tragic encounter with a man who was parked on a forlorn Vermont forest road and who shot the young man driving Sachs home. Sachs kills the man in self-defense, yet finds a fortune among his belongings and decides to trace him. Due to a coincidental connection Sachs indeed finds his victim's family, even becomes part of it, until he gets to know the man better through his writings—and decides to leave again and become the Phantom of Liberty, presumably to implement the dead man's plans. Yet what Sachs himself describes as the turning point does not satisfy Aaron, who seeks the explanation in the symbol Sachs attacks. The Statue of Liberty is probably *the* American icon and the one symbol which springs to any person's mind when he or she thinks about America. Sachs's attack against the replicas, however, is in Aaron's reading not an assault against the American idea or the idea of liberty, but rather a personal revenge, an attempt to liberate himself of the childhood memory he associates with the Statue. As Aaron learned during a meal with Sachs's family, an outing with his mother to the Statue ended with his recognition of parental vulnerability. The idea that her son might fall while climbing up to the top of the Statue's torch alone frightened Sachs's mother to an inexplicable degree:

> "It was my first lesson in political theory," Sachs said, turning his eyes away from his mother to look at Fanny and me. "I learned that freedom can be dangerous. If you don't watch out, it can kill you." (*Leviathan*, 35)

While the fall from the staircases within the Statue was only a fearful imagination of Mrs. Sachs, her son would later in life indeed fall, yet not within or from the Statue, but from the fire escape of a private apartment, notably during a party celebrating the Statue's one hundredth anniversary. And this fall will become, in Aaron's interpretation, the turning point in Sachs's life, the point where his life gets unhooked:

> His entire life flew apart in midair, and from that moment until his death four years later, he never put it back together again. (*Leviathan*, 107)

It is up to Peter Aaron to piece Sachs's story together, and he interprets the Statue of Liberty as the key symbol to understand the bombings, a highly political symbol for a seemingly arbitrary and apolitical act, or one for which the bomber delivers no other explanation than an ambiguous calling and project. The fragmentary nature of Sachs's identity and of the story itself becomes accentuated by the imagery evoked by the explosions, which pull things apart and leave everything in shreds and fragments. Explosions also let the reader's vision move back to Sachs's beginnings, which already show how the fragmentary nature leaves space for stories unverified, such as his allegation to have been "the original bomb child" (*Leviathan*, 23), the first child to be born after the explosion of the atomic bomb in Hiroshima. Whether this story was only "innocent mythologizing on his part[,]" (ibid.) the vivid imagination of one great "for turning facts into metaphors" (ibid.), remains hidden from the reader and Peter Aaron alike. However, it also opens the reader's eyes to the artistic in Sachs's bombings: the seemingly haphazard, the well-planned coincidence of his bombings, the ridiculous, yet disturbing target, and the silence on any motive betray more the hand of an artist, rather than a war-mongering terrorist who intends to spread fear. What other effect could a bombing series have which was planned by a man who studies another one's life, scolding his own hiding behind a typewriter, but in the next instance thinks to write something about the active part (*Leviathan*, 225)?

The artistic nature of Sachs's deed is accentuated by the presence and particular role of a character based on the French artist Sophie Calle, whose oeuvre encompasses installations, photography, and conceptual art.[57] "The author extends special thanks to Sophie Calle for permission to mingle fact with fiction[,]" reads the opening page of certain editions of *Leviathan*—"The author extends special thanks to Paul Auster for permission to mingle fiction with fact," reads the first page of Sophie Calle's *Double Game* (2007). In the latter, Calle reveals to what extent the artist Maria Turner, an artist friend of Aaron and later intimate friend of Sachs, is based on herself, or rather what projects described by Aaron have indeed been Calle's creations. One of the characteristics of Calle's works is the dissolution of fact and fiction, for she often creates new stories out of snapshots of life: be it by letting a detective shadow her and by assembling his photographs and reports, be it by reconstructing the image of a person by following all the notes in his lost address book, Calle dissolves the boundary between fact and fiction, thus she always dances on the threshold. Paul Auster's ideas for "further" projects for Maria Turner, projects not based on Calle's portfolio, presented an invitation to the existing artist to intensify the game of fact and fiction, and put Maria's projects into action. Another player in Maria's schemes was Benjamin Sachs, who must have found her method related to his own work as a writer, for Aaron's description could likewise be applied to literary endeavors, such as his own attempt to recapture the motives and movements of Sachs:

> When he handed in his report at the end of the week and she studied the photographs of herself and read the exhaustive chronologies of her movements, she felt as if she had become a stranger, as if she had been turned into an imaginary being. . . . Again she took photographs; again she invented life stories for them based on the evidence that was available to her. (*Leviathan*, 63)

Sachs's pursuit of his victim's alleged plans or mission thus resembles an artistic project à la Calle rather than a political act. Thereby, he can also feel in charge again, in charge of his life's story, for as the creator of such an inclusive art project he also becomes the creator of his self as part of this act. In a sense, Roth's Merry is a lot closer to Sachs than to the previously discussed apprentice terrorists, for her major aim can be seen as being to create a distinct identity, to establish who she really is. Her acts of self-invention, at least in Zuckerman's description, betray the perfectionism and diligence of an artist such as Maria/Sophie, the radical transformations and changes of directions are likewise only comprehensible from an artist's perspective.

Calle's/Maria's play with the factual and the fictional is intertwined with the blurring of the boundaries between the private and the public. For instance, by following an unknown person abroad and creating a piece of—public—art out of this manhunt, the private loses all intimacy, even the trivial becomes noteworthy. Terrorist acts likewise let the spheres of public and private collapse,[58] yet it is the public which becomes private in that it provokes an emotional response—a faculty which literature also possesses. Paul Auster's terrorist tale, however, has rather provoked the same reaction that we could witness before in Nathan Zuckerman: alienation and incomprehension. Thereby they both succeed in letting their readers consider terrorist acts in categories otherwise not touched in such a context—art and creation, self-creation by fragmentation at that.

4. Conclusion: Perpetual apprenticeship

> He had been taught much about what he didn't like; now he would embrace uncertainty. Maybe wisdom would come from what one didn't know, rather than from confidence. (*Album*, 227)
>
> How could anyone confine themselves to one system or creed? . . . Surely there was no fixed self; surely our several selves melted and mutated daily? There had to be innumerable ways of being in the world. He would spread himself out, in his work and in love, following his curiosity. (*Album*, 274)

Shahid's initiation story does not lead to his incorporation into a fundamentalist movement, but to his liberation as an artist. He has briefly frequented extremist circles, but on account of his doubt on the inerrancy in any text, his belief in the polyphony of any story, he withdraws from them and embraces the complexity of his own identity and the possibilities entailed by the indefinite.[59] Ahmad will still have to find an outlet to come to terms with his hybrid identity, yet he will not have to carry his search to the same extremes as Merry did.

Although Merry's story and the one of Benjamin Sachs are less "realistic" and "true to science" than both John Updike's and Hanif Kureishi's accounts of extremism, such incredible stories bear a special significance for political scientists, for they force them to consider a terrorist act from a rather uncommon angle. Both their stories lack the "classic" ingredients that Shahid's and Ahmad's initiations offer: to begin with, neither Merry nor Sachs are born into the position of outsiders to society, neither has to fight for acceptance. Groups or communities which seek to unite others at the margin of society do not appeal to them. This leaves them uninfluenced by mentors and demagogues. Like artists, however, they strive to reach the perfection of an idol, be it the purity of the Virgin Mary, the innocence of a Hollywood icon, or the imagined heroism of a killed activist and scholar. Instead of mere imitations, however, they produce their own variations of the idealized predecessors, variations which permit a complete rupture with their former selves.

The bomb they planted is no longer a tool of the terrorist, but it becomes the metaphor for their identities, yet not in the sense intended in clichéd media language: the fragments left from an explosion adequately describe the identity crisis of all the protagonists discussed, all of whom hunger for a consistent, holistic story of who they are. Their terrorist acts thus become a project of self-creation, which may be read and expressed in artistic terms, as in the case of Merry and Sachs. Violence is not a way to criticize the world around them—it is rather a way to piece together the fragments of their selves.

Part Four

De-Initiation

7

For Another Go: (Zucker)man as a Perpetual Initiand

1. Introduction

> "We are born innocent . . . we suffer terrible disillusionment before we can gain knowledge, and then we fear death – and we are granted only fragmentary happiness to offset the pain." (*Professor*, 94)

This is the final sentence of an essay written by David Kepesh's student, a statement which could likewise be represented as the essence of initiation and life's subsequent trials. The matter-of-fact manner of the young woman, who stirred fatherly as well as sexual feelings in Kepesh, stuns him, and lets him marvel as to whether she could have possibly learned this in his lectures: "How? *How*? I am only just beginning to learn it on this flight!" (*Professor*, 94). The fear of death, but more so of aging and physical decline, will occupy Kepesh's last appearance in *The Dying Animal* (2001), a novel that marks the beginning of Roth's literary interest in the struggles of old age. Although Roth had already let his readers witness the suffering of his father ten years earlier in *Patrimony: A True Story* (1991), it is only with Kepesh that he deals with the last stage of life in his fiction. Before returning with *Indignation* to a coming of age story, Roth further explores the mind of those facing the last threshold to cross in *Everyman* (2006) and *Exit Ghost* (2007).

This rather recent preoccupation of Philip Roth also leads to a new, fittingly last aspect to explore: the possibility of late maturation, and final attempts at assuming responsibility, on a personal as well as on a political level. So far, we have followed the development of classical initiation *topoi*, coming of age stories and the struggles of adolescence, with an additional emphasis on how identity is challenged by historical, spatial, racial, or religious forces. Typically, the final stages of life would not be taken into consideration in the context of initiation stories, which are usually associated with the turning points at younger age. Rather, old age only receives attention as a prolonged separation process, an extended farewell, or as the time individuals assume the role of mentors. Roth, however, shows how this stage of life can still prove to be a turning point—especially for characters of his making, who even at older age seem to be stuck in their younger, in certain ways still immature selves.

These stories do not fill gaps in political socialization research *strictu sensu*, but they rather cover new ground. Although political socialization research increasingly tries to adopt a lifespan view, studies still struggle in their efforts to deal with age and the political life of aging men.[1] While researchers in political socialization agree on the importance of adolescence with regard to changes of attitude, fittingly labeled the impressionable years hypothesis, results on later stages in life diverge.[2] Increasing persistence, disengagement, selective withdrawal[3]—these are diverse hypotheses which have also been tested, in view of politics' concern for this segment of the electorate,[4] which is growing in most industrial countries. Yet no convincing explanations of the elder's political behavior exist beyond the accumulated data, nor do researchers ask the question that becomes dominant in the minds of Roth's aging protagonists: why care about politics, if your health fails you? Why start to care now?

One might assume that those without an intention to grow wiser will remain stuck in their old ways, in spite of the platitude that age brings wisdom. Roth shows, however, that circumstances may induce change, and that an individual can always remain the creator of his own identity and opt for a life as a perpetual initiand. While *The Dying Animal* shows how a man can nearly find a new self even within the "chaos of eros" (20), *Everyman* presents a sober summoning of failed initiations. Forcibly, though, this part finishes with a reprise of Nathan Zuckerman's life, during which he embraces lasting immaturity in *Exit Ghost.*

2. Emotionally immature: Of masters and everymen

Roles reversed: The master as apprentice

David Kepesh, Roth's emblematic *Professor of Desire*, who once had turned in a Kafkaesque way into the very object of this desire, *The Breast*, is at the age of sixty-two at the height of his career and fame. As Kepesh frequently appears on radio and television, his university lectures attract students in masses, and among them, to his pleasure, many young women. It thus becomes an annual ritual for Kepesh to select among his fair disciples the one he will eventually have sex with—eventually, since he never starts an affair during the semester, but instead invites his class at the end of the term to a private party, which marks the beginning of his conquest. So far, none of these affairs had been of any consequence, although Kepesh resumed one at a later stage, with no emotional strings attached. This changes with *The Dying Animal* (2001) and Consuela Castillo's appearance in his class, a twenty-four-year old daughter of exiled Cubans. She captures Kepesh's attention from the very first moment thanks to her exquisite physique and the way she presents herself, shifting between overt confidence and a streak of insecurity about her effect on others.

As predicted, the closing party of his course marks the beginning of Kepesh's affair with Consuela, albeit a prolonged one which will introduce a transition in the professor's life, as Stephanie Cherolis pointedly observes: "from detachment to attachment, from the safety of solitude to the dangers of love and loss."[5] Both Cherolis and Aristie Trendel recognize the way that what is initially only a sexually motivated affair evolves into a parallel maturation of Kepesh, an emotional transformation usually expected in an adolescent but for once to be witnessed in an old man.[6] Whereas Trendel labels the novella as a *Bildungsroman*,[7] the story also contains, in my opinion, the ingredients of a classic initiation story. Emotionally detached at the outset, Kepesh develops feelings for Consuela, although he keeps reminding himself that a relationship between him and the younger woman lacks any perspective, that he has no means to bind her. What should have remained a mere sexual encounter, purely dedicated to pleasure, turns him into a suspicious, ever jealous, and possessive lover. While he considered himself her master in the beginning, her *Professor of Desire* so to speak, power quickly shifts to her side, as she bares her teeth after a demeaning episode on the bedstead: "Then something happened. The bite. The bite *back*. The biting back of life" (*Dying*, 30). Consuela thereby demonstrates how easily she can exercise her animalistic side and sexual power, and change the structure within their relationship, and the episode also indeed alters Kepesh's perception of her status and lets him forgo his assumed dominance:

> It was the true beginning of her mastery—the mastery into which my mastery had initiated her. I am the author of her mastery of me. (*Dying*, 32)

Formerly dominant, now dominated—as sexuality never permits equality in Kepesh's eyes (*Dying*, 20)—he recognizes his fragility, emotionally and physically. The woman he has initially described as excitable and unsure of how to employ her power, who increases through his mastership her knowledge of things both artistic and erotic, demands to be recognized in her strength. With his growing dedication to Consuela, which reaches the stage of obsession, his age becomes more of an uncomfortable reality to him:

> What do you do if you're sixty-two and the urge to take whatever is still takable couldn't be stronger? What do you do if you're sixty-two and you realize that all those bodily parts invisible up to now (kidneys, lungs, veins, arteries, brain, intestines, prostate, heart) are about to start making themselves distressingly apparent, while the organ most conspicuous throughout your life is doomed to dwindle into insignificance? (*Dying*, 33–4)

Ironically, though, it is less the latter organ that starts complicating Kepesh's relationship to Consuela, but it is rather his growing attachment to her. This is not only mirrored in the way he describes his confusion, but also becomes palpable in the discussions between the two lovers, for Kepesh hungers for a complete image of Consuela. Knowing her physically does not suffice; he even eagerly listens to her lectures on life and politics in Cuba. To express his devotion, he regularly plays the piano for her and hones his musical skills, a long abandoned habit. He becomes her guide through the world of art, introduces her to Diego Velázquez and promises to show her the paintings in the Prado. Despite all this, Kepesh is incapable of acknowledging his longing for a firm bond, as the difference in age leads him to the conviction that he could not offer her a joint future. However, given his age, he feels constantly captured by the limitations of his earthly existence, very much in the manner of Nathan Zuckerman at his last appearance in *Exit Ghost*:

> To those not yet old, being old means you've been. But being old also means that despite, in addition to, and in excess of your beenness, you still are. Your beenness is very much alive. You still are, and one is as haunted by the still-being and its fullness as by the having-already-been, by the pastness. Think of old age this way: it's just an everyday fact that one's life is at stake. (*Dying*, 36)

Unable to enter a relationship of a more formal, public nature, yet likewise no longer capable to keep it on a merely intimate level, Kepesh loses his poise and keeps torturing himself with fears of loss and obsessive jealousy. In this state of mind, he is bound to lose his grip not only on his reason, but also on Consuela, who puts him to a test: she invites Kepesh to her graduation party where she intends to present him to her whole family—yet as whom? Afraid of the uneasy position into which this event will force him, Kepesh escapes it, though with a thinly veiled excuse instead of an open discussion of his reservations. This puerile subterfuge stands for the once so self-assured scholar's incapability to deal with his emotions, and at the same time prompts Consuela to give up on him.

Trendel explains the young woman's decision as the one of a pupil who sought her master's acceptance, expressed by the invitation to her graduation party, but thus disappointed, her dominance loses all interest for her.[8] It could also be interpreted as Kepesh's initiation test, the instance to terminate his transition from his detached former self to the caring person who is willing to recognize his feelings publicly. The graduation party is Consuela's own initiation rite, a rite to conclude her years of academic discipleship and her entrance into professional life. At the same time, it is for her the moment her relationship with Kepesh is no longer designated as an intimate discipleship, but a public partnership which shall be recognized at this personal turning point. Yet for Kepesh the party becomes a trial he fails fatally, leaving an emotional vacuum and rendering him even less able to develop a healthy way of dealing with his feelings for Consuela: what remains is an obsession, a mind possessed by the thought of her. While Kepesh ridicules his son who cannot finish an extramarital affair light-headedly and is tormented by the pain he causes two women, the father is himself no longer in the position to shrug off a relationship and continue his past leisurely affairs. Although he failed the test with which Consuela confronted him, she succeeded in changing him irrevocably. The sexual animal in him is slowly dying.

Two years after the end of the affair, a phone call by Consuela proves Kepesh's lasting feelings for the young woman. While she had reaffirmed the permanent effect of her artistic discipleship with a postcard showing a Modigliani nude, he now expects and fears a reestablishment of the other aspect of their relationship. Asking him for a meeting in order to tell him something before anyone pre-empted her, Consuela puts Kepesh into commotion and lets his doubts and longing surface again. His feelings for her, which he describes as an obsession, but which the reader tends to think of as love, finally burst out when she reveals her scalp which testifies to prolonged chemotherapy. On the verge of major surgery to rid herself of breast cancer, she asks Kepesh to take photographs of her torso, the part of her body which he cherished the most, more than any other man she had met, and whose beauty she is forced to sacrifice. This time, Kepesh is capable of meeting her wish, proves worthy of her trust, and gives the reader the impression of a previously unknown intimacy. He even feels the age gap narrowing between himself and Consuela, as her sense of time must have changed due to her gloomy prospects:

> Time for the young is always made up of what is past, but for Consuela time is now how much future she has left, and she doesn't believe there is any. (*Dying*, 148)

In her filmic interpretation of Roth's novella, retitled *Elegy* (2008),[9] the Catalan director Isabel Coixet at this point takes the liberty to conclude Kepesh's initiation, sending him in the cinematically inevitable artificial rain to the hospital, driven by his own longing and not by a call from Consuela. Coixet even bridges the discrepancies between father Kepesh and son, who, as a member of the medical staff at the hospital in question, arranges for his father to visit Consuela.

Roth, in contrast, leaves it open as to whether Kepesh will assume responsibility for Consuela during these difficult times. While initially she does not want Kepesh at her bedside, the book finishes with his receiving another call from her, begging for his support and care. Although Kepesh seems determined to go, a voice of unknown origin, the voice of the person to whom he had been relating the whole story (a metaleptic interference by Roth? an anonymous friend?) and thus the link between Kepesh and the reader, this voice at the book's margin warns him not to yield to her imploring, for if he does, he will be "finished" (*Dying*, 156). Kepesh is unable to think of relationships, intimate or otherwise, beyond power relations, beyond submission or dominance. Any concerns beyond his own immediate desires become irrelevant. The individual body rules his every move; collective bodies, whether in a religious or a political sense, are left to obscurity.

It remains unclear whether Kepesh's transition, his initiation to a caring man capable of establishing a lasting bond, will be made whole in the end. In other words, he remains, for the reader's eyes, an initiand—yet one who proves that old age can be as trying a time as youth, trying in the sense of a time of trials and tests which might leave a definite mark.

A life more ordinary

> That was the end. No special point had been made. Did they all say what they had to say? No, they didn't, and of course they did. Up and down the state that day, there'd been five hundred funerals like his, routine, ordinary, and except for the thirty wayward seconds furnished by the sons—and Howie's resurrecting with such painstaking precision the world as it innocently existed before the invention of death, life perpetual in their father-created Eden, a paradise just

> fifteen feet wide by forty feet deep disguised as an old-style jewelry store—no more or less interesting than any of the others. But then it's the commonness that's most wrenching, the registering once more of the fact of death that overwhelms everything. (*Everyman*, 14–5)

Howie is the elder brother of the unnamed, titular *Everyman* (2006) and has to bury him at the very beginning of the second novel dominated by Roth's increasing preoccupation with mortality.[10] The main threshold to the text already announces thus, as the title quotes an English morality play from the fifteenth century, which is familiar to a German speaking readership in its adaptation *Jedermann* (1911) by Hugo von Hofmannsthal.[11] Roth stressed, however, that he did not intend to pay homage to the said play, and that his novel should not be read as an allegory or as a testimony of his personal frailty.[12] Leaving his protagonist nameless was, initially, only a coincidence, but in the end should merely highlight how people are defined much more by their relationships than by their name alone.[13] Still, the novel cannot deny a certain palimpsestic nature as it shares parallels with its English namesake as well as with its author's autobiographical book *Patrimony*—and, more importantly for our purpose, it shows that even at a later stage in life, self-recognition, a deep change in one's attitude to life, is possible.

The Summoning of Everyman, as is the complete title of the English morality play, opens with God bemoaning the disinterest of his earthly creatures toward their maker because of their preoccupation with pleasure and material satisfactions. Death subsequently appears and is asked to summon Everyman to heaven, for his final reckoning. Although Roth's *Everyman* does not have a comparable encounter with Death, reviewer Claudia Roth Pierpoint recognizes parallels between the summoning by Death and the unnamed Rothian hero's constant confrontation with medical warnings. Indeed, Roth's *Everyman* centers on illness, physical decay, and the constant attempt to preserve and recover health—in other words, to beat death:

> "The imperious summoning is done by Death ('A great enemy,' Everyman moans, 'that hath me in wait'), whom the medieval dramatist provides with a choice speaking role. Although this talkative personage arrives without warning, leaving Everyman—who has passed his life in pursuit of worldly pleasures—frantically unprepared to face the final reckoning, Roth's hero is beset by the kind of modern medical warnings that keep death ever present in one's mind. The question is whether these portents have left him any better prepared."[14]

While for the medieval Everyman a search ensues for a companion on his way to heaven, letting him plead in vain with Fellowship, Kindred, and Goods, Roth's Everyman starts contemplating his past and analyzing the decisions that brought him into his current situation, confined to solitude and illness. Born as the son of a jeweler and proprietor of "Everyman's Jewelry Store" in Elizabeth, New Jersey, he grew up to become a successful art director in a marketing agency in New York, where he also achieved domestic bliss in his second marriage. However, just like his first marriage, the second was sacrificed to an extramarital affair, this time leading to a less than happy marriage, which fell apart under the strain his illness imposed on the young third wife. Consequently, he is stranded on the shore of New Jersey, where he hopes to pass his final years as a painter, far from the danger he senses in post-9/11 New York. Yet instead of finding fulfillment in his art and the painting lessons he teaches, the one thing occupying his mind is his physical deterioration:

> He'd married three times, had mistresses and children and an interesting job where he'd been a success, but now eluding death seemed to have become the central business of his life and bodily decay his entire story. (*Everyman*, 71)

Thus isolated from his former healthy and successful self, he starts taking stock of his life. This often leads him back to comparing himself to his elder brother Howie, the eulogist met at the outset, who enjoys excellent health and a solid, monogamous life. Contrasting himself to his brother's polished surface, Roth's Everyman recognizes how he has lost his chance for happiness to his insatiable sexual lust. Although his second marriage had been the happiest time of his life, his wife Phoebe being a perfect match and reliable partner who would have helped him keep his dignity even in face of life-threatening surgery, he cheated on her for a Danish model, the preferred Rothian stereotype. Consequently, he feels forced to agree with his sons from the first marriage that he has failed in every way possible, except for one:

> As a father, he was an impostor. As a husband, even to the incomparable Phoebe, for whom he jettisoned their mother, he was an impostor. As anything but a cunthound, he was a fake through and through. (*Everyman*, 95–6)

"This is the man I have made!" (*Everyman*, 97) Roth's nameless protagonist exclaims as he looks back on his past. The exclamation is thereby ambiguous, for it is on the one hand a play on the idea of the self-made man and testifies to an increased awareness of our capacities to create, to "make" our identity and define the way we want to be perceived by others. On the other hand, it opens again the view of the double constructiveness of fictional characters, namely that the reader can no longer rely on the fictional pact with the writer, that is that the reader is no longer willing to suspend his disbelief, as Samuel Taylor Coleridge once described the condition for fiction to work its magic.[15] In this instance, however, the former idea is dominant, for, in spite of Roth's predilection for unreliable narrators, he now leaves the reader in trustworthy hands. Hands, though, which draw the picture of a man who is, in the end, just as isolated and desperate as his medieval counterpart.

In a similar vein, the nameless protagonist recognizes his past mistake, yet redemption is not foreseen in his book: existence, the belief forced upon him by his author, does not go beyond our earthly, bodily reality.[16] Although a visit to the cemetery, a scene reminding the reader of Roth's own accidental visit to the burial ground of his mother in *Patrimony*, reveals that he clings to the idea that his dead parents might in some form still be present, he can for himself only believe in the Now. Old age must therefore be seen as a "massacre" (*Everyman*, 156), since it claims no winners and no after, as the idea of a "battle" would. Yet in the case of Roth's Everyman old age at least offered an initiation to self-recognition and self-reflection, endeavors only attempted by his protagonist at the final stage of his life.

The plot of *Everyman* lacks the clear structure of an initiation story, and it does not consider a political coming of age—and yet I put it under such a heading. While the initiatory elements have already been touched upon, the political dimension remains well hidden. Indeed, it is its very obscurity which makes it relevant: *Everyman* asks, in a way, whether politics can still be of any concern to an individual when his or her predominant need, health, is no longer met. The answer is sobering, as the worldly affairs no longer touch any of those paying the physical toll of old age around the nameless protagonist. "Once upon a time I was a full human being[,]" (*Everyman*, 130) but given his current state he cannot reach beyond his own ambit. Politics is reduced to a diffuse source of threat, palpable in the events of 9/11, which induce Roth's protagonist to flee the city and seek refuge in a beach resort populated by the elderly. Thereby, he turns into a hermit, shunned from anything that might remind him of the minuteness of his suffering compared to the political events taking place on a larger stage. He hopes to find quiet and satisfaction in art. However, as he already betrayed his vocation as an artist by submitting it to commercial use, he is now unable to be creative, and even his painting lessons force him to face his frailty, as he surrounds himself with equally weak coevals.

While Kepesh remained in the center of New York, at the pulse of time, and even increased his political knowledge, even if mainly inspired by Consuela, the central character in *Everyman* can no longer move the focus from his own bodily self. His self-chosen hermitage on the sea-shore thereby reminds the reader of another Rothian character who decided to withdraw from society and opted for total remoteness, the solitude of the Berkshires: Nathan Zuckerman.

3. Rash moments in the final years

In 1917, Joseph Conrad lent his voice to a nameless young sailor who leaves his ship in a South Asian port, without any reason or further plans: "My action, rash as it was, had more the character of divorce – almost of desertion" *(Shadow-Line,* 4). A rash action in a rash moment. This mere adjective haunts Nathan Zuckerman's last appearance as Philip Roth's writer-protagonist in *Exit Ghost* (2007), a title indebted to Shakespeare's *Macbeth*. In fact, it becomes the formula by which he transcends his past experiences and it inspires him to write an erotic, maybe even rash, playlet:

> HE
>
> Did you ever read a short novel called *The Shadow-Line*?
>
> . . .
>
> The opening line goes, "Only the young have such moments." These are moments Conrad describes as "rash." In the first few pages he lays everything out. "Rash moments"—the two words make up the entire sentence. He goes on,

> "I mean moments when the still young are inclined to commit rash actions, such as getting married suddenly or else throwing up a job for no reason." It goes like that. But these rash moments don't just happen in youth. Coming here last night was a rash moment. Daring to return is another. With age there are rash moments too. My first was leaving, my second is returning. (*Exit*, 137–8)

"Rash moments" involve thoughtlessness and reflect a tendency to act upon whims; in short, they are signs of immaturity. As indicated by the subtitle of his monograph *Philip Roth's Rude Truth: The Art of Immaturity* (2006), Ross Posnock perceives "immaturity" as a central characteristic of Roth's writing, albeit in a creative sense: Posnock locates Roth alongside writers who have shared his sense for provocation and obscenity, refining their immature surface, so to speak. Posnock argues that after serious beginnings, particularly with *Letting Go* (1962) and *When She was Good* (1966), Roth started working on his frivolous art, trying to capture the anarchic spirit of immaturity, and celebrating the abandon of his protagonists.[17] Yet "immaturity" is not only to be identified as Roth's artistic credo, he is also concerned by more profane aspects of the characteristic, as signaled by Zuckerman's reference to Conrad. In fact, the reference reveals one of the themes dominating the Zuckerman series, as Conrad's protagonist is the prototype of a very specific *immaturus*, his immaturity being that of an initiand. *The Shadow-Line* is an initiation story in that it shows its nameless protagonist undergoing a lasting change in experience and character, which leads him permanently to an adult world[18]—a path Nathan Zuckerman never walks to its end, and thus remains a perpetual initiand.

Awakening beyond The Shadow-Line

> "I . . . felt myself a mere bird of passage in that port. In fact, it might have been said that I had already broken off my connection. (*Shadow-Line*, 23)

This key line from *The Shadow-Line* describes the condition of Conrad's protagonist after he quits his employer's ship. His first instinct, albeit not his firm plan, is simply to wait for the first passage back to his home country. Yet the experienced Captain Giles, whom he encounters in this unnamed transit harbor, gingerly persuades him to assume the post of successor to a recently deceased captain. In hindsight, Conrad's novice-captain sees himself claiming the command of his ship with a relative naïveté, unaware of the challenges lying ahead: "My education was far from being finished, though I didn't know it. No! I didn't know it" (39). When he first sets foot on the deck of his purported dominion, he encounters a crew wrecked by illness and a first mate still haunted by the image of the captain's predecessor. The journey to the safety of Singapore's harbor will thus challenge the nameless youth on several levels, demanding that he not only learn to lead his crew and to fight superstitious premonitions, but also live with his weaknesses and surmount them in times of crisis, such as a storm:

> And what appalls me most of all is that I shrink from going on deck to face it. It's due to the ship, it's due to the men who are there on deck – some of them,

> ready to put out the last remnant of their strength at a word from me. And I am shrinking from it. From the mere vision. My first command. Now I understand that strange sense of insecurity in my past. I always suspected that I might be no good. And here is proof of the positive. I am shirking it. I am no good. (*Shadow-Line,* 88)

The recognition of his own shortcomings finally prepares him to overcome the feeling of being "no good." He becomes aware of his dependence on the crew—the intricate links between his own destiny and those of other people. This enables him to accept individual weakness and teaches him compassion. Therefore, he does not scorn being left by his reliable, but, in the end, worn-out cook when they reach their destination: definitive proof of—as Carl Benson put it poignantly—his "passage from egocentric youth to human solidarity."[19] When at last he reencounters his furtive mentor Captain Giles, the latter acknowledges the erstwhile novice among the ranks of experienced men.[20]

In light of Conrad's tale, the word "passage" again assumes several meanings: on the one hand, it is simply a passage to Singapore, a voyage on the sea with a point of departure, time on the open sea, and eventual arrival at the destined port. More importantly, though, the story traces a passage in the sense coined by van Gennep.[21] It can indeed be read as a classic, nearly ideal-typical initiation story, as it follows van Gennep's threefold pattern in that it is split into the triad "point of origin - open sea - destination." Each of these three geographic locations in fact mirrors one of the three phases of initiation: at the unnamed point of origin, the still ingenuous youth breaks with his routine and is virtually ushered by a third person into forsaking the known destination of home for the insecurity of being a captain, that is for a *separation*. The mind behind it, Captain Giles, intended thereby to let the young man undergo a first true test, a phase of *transition*, which forces the youth to wake up to the realities of adult life. On the sea, during his mental transition, we can grasp this dramatic awakening by the entries in the captain's diary, in which he records his reaction to every test the journey presents. Finally, with his feet on the ground of Singapore, he is welcomed—*incorporated*—by Captain Giles among his equals.

Although the pattern is less clear, we can identify similarities in the case of a very late initiate, namely Henry James's Dencombe in "The Middle Years" (1893). An illness forces Dencombe, an author of repute, to *separate* from his usual environment and seek recovery on the English seaside. Unexpectedly, a relapse will turn out to be his *transitory phase*, as it brings an ardent admirer, young Dr Hugh, to his bedside. Thanks to the youth's devotion, the writer recognizes that he himself had sacrificed his life for art, that "[h]e had done all that he should ever do, and yet he had not done what he wanted" (213). One could therein see his *incorporation* among the wise, although it is immediately followed by his death, making him a neophyte at the last moment possible.

Both James's initiation at the verge of death and the Conradian initiation journey further accentuate the liminality of their protagonists' development by the locations chosen. While in James's short story the bed, the connection between wake and sleep, and the beach, the transitory space between land and water, are central places, Conrad captures the liminality of the young captain's initiation journey by first setting the story in a harbor, a typical space of transit and second meaning of the Greek word *limén*, and by letting it further evolve on a ship. Ships have, as Cesare Casarino pointed out in reference to Conrad's preceding work, *The Secret Sharer* (1910), a distinct meaning in terms of Michel Foucault's concept of *heterotopia*,[22] "other place":

> "[I]f we think, after all, that the boat is a floating piece of space, a place without a place, that exists by itself, that is closed in on itself and at the same time is given over to the infinity of the sea and that, from port to port, from tack to tack, from brothel to brothel, it goes as far as the colonies in search of the most precious treasures they conceal in their gardens, you will understand why the boat . . . has been . . . the greatest reserve of the imagination. The ship is the heterotopia par excellence. In civilizations without boats, dreams dry up, espionage takes the place of adventure, and the police take the place of pirates."[23]

The liminal space occupied by Conrad's initiation story is moreover stressed by what Benson calls a "dream-like unreality" conveyed by the mode in which the young captain tells his story.[24] There are times when he feels inclined to yield to the superstitious warnings of his first mate and he seems to surrender his rationality to haunting fears. His language often slides into the voice of fairy tales, as Michael C. Kotzin observes,[25] and reminds us of our initiands Marcus Messner and "Philip Roth": "I was very much like people in fairy tales. Nothing ever astonishes them" (*Shadow-Line*, 33). In contrast, fairy tales astonish their audience, which generally consists of children, who should be not only entertained by them, but instructed by them as well. Fittingly, Conrad's narrator is the one gaining most in knowledge from the tale, and is transformed by the "strong magic" of command (24). Although the tune of fairy tales and the wonders of magical beliefs are alien to Nathan Zuckerman, he likewise uses narrative devices to highlight the liminality of his experiences—and his constant challenges as an initiand.

Zuckerman along The Shadow-Line

Zuckerman might regard himself as part of a conspiracy, burlesque or tragedy, rather than as the hero of a fairy tale; his tales, however, are likewise haunted, as Alexis Kate Wilson showed.[26] While the ghost of his predecessor troubles Conrad's captain on board, Zuckerman feels doomed by his Jewish roots and the collective memory linked to them. This leads to his being persecuted by the effects his writing has on both those who are close to him and his readers. Yet different from the Conradian protagonist, Zuckerman will not even in the exorcism of *Exit Ghost* be able to banish these specters from his life, just as the quest for his self never reaches an end. This is somewhat ironic, given the fact that the Zuckerman series starts with what Zuckerman presents as an example of the genre, which usually requires stories to culminate in self-recognition, or at least a leap toward this goal: the *Bildungsroman*. Alas, neither the desired maturation nor the sought-after mentor truly materializes in *The Ghost Writer*, although Zuckerman optimistically begins his odyssey as an artist and man with a visit to the writer E. I. Lonoff, in whom he hopes to find, according to David Brauner, "a father/confessor, a benign judge who will acquit him of all charges of betraying his real father and exploiting his family history for the purposes of furthering his career."[27] Although the detached and solitary lifestyle, dedicated solely to "turning sentences around," appeals to Zuckerman, Lonoff points out that life in the midst of society actually nourished the young writer's prose, and living as a recluse would only have deprived him of this fountain.[28] (Little could Lonoff know at that time that Zuckerman was equally productive in the solitude of the Berkshires, even though his creative power still depended upon external stimuli.)

Thus the chosen mentor refuses to assume his assigned role, and, for his part, cannot draw anything from the admiration and energy brought to him. Instead of following the example of the often-cited Dencombe, who finally realizes what limits he had imposed on himself, Lonoff remains within his confinement.[29] Unwittingly, Lonoff thus becomes not Dencombe, but a clueless Captain Giles in Zuckerman's life, as after his visit, the youth will further pursue his initiatory quest. He will actually explore a first path toward maturation during the night spent at the master's house, although only toward an imagined process: eavesdropping on Lonoff and Amy Bellette, student and temptress, Zuckerman mentally writes the story of the young woman reconceived as Anne Frank, the clandestine survivor, perfectly suited to become his future wife. For how else could he redeem himself, he who had been accused of Jewish self-hatred and of stimulating fascist fancies, than by marrying the one Jewish icon of victimization and courage?

Hence, Zuckerman embarks upon his artistic initiation journey, separating himself from his family and seeking to undergo his transition under the wings of a mentor, but, to no avail, at least if we take the initial motives as the benchmark. As an artist, he will succeed beyond his hope, as we witness in *Zuckerman Unbound* (1981), in which he tries to restrain the ghosts of his success: "The only book that seemed to exist was his own. And whenever he tried to forget it, someone reminded him" (50). Worse, his scandalously carnal novel *Carnovsky*, in the fashion of *Portnoy's Complaint* (1969), puts him in the similarly strained situation within his family that he confronts at the outset of *The Ghost Writer*. Thus, he is exposed to the same trial; the story, though, will not repeat itself, but rather presents us a dim variation of the primary odyssey, a heedless one with a sole objective, to escape. Instead he encounters yet another would-be resurrection of Anne Frank, for the first time embodied in an actress whose most important role was this icon of Jewishness. Again, Zuckerman's trials do not culminate in his acquittal by recovering his self, and in lieu of this acquittal, he becomes separated once more from his known spheres:

> "No one," replied Zuckerman, and that was the end of that. You are no longer any man's son, you are no longer some good woman's husband, you are no longer your brother's brother, and you don't come from anywhere anymore, either. (*Unbound*, 224–5)

"Bastard," was the last word Nathan heard his father utter. "Bastard," is what his brother Henry calls him for having ridiculed the family in his bestseller. Thus unbound by his family ties, Zuckerman still does not feel liberated. Rather, with the last abuse still haunting him, Roth not only ends *Zuckerman Unbound* on a note of defeat and forsakenness, but also keeps this tune in *The Anatomy Lesson* (1983). The novel shows Zuckerman tormented by physical pain, which he interprets as his penalty, a penalty only aggravated by his brother's firm wish to keep him out of all the planning of the last rites accompanying the recent death of their mother. Nathan may attend the funeral, but being deprived of any role during this time of mourning, he cannot even go through this particular rite of passage, or, more precisely, this rite of separation.[30] His exclusion and his sudden mentioning of past marriages and subsequent divorces heighten the reader's awareness for the lacunae in his story, namely the lack of Zuckerman's undergoing any classical rite of passage. No such rite merits Zuckerman's further description, none has left a definite mark in his memory, a short moment of recelebration. His marriages happened; his Bar Mitzvah happened; his first sex happened; but none of these events has led him truly through a phase of transition. None of them has led to his incorporation as a neophyte.

Again Zuckerman seeks redemption, this time by cherishing the idea of going to medical school and becoming a worthy man, and again this attempt comes to naught. The paralysis of his writing is only paralleled by the paralysis of his speaking ability. Like the observers grouped around Rembrandt's image of Dr Tulp, the original *Anatomy Lesson*, the reader stares at Zuckerman's viscera, yet he does not find the remedy for his suffering. Neither does Zuckerman. Instead, in his following appearances he embarks on journeys that, at the outset, might be perceived as political initiation journeys in conflict zones: in *The Prague Orgy* (1985) he follows the footsteps of David Kepesh by traveling to Prague, albeit on the lookout for a lost manuscript. In *The Counterlife* (1986) Zuckerman's several invented selves find their way to Israel and England. Although these journeys broaden his perspective of potential selves and responsibilities, none of them will truly alter him—although one will make it undesirably clear which part of his identity cannot be redefined.

The journeys both to Prague and to Israel entail a political education, for they introduce Zuckerman to regimes obeying codes other than those known to him. In this vein, from his Czech guide and fellow-writer Bolotka he learns the rules of artistic survival in a totalitarian regime, while the fanatic and fundamentalist Lippman colors Israel in Hobbesian and Machiavellian shades. They present him with a distorting mirror, letting him get a glimpse of what he believes he is not, as an artist and as an American Jew. As an artist, he does not see himself politically compelled to write, to write as a form of resistance; as an American and a Jew, he does not feel tied to Israel, even though his brother would want him to feel that way. Yet his Jewishness becomes an inescapable reality on the uncontested grounds of England: "England made a Jew of me in only eight weeks, which, on reflection, might be the least painful method" (*The Counterlife*, 273). In Israel, Zuckerman feels that he cannot escape his roots. However, while he could distance himself from Lippman's frantic soliloquy, his friend Shuki's question whether his English partner would agree to have a son circumcised cannot be refuted so easily:

> "Why do you pretend to be so detached from your Jewish feelings? In the books all you seem to be worrying about is what on earth a Jew is, while in life you pretend that you're content to be the last link in the Jewish chain of being." (*Counterlife*, 77)

Shuki's reminder of the covenant between God and Israel induces Zuckerman to ponder, for the first and last time, an actual initiation ritual, which he interprets not as an incorporation into the group and thus a gain, but rather as a story of loss: like any integration rite by mutilation, circumcision is an irreversible mark that is, as Zuckerman explains, inescapable in that it leaves no possibility of defining oneself without reference to the mark, to Judaism.[31] Whether the mark carries any meaning for oneself, whether one would have chosen freely to be singled out in this manner, is irrelevant: circumcision turns into a predicament, the one sign locking the individual into Judaism. Maybe this perceived entrapment explains why Zuckerman later will fail to take on any other role, and why he even rewrites his possible initiation journeys. For in Zuckerman's hands, both Israel and Prague turn into utopias, unreal zones mocking any differentiated viewpoint. Be it the burlesque personnel populating the Czech nightlife or the ideal-typical extremists jeopardizing Israel, be it the suffocating imprisonment under socialism or the frantic fundamentalism instilled at the Wailing Wall, the absurdity of both contexts can hardly serve Zuckerman as a place of rebirth. Rather, we see him wandering through liminal zones that oscillate between fiction and madness.

The aimlessness of Zuckerman's wanderings only becomes understandable when we read in *I Married A Communist* (1998) memories of his adolescence. They are primarily memories of the Ringold brothers Ira and Murray. Even a story which contains classic ingredients, images, and plotlines of a (political) initiation is in the end only a herald of later odysseys and the subsequent de-initiation from all societal responsibilities. Zuckerman remembers his friendship with the Ringold brothers as a mentorship, casting himself in the role of the disciple introduced, predominantly by Ira, to socialist ideology and the political instrumentalization of art. The brothers, archetypically for the genre of the initiation story, gain the position his father once held, though with the implicit promise of a new role for young Nathan. The rupture of filial ties, a transitional vacation in Ira's shack, and the political indoctrination by means of literature are elements that hint at a classic initiation story, and let us expect an ideologically invigorated grown-up Nathan Zuckerman. Yet, as we already know from earlier novels, he will assume quite a different path: art recaptures him. The show to join will be the literary circus, which induces him to leave ideological battles behind and instead indulge in the pleasures of immaturity.

His retreat will be finalized after his odysseys through the liminal zones of world politics during which Zuckerman chooses, like Rousseau, Thoreau, and Ira Ringold before him, to seek solitude in a small house in the Berkshires, a classic symbolically laden location chosen for initiation rites. Zuckerman, however, seems to see his retreat first and foremost as what its name promises, a place permitting him to evade life, as well as the pleasures and responsibilities tied to life. Not for the potential injustices around him, nor for any person's doings, would he assume responsibility. No one seeking his support will find it. As someone who never reached the fruition of an initiation process, he will not become a mentor himself, and even misses the last chance to make this transition: *Exit Ghost*, our final literary encounter with Zuckerman, offers him the opportunity not only to revisit his beginnings and finally close that chapter of his life, but also to become a mentor. Instead, he aims for a position midway between Lonoff's stance and the one taken by Dencombe in Henry James's "The Middle Years."

Zuckerman, a perpetual initiand

After years of rarely interrupted seclusion, Zuckerman returns in *Exit Ghost* for a longer stay in New York. Here he consigns himself into the hands of a physician who cannot promise him a bath in the fountain of youth, but at least a chance for more dignity, specifically relief from incontinence. While trying to get back at least a bit of his former physical assuredness, Zuckerman will see his younger self as depicted in *The Ghost Writer* through a distorting mirror, and he will be reminded of his past in two ways: on the one hand by encountering Amy Bellette, the former seducer and now widow of E. I. Lonoff, and on the other hand, by recognizing himself in an aspiring young writer.

And again, Zuckerman encounters a young woman who will stir his desires and his imaginative powers so that he creates a plot involving him and her, "He and She", as a couple. However, other than his once dreamed up marriage to Amy Bellette/Anne Frank, the affair outlined in the short play shall not redeem him. Rather, he dreams of once more indulging in a moment of sexual rashness and thus reclaiming his former self. While the earlier marriage fantasy should have led to his maturation, he now embraces immaturity; the collective is of no consequence anymore. Instead, Zuckerman mourns the loss of the vigor needed to savor the pleasures to which his immaturity might eventually lead. At times, the reader can imagine him repeating the sigh of Henry James's dying novelist Dencombe in "The Middle Years": "Ah for another go!—ah for a better chance!" (214).

In Richard Kliman, E. I. Lonoff's ambitious would-be biographer, Zuckerman sees the one who will indeed have more than just another go at life, who does not yet feel alienated from and betrayed by his body, as he exclaims in a fashion reminding us of David Kepesh:

> All of us are now "no-longers" while the excited mind of Richard Kliman believes that his heart, his knees, his cerebrum, his prostate, his bladder sphincter, his everything is indestructible and that he, and he alone, is not in the hands of his cells. Believing this is no soaring achievement for those who are twenty-eight,

> certainly not if they know themselves to be beckoned by greatness. They are not "no-longers," losing faculties, losing control, shamefully dispossessed from themselves, marked by deprivation and experiencing the organic rebellion staged by the body against the elderly; they are "not-yets," with no idea how quickly things turn out another way. (*Exit*, 256)

Although Kliman offers Zuckerman a last chance to influence another's path as a mentor, the elder novelist refuses this task. Amy had pleaded with him to dissuade Kliman from uncovering her late husband's alleged incestuous relationship, hoping that Zuckerman would be more successful than her. To the reader's surprise, the latter seems willing to act as Amy's messenger, even though Roth once let a writer envision the plight of a Lonoff biographer in *Deception* (1990). While then it seemed ridiculous that a literary hermit like Lonoff might "in secret [have] the remissive history of Jean Genet" (*Deception*, 98), which let the biographer scorn the Lonoff family and its desire for a "pious monument" (98) to the deceased, Zuckerman now shows sympathy for similar wishes. Yet he stumbles over his former self, as Kliman constantly reminds him that he, Zuckerman, had once also been brash and rash in his writing. Kliman becomes a projection surface for Zuckerman's old self,[32] and can indeed instill in him the desire once felt by Dencombe.

When Lonoff was confronted with Zuckerman's ardency, he referred to the protagonist in James's tale, yet failed to take him as an example. Zuckerman, however, would become a better disciple of Dencombe, a disciple who prefers to reread a tale of awakening rather than a tale of death when confronted with his physical decline. The chiastic relationship between these two central intertexts, "The Middle Years" and *The Shadow-Line*, and the two Zuckerman novels featuring them, *The Ghost Writer* and *Exit Ghost*, thereby becomes palpable. While, in the novels explicitly referring to them, these texts grasp the situation of one of the minor characters, Lonoff and Kliman respectively, they only unfold their significance with regard to Zuckerman in the opposite novel: whereas James defines the tune of *Exit Ghost*, Conrad defines the motif of Zuckerman's existence. By turning to Conrad rather than to James during his final appearance, Zuckerman even seems to acknowledge his fate as the perpetual initiand, who cannot become anyone's mentor, for his own art is nourished by the constant rashness of his existence, an art, in the words of Posnock once more, celebrating "the art of immaturity." Zuckerman's *vita* seems to suggest that a writer can only "reach" immaturity in his art, can only liberate himself from bourgeois constraints, if he remains captured in the ambiguous status of the initiand: only when he is enjoying the liberty of the initiand, who may break society's rules and put his own abilities constantly to the test, can the artist exemplify the art of immaturity.

Immaturity, however, here also means indifference toward the political sphere. Once struggling with political ideas and his commitment to the Jewish community, later at least following the turnings of international conflicts, Zuckerman prefers to keep a child's distance from the recent history of New York. While Roth's Everyman fled the city to escape the sense of dread and uncertainty after 9/11, Zuckerman finds even within the city's boundaries spaces where time stopped still and he can picture himself again wandering around as a young man:

> I started toward the subway to take a train downtown to Ground Zero. Begin there, where the biggest thing of all occurred; but because I've withdrawn as witness and participant both, I never made it to the subway. That would have been wholly out of character for the character I'd become. Instead, after crossing the park, I found myself in the familiar rooms of the Metropolitan Museum, wiling away the afternoon like someone who had no catching up to do. (*Exit*, 15)

Why it would have been "wholly out of character" at first seems incomprehensible to the young couple to whom he intends to let his house in the Berkshires. While their attention is focused on the 2004 Presidential election, which they follow as ardent, at times ridiculously so, opponents of the incumbent President, Zuckerman remains completely detached and explains to the incredulous couple that

> "I've served my tour as exasperated liberal and indignant citizen . . . . I don't wish to register an opinion, I don't want to express myself on "the issues"—I don't even want to know what they are. It no longer suits me to know, and what doesn't suit me, I expunge. That's why I live where I do. That's why you want to live where I do." (*Exit*, 36–7)

Consequently, the exasperation displayed by the two upcoming writers in view of the election's outcome no longer concerns him. He may be acquainted with "the theatrical emotions that the horrors of politics inspire" (*Exit*, 94), but he now remains simply an "onlooker" to this "public drama" (ibid.). As Murray Ringold had once predicted, the years of recluse had finally given Zuckerman the feeling that he did not need to participate anymore, the "moral pass" seemed to have been granted. While the unnamed protagonist of *Everyman* could no longer dedicate his time for political questions due to his increasing preoccupation with his physical frailty, Zuckerman voluntarily and consciously decides to stay out of political issues, to regain the political innocence of a child, and to live only for art, a true disciple of his former college mentor Leo Glucksman. His hesitance and the brief moment of considering visiting Ground Zero betray, however, that he knows that the initial natural cluelessness is only a mask and that he could quickly be drawn into political thought again. Escapes from History, this much "Philip Roth" in *The Plot Against America* already learned, are impossible, for it eventually claims us all.

4. Conclusion: Perpetually tried, perpetually in transit

In contrast to Henry James's writer Dencombe, Zuckerman is denied the final passage; Roth has refused Zuckerman the completion of any rite of passage, and, consequently, also refuses to bury him. Nathan Zuckerman will remain the perpetual initiand, tried and tired, never whole, but always creating new ways to fill the voids. This pattern of perpetual initiations, figures kept in transit, figures who are not capable of completing their personal development, is identifiable in Roth's other works, namely *The Dying Animal* and *Everyman*, but also in his younger protagonists like Marcus Messner in *Indignation*, who died before he comprehended the stakes of adult life. While it is easy to forgive the young their failures, the elder *immaturi* are eyed suspiciously. What they prove, however, is that the terms age and initiation should not be disconnected: even at later stages of our lives we might be able to tell a new initiation story, if maybe only a failed one.

The genre of the initiation story and the term of initiation as such are usually reserved for the experiences of adolescents or children, even though the reader can unravel elements of initiation in the stories of older age. Extending the usage of the term to these later instances opens the view to aspects otherwise neglected, namely the recurrent nature of initiation and the permanent possibility of change—or the conscious decision to stay in limbo. The latter particularly concerns the political question in the lives of the three protagonists: Kepesh shows interest in political matters only as a means to comprehend his lover or to reflect the power structure within sexual relationships; the ailing Everyman flees the grounds where world politics touched his life and became all too present in his life; and Zuckerman remains above political events, even when they are forced upon his attention: three elderly men who have practically banished the political from their lives—three elderly men whose behavior is not met by a plausible narrative by political socialization research. They have consciously disconnected themselves from collective concerns, and decided that they have no duty remaining toward society as a whole, but rather prefer to focus on their own bodily reality and physical struggles.

While the three men would serve as perfect examples of political disengagement theories, they are still preoccupied with one aspect of human existence that might surprise a clichéd view of age: sexual desire. Of the three, however, only Kepesh is still physically fit enough to have his sexual needs fulfilled, the other two require substitutes. Since neither politics nor religion can satisfy him, Zuckerman finds his outlet in art. The medium which helped him as a youth to give his political ideas a shape, the medium which once brought him to loggerheads with Judaist notables, this very medium is now the last space wherein he can enact his sexual needs. The nameless Everyman, in contrast, had abandoned art too early and sought it again too late for it to constitute a final chance to grasp life.

Epilogue

All the world's a stage,
And all the men and women merely players:
They have their exits and their entrances;
And one man in his time plays many parts,
His acts being seven ages. At first the infant,
Mewling and puking in the nurse's arms.
And then the whining school-boy, with his satchel
And shining morning face, creeping like snail
Unwillingly to school. And then the lover,
Sighing like furnace, with a woeful ballad
Made to his mistress' eyebrow. Then a soldier,
Full of strange oaths and bearded like the pard,
Jealous in honour, sudden and quick in quarrel,
Seeking the bubble reputation
Even in the cannon's mouth. And then the justice,
In fair round belly with good capon lin'd,
With eyes severe and beard of formal cut,
Full of wise saws and modern instances;
And so he plays his part. The sixth age shifts
Into the lean and slipper'd pantaloon,
With spectacles on nose and pouch on side,
His youthful hose, well saved, a world too wide
For his shrunk shank; and his big manly voice,
Turning again toward childish treble, pipes
And whistles in his sound. Last scene of all,
That ends this strange eventful history,
Is second childishness and mere oblivion,
Sans teeth, sans eyes, sans taste, sans everything.

William Shakespeare, *As You Like It*,
Jacques in Act 2, Scene 7, Lines 139–66

Ending with Shakespeare is nearly as trite as beginning with Spielvogel, the doctor in *Portnoy's Complaint* quoted in the prologue. Yet the passage fits the core of this study too well to ignore it, and it also resounds in one of Roth's more recent works. *The Humbling* (2009) could be paired with *The Dying Animal*, *Everyman*, and *Exit Ghost*, since it centers on the final stage of life, or to apply Shakespearian diction, on the seventh age of man. To choose Shakespeare is even more fitting since the protagonist of *The Humbling*,

Simon Axler, had once captivated theater audiences in the roles of Hamlet or Prospero. He had mastered the art of acting like few before him. The first sentence of the novel, however, announces the end of this glorious career: "He'd lost his magic" (*Humbling*, 2). The former lead actor no longer knows how to act, to pretend, and to impersonate; no role suits him anymore, except for one: "The only role available to him was the role of someone playing a role. A sane man playing an insane man" (*Humbling*, 6). Although the second chapter shows, as its title indicates, a "Transformation," when Axler rediscovers his lust for life together with the recurrence of sexual desire and the fleeting wish to father a child, it all comes to naught with "The Final Act." In that last chapter, Axler declares Konstantin Gavrilovich as his paragon, the young playwright in Anton Chekhov's *The Seagull*, and shoots himself in the head. He thus takes Shakespeare's idea of man playing many parts literally, and chooses the suitable script to terminate his seventh stage.

It is not hard to guess that politics and collective concerns have been further away from Axler's thoughts than his immediate needs and sexual gratification. Therein, he resembles the nameless protagonist in *Everyman* and Zuckerman in *Exit Ghost*. Yet both of these earlier characters have still heeded echoes of the political, either by fleeing the suspenseful atmosphere of post-9/11 New York, or by being forced to follow the 2004 Presidential Election. With Axler, Philip Roth has completed the image of the politically dissociated elderly man, and thus his many variations on the creation of political identities: the final being the apolitical individual. Roth's works lead the reader through many of the stages described by Shakespeare, but, more importantly, they present a view of one aspect of the "seven ages of man" neglected by the British poet: times of ambiguity and limbo, the transitions and thresholds between these allegedly distinct phases. In and between all these stages, the reader can detect moments of initiation, and elements regularly associated with initiation, which become important to comprehend how Roth's characters develop their self, and eventually (re)create their identity, defining the way they will be perceived by the outside world.

In some instances, Roth's depictions of initiations come close to an exact illustration of the findings in political socialization research, for instance in his account of "Philip's" development in *The Plot*, where the schoolboy slowly learns to think of politics as a force that may concern him. The reading experience, however, goes beyond a mere gathering of facts. The aesthetic pleasure aside, even plotlines that may serve as simple illustrations of known facts—one could even use the term "case studies"—offer more in that they urge the reader, particularly if he or she is a political scientist, to consider the character's development in context, to decipher his or her dependence on the behavior of other figures, and to focus on the whole picture. Similarly, the researcher has to ponder metaphors, symbols, the way voices and spaces are employed, which may contain hidden keys to unlock another level of the plot.

The immediate merit of fiction for political science becomes palpable in instances in which political science has reached an impasse or has not yet established a consensus. In other words, a writer such as Roth can confront political scientists with puzzling counter-worlds and counter-realities. This is particularly the case in his account of Merry Levov's fanatic descent in *American Pastoral*. Roth emphasizes the artistic side in an individual's identity development, which he indeed presents in his novels as an act of creation, sometimes a conscious act, sometimes a forced one: an act which leaves it up to the protagonist to choose the appropriate narrative. More generally, whenever Roth confronts the political scientists with his self-inventive characters, he presents them with a phenomenon unknown to political socialization research. Thus, literature not only helps political science to connect the dots drawn by its empirical research, but it may also, so to speak, highlight certain dots that have been invisible for political science up to now.

"A novel is not evidence," Zuckerman stressed in *Exit Ghost* and thereby recounted the *l'art pour l'art* stance presented in the second chapter of Part II, "a novel's a novel" (265). Yet as Roth himself showed and argued at numerous instances, "the impenetrable line dividing fiction from reality" that Kliman ridicules (*Exit*, 267) is not as impenetrable that it should keep social sciences constrained empirical data. Fiction may not provide hard evidence, but it is, more often than not, "the not-so that reveals the so" (*Exit*, 120).

ambiguous *undefined* *unsettled*
suspenseful *faltering*
in limbo *transitory* *insecure*
fragmentary *contested*

These words express the ambiguity of transitional moments, the theme connecting political science, literature, and anthropology. They likewise serve to describe the nascence of this book, the circumstances under which it was written, and the choices it involved: balancing along the threshold between literary theory and political science, between art and science often puts the imaginary scales at risk of tipping all too heftily to one side. At times it turned into a work of translation, for the two disciplines pursue different cognitive interests and thus often require the interdisciplinary worker to focus on distinct points. As a consequence, the political scientist who learns to read fiction differently, who takes a peek through the lens of a literary theorist, may learn to approach his own subject differently. In the end, literature as the Great Particularizer and politics as the Great Generalizer might not have found harmony—but fruitful frictions.

Notes

Prologue

1 For instance Irina Livezeanu, "Journal 1935–1944: The Fascist Years," *Holocaust and Genocide Studies* 16, 3 (2002); Linda M. G. Zerilli, "Machiavelli's Sisters: Women and 'The Conversation' of Political Theory," *Political Theory* 19, 2 (1991).
2 Simon Stow, "Written and Unwritten America: Roth on Reading, Politics and Theory," *Studies in American Jewish Literature* 23 (2004).
3 Anthony Hutchison, "Purity is Petrefaction: Liberalism and Betrayal in Philip Roth's *I Married a Communist*," *Rethinking History* 9, 2 (2005); Anthony Hutchison, *Writing the Republic: Liberalism and Morality in American Political Fiction* (New York: Columbia University Press, 2007).
4 Maureen Whitebrook, *Identity, Narrative and Politics* (London: Routledge, 2001).
5 David Brauner, *Philip Roth* (Manchester and New York: Manchester University Press, 2007).
6 Sigurd Burckhardt, "English Bards and APSR Reviewers," *The American Political Science Review* 4, 1 (1960), 158.

Chapter 1

1 Warren Rosenberg, *Legacy of Rage: Jewish Masculinity, Violence, and Culture* (Amherst, MA: University of Massachusetts Press, 2001), 192; Lawrence E. Ziewacz, "Holden Caulfield, Alex Portnoy, and Good Will Hunting: Coming of Age in American Films and Novels," *The Journal of Popular Culture* 35, 1 (2001): 216.
2 Barry Gross, "Seduction of the Innocent: *Portnoy's Complaint* and Popular Culture," *MELUS* 8, 4 (1981): 83–4; Ziewacz, "Holden Caulfield, Alex Portnoy, and Good Will Hunting: Coming of Age in American Films and Novels," 215.
3 Rosenberg, *Legacy of Rage: Jewish Masculinity, Violence, and Culture*, 194; Alan Segal, "*Portnoy's Complaint* and the Sociology of Literature," *The British Journal of Sociology* 22, 3 (1971): 266.
4 Eileen Z. Cohen, "Alex in Wonderland, Or 'Portnoy's Complaint'," *Twentieth Century Literature* 17, 3 (1971): 163.
5 Karen R. Tolchin, *Part Blood, Part Ketchup: Coming of Age in American Literature and Film* (Lanham, MD and Plymouth: Lexington Books, 2007), 28–9.
6 Barbara B. Aponte, "El rito de la iniciación en el cuento hispanoamericano," *Hispanic Review* 51, 2 (1983): 129.
7 Arno Heller, *Odyssee zum Selbst. Zur Gestaltung jugendlicher Identitätssuche im neueren amerikanischen Roman* (Innsbruck, 1973), 24.
8 Winther, *Weibliche Initiation in den Romanen von Virginia Woolf und Doris Lessing*, 45.

9 Arnold van Gennep, *Übergangsriten*, trans. Klaus Schomburg and Sylvia M. Schomburg-Scherff, Studienausg. ed. (Frankfurt a.M.: Campus, 1999), 15. Cf. also Ronald L. Grimes, *Deeply into the Bone: Re-Inventing Rites of Passage* (Berkeley, CA, Los Angeles and London: University of California Press, 2000), 103.

10 See also Alan Morinis, "The Ritual Experience: Pain and the Transformation of Consciousness in Ordeals of Initiation," *Ethos* 13, 2 (1985): 152.

11 Van Gennep, *Übergangsriten*, 21.

12 Grimes, *Deeply into the Bone: Re-Inventing Rites of Passage*, 104.

13 Alice Schlegel and Herbert Barry III, "The Evolutionary Significance of Adolescent Initiation Ceremonies," *American Ethnologist* 7, 4 (1980): 696.

14 Mircea Eliade, *Das Mysterium der Wiedergeburt – Initiationsriten, ihre kulturelle und religiöse Bedeutung* (Zürich: Rascher, 1961), 17.

15 The majority of the reviewed literature associates initiation with the symbolism of death and rebirth respectively and demonstrates that this symbolic interpretation indeed stands behind many initiation rites observed by small-scale societies. Yet this view is contradicted by Alice Schlegel and Herbert Barry III, "Adolescent Initiation Ceremonies: A Cross-Cultural Code," *Ethnology* 18, 2 (1979): 204.

16 Peter Freese, *Die Initiationsreise: Studien zum jugendlichen Helden im modernen amerikanischen Roman* (Tübingen: Stauffenburg-Verlag, 1998), 106.

17 Eliade, *Das Mysterium der Wiedergeburt – Initiationsriten, ihre kulturelle und religiöse Bedeutung*, 13–4.

18 Van Gennep, *Übergangsriten*, 112; Victor Turner, *From Ritual to Theatre: The Human Seriousness of Play* (New York: PAJ Publications, 1982), 27.

19 Stefanie Winther, *Weibliche Initiation in den Romanen von Virginia Woolf und Doris Lessing*, Universität Trier (Trier: WVT Wissenschaftlicher Verlag Trier, 2005), 29.

20 Victor Turner, "Betwixt and Between: The Liminal Period in Rites of Passage," in *Betwixt & Between: Patterns of Masculine and Feminine Initiation*, eds, Steven Foster and Meredith Little Louise Carus Mahdi (La Salle, IL: Open Court, 1987), 9.

21 Elmer John Thiessen, "Initiation, Indoctrination, and Education," *Canadian Journal of Education/Revue canadienne de l'éducation* 10, 3 (1985): 243. See also Turner, "Betwixt and Between: The Liminal Period in Rites of Passage," 11.

22 Thiessen, "Initiation, Indoctrination, and Education," 234–5.

23 Van Gennep, *Übergangsriten*, 76.

24 J. M. Glass, "Religious Circumcision: A Jewish View," *BJU International* 83, 1 (1999): 17–21.

25 Abraham Gross, "The Blood Libel and the Blood of Circumcision: An Ashkenazic Custom that Disappeared in the Middle Ages," *The Jewish Quarterly Review* 86, 1/2 (1995): 171.

26 Leonard B. Glick, "Jewish Circumcision. An Enigma in Historical Perspective," in *Understanding Circumcision: A Multi-Disciplinary Approach to a Multi-Dimensional Problem*, eds, George C. Denniston, Frederick Mansfield Hodges, and Marylin Fayre Milos (New York, Boston, Dordrecht, London, Moscow: Kluwer Academic/Plenum Publishers, 2001), 22.

27 Van Gennep, *Übergangsriten*, 78.

28 Grimes, *Deeply into the Bone: Re-Inventing Rites of Passage*, 298.

29 Tamar A. Levinson and Susan Zoline, "Impact of Summer Trip to Israel on the Self-Esteem of Jewish Adolescents," *Journal of Psychology and Judaism* 21, 2 (1997): 92–3; Norman Solomon, *Judentum: Eine kurze Einführung* (Stuttgart: Reclam, 1999), 110.

30 Grimes, *Deeply into the Bone: Re-Inventing Rites of Passage*, 100; Levinson and Zoline, "Impact of Summer Trip to Israel on the Self-Esteem of Jewish Adolescents," 92–3; Schlegel and Barry III, "Adolescent Initiation Ceremonies: A Cross-Cultural Code," 199.
31 Grimes, *Deeply into the Bone: Re-Inventing Rites of Passage*, 94–5.
32 Turner, "Betwixt and Between: The Liminal Period in Rites of Passage," 14.
33 Here and in the following see Turner, *From Ritual to Theatre: The Human Seriousness of Play*, 24, 41–2.
34 Victor Turner, *The Ritual Process: Structure and Anti-Structure* (New York: Aldine de Gruyter, 1969), 95.
35 Grimes, *Deeply into the Bone: Re-Inventing Rites of Passage*, 103; Turner, *From Ritual to Theatre: The Human Seriousness of Play*, 25; van Gennep, *Übergangsriten*, 184.
36 Adéle Nel, "The Poet in Transit: Travel Poems and Liminality in *Lykdigte* (Elegies) and *Ruggespraak* (Consultation) by Joan Hambridge," in *Beyond the Threshold: Explorations of Liminality in Literature*, eds. Hein Viljoen and Chris N. van der Merwe (New York: Peter Lang, 2007), 224–5.
37 Alan Roughley, "Liminal Paperspaces: Writing between Derrida and Joyce and Being and Writing," in *Mapping Liminalities: Thresholds in Cultural and Literary Texts*, eds. Lucy Kay, et al. (Bern: Peter Lang, 2007), 209.
38 Kathy Smith, "The Emptiness of Zero: Representations of Loss, Absence, Anxiety and Desire in the Late Twentieth Century," *Critical Quarterly* 46, 1 (2004): 49.
39 Schlegel and Barry III, "The Evolutionary Significance of Adolescent Initiation Ceremonies," 696.
40 Ihab Hassan, *Radical Innocence: Studies in the Contemporary American Novel* (Princeton, NJ: Princeton University Press, 1961), 41.
41 Freese, *Die Initiationsreise: Studien zum jugendlichen Helden im modernen amerikanischen Roman*, 92.
42 This quotation as well as the preceding information are taken out of Hassan, *Radical Innocence: Studies in the Contemporary American Novel*, 223.
43 Freese explains this typology in *Die Initiationsreise: Studien zum jugendlichen Helden im modernen amerikanischen Roman*, 95–102.
44 Cohen, "Alex in Wonderland, Or 'Portnoy's Complaint,'" 163–4.
45 Debbie Lisle, *The Global Politics of Contemporary Travel Writing* (Cambridge: Cambridge University Press, 2006), 93.
46 My translation. For the quotation see Régine Camps-Robertson, "Les seuils infranchissables dans *Portnoy's Complaint*," in *Profils Américains: Philip Roth*, eds. Paul Lévy and Ada Savin (Montpellier: Presses de l'Université Paul-Valéry Montpellier III, 2002), 63. For the following observations, see Camps-Robertson, 63–5.
47 Debra Shostak, *Philip Roth: Countertexts, Counterlives* (Columbia, SC: University of South Carolina Press, 2004), 83.
48 Gérard Genette, *Palimpseste. Die Literatur auf zweiter Stufe*, trans. Wolfram Bayer and Dieter Hornig (Frankfurt a.M.: Suhrkamp, 1993), 9. The further types of transtexts are a. metatexts, texts which can be read as comments on another text; b. architexts, a transtextual relation which is generally based on belonging to the same genre; and c. hypertexts, i.e. texts which have been derived from other texts, for instance by transforming the original one.
49 Cohen, "Alex in Wonderland, Or 'Portnoy's Complaint,'" 165.

50 Patricia Waugh, *Metafiction: The Theory and Practice of Self-Conscious Fiction* (London: Routledge, 1984), 2.

51 Debra N. Malina, *Breaking the Frame: Metalepsis and the Construction of the Subject* (Columbus: The Ohio State University Press, 2002), 2.

52 Needless to say, a myriad of examples for metalepses could be forwarded, if the reader consults writers beyond Philip Roth. An example is Paul Auster whose detective-protagonist in *City of Glass* (1985) rings at the author's door, a tension which becomes even more palpable in the novel's adaptation as a graphic novel by Peter Karasik and David Mazzucchelli (New York: Picador, 2004). Classic examples of metalepsis are, to name but a few, Cervantes *Don Quixote* (1605/1615), Miguel de Unamuno's *Mist* (1914), or Primo Levi's *If on a Winter's Night a Traveller* (1979). The concept of the metalepsis becomes, however, more plastic if we consider a filmic example. In Marc Forster's comedy drama *Stranger than Fiction* (2006), protagonist Harold Crick one day suddenly hears a female voice describing his every move. He later finds out that the voice belongs to writer Karen Eiffel, and that he is in fact her creation. A classic filmic example thereof would be Woody Allen's *The Purple Rose of Cairo* (1985).

53 Hein Viljoen and Chris N. van der Merwe, "A Poetics of Liminality and Hybridity," in *Beyond the Threshold: Explorations of Liminality in Literature*, eds, Hein Viljoen and Chris N. van der Merwe (New York: Peter Lang, 2007), 11.

54 Ottmar Ette, *Literatur in Bewegung: Raum und Dynamik grenzüberschreitenden Schreibens in Europa und Amerika* (Weilerswist: Velbrück Wissenschaft, 2001), 448.

55 Herbert H. Hyman, *Political Socialization: A Study in the Psychology of Political Behavior* (London: Collier-Macmillan, 1969).

56 Richard M. Merelman, "The Adolescence of Political Socialization," *Sociology of Education* 45, 2 (1972): 135.

57 David Easton and Robert Hess, "The Child's Political World," *Midwest Journal of Political Science* 6, 3 (1962): 235.

58 Again David Easton and Robert Hess, "The Child's Political World," 230.

59 Anna Emilia Berti, "Children's Understanding of Politics," in *Children's Understanding of Society*, eds. Martyn and Eithne Buchanan-Barrow Barrett (Hove, England: Psychology Press, 2005), 69–70. As an example of the beginnings: David Easton and Jack Dennis, "The Child's Acquisition of Regime Norms: Political Efficacy," *The American Political Science Review* 61, 1 (1967).

60 Martha Cottam et al., *Introduction to Political Psychology* (Mahwah, NJ: Lawrence Erlbaum Associates, 2004), 143; Robert L. Dudley and Alan R. Gitelson, "Political Literacy, Civic Education, and Civic Engagement: A Return to Political Socialization?," *Applied Developmental Science* 6, 4 (2002): 176; Richard G. Niemi and Mary A. Hepburn, "The Rebirth of Political Socialization," *Perspectives on Political Science* 24, 1 (1995): 8.

61 Emphasis added. Easton and Hess, "The Child's Political World," 232.

62 On this development and the following observations see Berti, "Children's Understanding of Politics," 72.

63 Timothy E. Cook, "The Bear Market in Political Socialization and the Costs of Misunderstood Psychological Theories," *The American Political Science Review* 79, 4 (1985): 1080.

64 David O. Sears, "Whither Political Socialization Research? The Question of Persistence," in *Political Socialization, Citizenship Education, and Democracy*, ed. Orit Ichilov (New York and London: Teachers College Press, 1990), 71.

65 Constance Flanagan and Leslie S. Gallay, "Reframing the Meaning of 'Political' in Research with Adolescents," *Perspectives on Political Science* 24, 1 (1995): 35. Cf. also Niemi and Hepburn, "The Rebirth of Political Socialization," 7; Shawn W. Rosenberg, "Sociology, Psychology, and the Study of Political Behavior: The Case of the Research on Political Socialization," *The Journal of Politics* 47, 2 (1985): 716; Roberta S. Sigel, "New Directions for Political Socialization Research: Thoughts and Suggestions," *Perspectives on Political Science* 24, 1 (1995): 17.

66 Berti, "Children's Understanding of Politics," 72.

67 Cf. inter alia R. W. Connell, "Political Socialization in the American Family: The Evidence Re-Examined," *The Public Opinion Quarterly* 36, 3 (1972); Eleanor E. Maccoby, Richard E. Matthews, and S. Morton Anton, "Youth and Political Change," *The Public Opinion Quarterly* 18, 1 (1954). For a more recent article cf. Boris Wernli, "La transmission intergénérationnelle de l'orientation idéologique en Suisse dans les familles à plusieurs générations," *Swiss Political Science Review* 13, 2 (2007).

68 Robert E. Lane, "Fathers and Sons: Foundations of Political Belief," *American Sociological Review* 24, 4 (1959): 502.

69 The same Declaration of Independence will be hanging in the home of the fictive replica of the Roth family in *The Plot Against America*, as you will see in Chapter 2.

70 M. Kent Jennings and Richard G. Niemi, "The Transmission of Political Values from Parent to Child," *The American Political Science Review* 62, 1 (1968): 183.

71 Russell Middleton and Snell Putney, "Political Expression of Adolescent Rebellion," *The American Journal of Sociology* 68, 5 (1963): 528–9.

72 Niemi and Hepburn, "The Rebirth of Political Socialization," 14.

73 Judith Torney-Purta, "Psychological Theory as a Basis for Political Socialization Research: Individuals' Construction of Knowledge," *Perspectives on Political Science* 24, 1 (1995): 23.

74 Sigel, "New Directions for Political Socialization Research: Thoughts and Suggestions," 18.

75 Torney-Purta, "Psychological Theory as a Basis for Political Socialization Research: Individuals' Construction of Knowledge," 23. See also McDevitt and Chaffee, "From Top-Down to Trickle-up Influence: Revisiting Assumptions About the Family in Political Socialization," 282–3.

76 Niemi and Hepburn, "The Rebirth of Political Socialization," 8.

77 Sigel, "New Directions for Political Socialization Research: Thoughts and Suggestions," 19.

78 Niemi and Sobieszek, "Political Socialization," 227; Niemi and Hepburn, "The Rebirth of Political Socialization," 7.

79 Sigel, "New Directions for Political Socialization Research: Thoughts and Suggestions," 19.

80 Maureen Whitebrook, *Identity, Narrative and Politics* (London: Routledge, 2001), 9.

81 Catherine H. Zuckert, "On Reading Classic American Novelists as Political Thinkers," *The Journal of Politics* 43, 3 (1981): 688. See also Zuckert, "Why Political Scientists Want to Study Literature," 89.

82 William Lowell Randall, *The Stories We Are: An Essay on Self-Creation* (Toronto, Buffalo, Canada: University of Toronto Press, 1995), 111.

83 Paul Ricœur, "Life in Quest of Narrative," in *On Paul Ricœur: Narrative and Interpretation*, ed. David Wood (London and New York: Routledge, 1991), 32.

84 Whitebrook, *Identity, Narrative and Politics*, 10. Similarly Nira Yuval-Davis, "Belonging and the Politics of Belonging," *Patterns of Prejudice* 40, 3 (2006): 202.

Chapter 2

1 On the origins of the "hyphenated American," see Chapter 4.
2 Alan Cooper, "It Can Happen Here, or All in the Family Values: Surviving *The Plot Against America*," in *Philip Roth: New Perspectives on an American Author*, ed. Derek Parker Royal (Westport, Connecticut, London: Praeger, 2005), 243.
3 Ross Posnock, *Philip Roth's Rude Truth: The Art of Immaturity* (Princeton, NJ: Princeton University Press, 2006), 29.
4 Brauner, *Philip Roth*, 205.
5 See Part I.
6 Jeffrey L. Geller, "*Indignation: A Novel.* Book Review," *Psychiatric Services* 59, 12 (2008): 1476.
7 Andrea Köhler, "Der endlose Strom des Blutes: Philip Roth erzählt von jenseits des Grabes," *Neue Zürcher Zeitung*, 10 February 2009, 37.
8 He said this during a webcast interview which was shown in different bookstores around the United States, when *Indignation* was first sold on 16 September, 2009. I watched the webcast at the Eck Center, located on the campus of the University of Notre Dame, Indiana.
9 Edwin Fussell, "*Winesburg, Ohio*: Art and Isolation," in *Sherwood Anderson: A Collection of Critical Essays*, ed. Walter B. Rideout (Englewood Cliffs, NJ: Prentice-Hall, Inc., 1974), 41. Cf. also Monika Fludernik, "*Winesburg, Ohio*: The Apprenticeship of George Willard," *Amerikastudien/American Studies* 32, 4 (1987): 433. Although Stouck basically agrees with the reading of *Winesburg, Ohio* as a *Bildungsroman*, he has a few objections to make against Fussell's overall analysis of the novel, see: David Stouck, "*Winesburg, Ohio* and the Failure of Art," *Twentieth Century Literature* 15, 3 (1969): 146–51.
10 Fludernik, "*Winesburg, Ohio*: The Apprenticeship of George Willard," 447; Stouck, "*Winesburg, Ohio* and the Failure of Art," 148.
11 Marc C. Conner, "Fathers and Sons: *Winesburg, Ohio* and the Revision of Modernism," *Studies in American Fiction* 29, 2 (2001): 214–5.
12 David Stouck, "*Winesburg, Ohio* as a Dance of Death," *American Literature* 48, 4 (1977): 537.
13 Conner, "Fathers and Sons: *Winesburg, Ohio* and the Revision of Modernism," 220; Fussell, "*Winesburg, Ohio*: Art and Isolation," 46; Mark Whalan, "Dreams of Manhood: Narrative, Gender, and History in *Winesburg, Ohio*," *Studies in American Fiction* 30, 2 (2002): 230.
14 Conner, "Fathers and Sons: *Winesburg, Ohio* and the Revision of Modernism," 220.
15 Fludernik, "*Winesburg, Ohio*: The Apprenticeship of George Willard," 433.
16 Freese, *Die Initiationsreise: Studien zum jugendlichen Helden im modernen amerikanischen Roman*, 92; van Gennep, *Übergangsriten*, 72; Charles Harrington, "Sexual Differentiation in Socialization and Some Male Genital Mutilations," *American Anthropologist* 70, 5 (1968): 951.
17 For a brief introduction to Lacan's theory, see Robert Dale Parker, *How to Interpret Literature: Critical Theory for Literary and Cultural Studies* (New York, Oxford: Oxford University Press, 2008), 126–35.
18 Cf. Chapter 3.

19 Freese, *Die Initiationsreise: Studien zum jugendlichen Helden im modernen amerikanischen Roman*, 135.

20 A recent publication by Thomas Macho gives a brief and highly readable introduction to rituals of yesterday and today, albeit only in German: Thomas Macho, *Rituale*, vol. 1750, Vontobel-Schriftenreihe (Zürich: Vontobel-Stiftung, 2006).

21 Yvette Sánchez, *Coleccionismo y literatura* (Madrid: Cátedra, 1999), 41–2.

22 The educational and political aspect of Philip's stamp collection will be considered below.

23 According to genealogical sources, the German surname Messner is derived from the city of Meissen, yet Roth might have chosen it for the name's orthographic similarity to the German word for "knife," "Messer." This, however, is simply an educated guess.

24 Morinis, "The Ritual Experience: Pain and the Transformation of Consciousness in Ordeals of Initiation," 151.

25 On indoctrination and formation, cf. Daniel G. Scott, "Rites of Passage in Adolescent Development: A Reappreciation," *Child and Youth Care Forum* 27, 5 (1998): 324–335.

26 Further differentiation of the types of initiation journeys follows in Chapter 4. Freese, *Die Initiationsreise: Studien zum jugendlichen Helden im modernen amerikanischen Roman*, 108–9; Lisle, *The Global Politics of Contemporary Travel Writing*, 35.

27 Cf. Part I.

28 Lauren Berlant, *The Queen of America Goes to Washington City. Essays on Sex and Citizenship* (Durham and London: Duke University Press, 1997), 28–9.

29 Gaston Bachelard, *Poetik des Raumes*, trans. Kurt Leonhard, 7th ed. (Frankfurt am Main: Fischer Taschenbuch Verlag, 2003), 43.

30 Ross Posnock, "On Philip Roth's *The Plot Against America*," *Salmagundi: A Quarterly of the Humanities & Social Sciences*, 150/151 (2006): online; Elaine B. Safer, *Mocking the Age: The Later Novels of Philip Roth*, 152; Philip Roth, "The Story Behind 'The Plot Against America,'" *The New York Times*, 19 September 2004, online; Jeffrey Severs, "'Get Your Map of America': Tempering Dystopia and Learning Topography in *The Plot Against America*," *Studies in American Fiction* 35, 2 (2007): 236.

31 Widmann interprets the role of the stamp collection differently: he sees in the loss of the collection a specular image to Lindbergh's disappearance at a later point of the novel. Personally, I regard the significance of this loss for the development of Philip as more important, as it fits more neatly in the overall direction of the novel as an early *Entwicklungs-* or *Initiationsroman*. [See Andreas Martin Widmann, *Kontrafaktische Geschichtsdarstellung. Untersuchungen an Romanen von Günter Grass, Thomas Pynchon, Thomas Brussig, Michael Kleeberg, Philip Roth und Christoph Ransmayr*, vol. 4, Studien zur historischen Poetik (Heidelberg: Universitätsverlag Winter, 2009), 306.]

32 Ekaterina V. Haskins, "'Put Your Stamp on History': The USPS Commemorative Program *Celebrate the Century* and Postmodern Collective Memory," *Quarterly Journal of Speech* 89, 1 (2003): 1–3.

33 Pierre Nora, "Between Memory and History: *Les lieux de mémoire*," *Representations*, 26 (1989): 19.

34 Brett Ashley Kaplan, "Contested, Constructed Home(lands): Diaspora, Postcolonial Studies and Zionism," *Journal of Modern Jewish Studies* 6, 1 (2007): 88.

35 Brauner, *Philip Roth*, 202.
36 As said in the webcast interview on 16 September 2009.
37 Brauner, *Philip Roth*, 179.
38 Cited by Michael Hanne, *The Power of the Story: Fiction and Political Change* (Providence etc.: Berghahn Books, 1994), 11.
39 Horst Steinmetz, *Literatur und Geschichte* (München: Iudicum Verlag, 1988), 29–30.
40 Martin J. Plax, "Thoughts on *The Plot Against America*," *Society* 42, 4 (2005): 81.
41 Roth, "The Story Behind 'The Plot Against America.'"
42 Extensively on the subject: Widmann, *Kontrafaktische Geschichtsdarstellung. Untersuchungen an Romanen von Günter Grass, Thomas Pynchon, Thomas Brussig, Michael Kleeberg, Philip Roth und Christoph Ransmayr*. He therein also deals with The Plot as an example of a counterfactual historical novel (273–308).
43 Thematized by Brauner, *Philip Roth*, 192; Plax, "Thoughts on *The Plot Against America*," 77; Safer, *Mocking the Age: The Later Novels of Philip Roth*, 147.
44 Roth, "The Story Behind 'The Plot Against America.'"
45 Ross Douthat, "It Didn't Happen Here," *Policy Review*, February/March (2005), online. On the parallels between the Lindbergh Administration as portrayed by Roth and the actual Bush Administration, see Kaplan, "Contested, Constructed Home(lands): Diaspora, Postcolonial Studies and Zionism," 87. It is particularly interesting to learn what similarities can be seen in the way the two figures stage their presidency, what images they apply, et cetera. See also Aimee Pozorski, *Roth and Trauma: The Problem of History in the Later Works (1995–2010)* (London and New York: Continuum, 2011), 120–1, who reminds readers to consider the novel's publishing year and thus its implied critique of the Bush Administration.
46 Charles Lewis, "Real Planes and Imaginary Towers: Philip Roth's *The Plot Against America* as 9/11 Prosthetic Screen," in *Literature after 9/11*, eds. Ann Keniston and Jeanne Follansbee Quinn (New York, London: Routledge, 2008), 247–8.
47 Hayden White, "Introduction: Historical Fiction, Fictional History, and Historical Reality," *Rethinking History – The Journal of Theory and Practice* 9, 2/3 (2005): 150; Hayden White, *Metahistory: The Historical Imagination in Nineteenth-Century Europe*, 4th printing ed. (Baltimore, MD: Johns Hopkins University Press, 1983); Lisle, *The Global Politics of Contemporary Travel Writing*, 31–2; briefly Hanne, *The Power of the Story: Fiction and Political Change*, 7. For a very short overview on White's theory, see "White, Hayden V.," in *Metzler Lexikon: Literatur- und Kulturtheorie. Ansätze – Personen – Grundbegriffe*, ed. Ansgar Nünning (Stuttgart, Weimar: Verlag J.B. Metzler, 2008), 764–65.
48 Hayden White, "The Value of Narrativity in the Representation of Reality," *Critical Inquiry* 7, 1 (1980): 6.
49 Stephan Jaeger, "Erzähltheorie und Geschichtswissenschaft," in *Erzähltheorie transgenerisch, intermedial, interdisziplinär*, eds. Vera Nünning and Ansgar Nünning (Trier: WVT Wissenschaftlicher Verlag, 2002), 237.
50 White, "Introduction: Historical Fiction, Fictional History, and Historical Reality", 150.
51 Hanne, *The Power of the Story: Fiction and Political Change*, 12–3.
52 Post-historicism is not to be confused with the so-called "Posthistoire," as termed by Lutz Niethammer, see Jane Caplan, "Postmodernism, Poststructuralism, and Deconstruction: Notes for Historians," *Central European History* 22, 3/4 (1989):

263. On Posthistoire see: Peter Seixas, “Lutz Niethammer. Posthistoire: Has History Come to an End?,” *Historical Studies in Education/Revue d’histoire de l’éducation* 6, 1 Spring/Summer (1994): 121–4.

53 Moritz Bassler, “Einleitung: New Historicism – Literaturgeschichte als Poetik der Kultur,” in *New Historicism*, ed. Mario Bassler (Tübingen; Basel: Francke/Uni-Taschenbücher, 2001), 10.

54 Roth, “The Story Behind ‘The Plot Against America.’”

55 Gérard Genette, “Fictional Narrative, Factual Narrative,” *Poetics Today* 11, 4 (1990): 758–9 and 766–7.

56 White, “Introduction: Historical Fiction, Fictional History, and Historical Reality,” 153.

57 Roth, “The Story Behind ‘The Plot Against America.’”

58 Brauner, *Philip Roth*, 212–3.

Chapter 3

1 Ansgar Nünning, “Welten – Weltbilder – Weisen der Welterzeugung: Zum Wissen der Literatur und zur Aufgabe der Literaturwissenschaft,” *Germanisch-Romanische Monatsschrift* 59, 1 (2009): 66.

2 For a detailed analysis of the dialogs between Zuckerman and Murray Ringold see: Robert Chodat, “Fictions Public and Private: Philip Roth,” *Contemporary Literature* 46, 4 (2005): 689–90.

3 Hutchison, “Purity Is Petrefaction: Liberalism and Betrayal in Philip Roth’s *I Married a Communist*,” 317.

4 Brauner, *Philip Roth*, 153, Hutchison, “Purity Is Petrefaction: Liberalism and Betrayal in Philip Roth’s *I Married a Communist*,” 319; Hutchison, *Writing the Republic: Liberalism and Morality in American Political Fiction*, 102; Ellen Lévy, “Non-Genetic Genealogies in *I Married a Communist*,” in *Profils Américains: Philip Roth*, eds. Paul Lévy and Ada Savin (Montpellier: Presses de l’Université Paul-Valéry Montpellier III, 2002), 174.

5 Ina Bergmann, *And Then the Child Becomes a Woman. Weibliche Initiation in der amerikanischen Kurzgeschichte 1865–1970*, vol. 110, American Monograph Series (Heidelberg: Universitätsverlag Winter, 2003), 37–8.

6 Bachelard, *Poetik des Raumes*, 55.

7 Posnock, *Philip Roth’s Rude Truth: The Art of Immaturity*, 46.

8 Till Kinzel, *Die Tragödie und Komödie des amerikanischen Lebens. Eine Studie zu Zuckermans Amerika in Philip Roths Amerika-Trilogie*, Vol. 137, American Studies Monograph Series (Heidelberg: Universitätsverlag Winter, 2006), 61; Posnock, *Philip Roth‘s Rude Truth: The Art of Immaturity*, 46.

9 See Thiessen, “Initiation, Indoctrination, and Education,” 234–5.

10 Kinzel, *Die Tragödie und Komödie des amerikanischen Lebens. Eine Studie zu Zuckermans Amerika in Philip Roths Amerika-Trilogie*, 89.

11 Reminder of Claire Bloom’s biography: Claire Bloom, *Leaving a Doll’s House. A Memoir* (Boston, New York, Toronto, London: Little, Brown and Company, 1996).

12 Cristina Grasseni, “Taxidermy as Rhetoric of Self-Making: Charles Waterton (1782–1865), Wandering Naturalist,” *Studies in History and Philosophy of Biology and Biomedical Sciences* 29, 2 (1998): 286–7.

13 Kinzel, *Die Tragödie und Komödie des amerikanischen Lebens. Eine Studie zu Zuckermans Amerika in Philip Roths Amerika-Trilogie*, 84.
14 Lévy, "Non-Genetic Genealogies in *I Married a Communist*," 172.
15 Hutchison, "Purity Is Petrefaction: Liberalism and Betrayal in Philip Roth's *I Married a Communist*," 325.
16 Eric Schocket, "Redefining American Proletarian Literature: Mexican Americans and the Challenge to the Tradition of Radical Dissent," *The Journal of American Culture* 24, 1–2 (2001): 59–60.
17 Lévy, "Non-Genetic Genealogies in *I Married a Communist*," 171–2.
18 Maureen Whitebrook, *Real Toads in Imaginary Gardens: Narrative Accounts of Liberalism* (Lanham, Maryland etc.: Rowman & Littlefield, 1995), 2.
19 Stow, "Written and Unwritten America: Roth on Reading, Politics and Theory," 80.
20 Ethan Fishman, "Saul Bellow's 'Likely Stories,'" *The Journal of Politics* 45, 3 (1983): 616.
21 Joseph Blotner, *The Political Novel*, reprint ed. (Westport, Conn: Greenwood Press, 1979), 63; Alex Gottfried and Sue Davidson, "Utopia's Children: An Interpretation of Three Political Novels," *The Western Political Quarterly* 15, 1 (1962): 19; Whitebrook, *Identity, Narrative and Politics*, 11; Zuckert, "Why Political Scientists Want to Study Literature," 189.
22 For a review on a recent monograph covering the remains of Hitler's library see John Gross, "A Constant Reader," *The New York Review of Books*, 14 May 2009, 8–10.
23 Eleonora Belfiore and Oliver Bennett, "Rethinking the Social Impacts of the Arts," *International Journal of Cultural Policy* 13, 2 (2007): 139. For a recent study on the conflicts between art and democracy see Caroline Levine, *Provoking Democracy: Why We Need the Arts* (Malden, MA, Oxford and Victoria: Blackwell Publishing Ltd., 2007).
24 Martha Craven Nussbaum, *Poetic Justice: The Literary Imagination and Public Life* (Boston, MA: Beacon Press, 1995), 5.
25 Simon Stow, *Republic of Readers? The Literary Turn in Political Thought and Analysis* (Albany, NY: State University of New York Press, 2007), 41.
26 Nussbaum, *Poetic Justice: The Literary Imagination and Public Life*, xii. Ideas previously developed in Martha C. Nussbaum, "The Literary Imagination in Public Life," *New Literary History* 22, 4 (1991).
27 Stow, *Republic of Readers? The Literary Turn in Political Thought and Analysis*, 41.
28 Nussbaum, *Poetic Justice: The Literary Imagination and Public Life*, 6.
29 Again Nussbaum, *Poetic Justice: The Literary Imagination and Public Life*, 74. See also Stow, *Republic of Readers? The Literary Turn in Political Thought and Analysis*, 44; Maureen Whitebrook, "Compassion as a Political Virtue," *Political Studies* 50, 3 (2002).
30 Jane B. Baron, "Law, Literature, and the Problems of Interdisciplinarity," *The Yale Law Journal* 108, 5 (1999): 1064.
31 Ian Ward, *Law and Literature: Possibilities and Perspectives* (Cambridge: Cambridge University Press, 1995), 4.
32 Stow, *Republic of Readers? The Literary Turn in Political Thought and Analysis*, 61.
33 In her influential essay "The Liberalism of Fear," Judith Shklar bases the legitimacy of liberalism on the idea of a *summum malum*, which she sees in cruelty and the fear of cruelty, the latter being the one thing shared by all human beings. A just regime

thus has to ascertain that no one has to be afraid of systematic cruelty. For the complete essay see: Judith Shklar, *Political Thought and Political Thinkers* (Chicago, IL: University of Chicago Press, 1998).

34 Stow, *Republic of Readers? The Literary Turn in Political Thought and Analysis*, 64.

35 The significance of Eve's chosen alias will be further discussed in Chapter 5.

36 Colin Radford and Michael Weston, "How Can We Be Moved by the Fate of Anna Karenina?," *Proceedings of the Aristotelian Society* 49 (1975).

37 John Wilcox, "The Beginnings of L' Art Pour L' Art," *The Journal of Aesthetics and Art Criticism* 11, 4 (1953): 363.

38 Cited by Wilcox, "The Beginnings of L' Art Pour L' Art," 364.

39 Belfiore and Bennett, "Rethinking the Social Impacts of the Arts," 145; Frederick Burwick, "'Art for Art's Sake' and the Politics of Prescinding: 1790s, 1890s, 1990s," *Pacific Coast Philology* 34, 2 (1999): 122.

40 Hermione Lee, "Age Makes a Difference. Hermione Lee Talks with Philip Roth About His New Novel, 'Exit Ghost,'" *The New Yorker*, 1 October 2007, online.

41 Lee, "Age Makes a Difference. Hermione Lee Talks with Philip Roth About His New Novel, 'Exit Ghost,'" online.

42 For an overview and an additional study see Eirini Tsiknaki, *Literatur und Persönlichkeitsentwicklung. Eine empirische Untersuchung zur Erfassung des Zusammenhangs zwischen literarischem Lesen und emotionaler Intelligenz*, Forum Europäische Literatur 5 (München: M-Press, Meidenbauer, 2005), 145.

43 Raymond A. Mar et al., "Bookworms versus Nerds: Exposure to Fiction Versus Non-Fiction, Divergent Associations with Social Ability, and the Simulation of Fictional Social Worlds," *Journal of Research in Personality* 40 (2006); Christine Pappas, "'You Hafta Push': Using Sapphire's Novel to Teach Introduction to American Government," *Journal of Political Science Education* 3, 1 (2007); Howard Sklar, "Narrative as Experience: The Pedagogical Implications of Sympathizing with Fictional Characters," *Partial Answers* 6, 2 (2008). For an extensive exploration of the relationship between empathy and literature, see Suzanne Keen, *Empathy and the Novel* (Oxford, New York: Oxford University Press, 2007).

44 Mary Sigler, "Review: A Sneeze and a Cup of Sugar: A Cautionary Tale of Narrative and the Law," *Law and Philosophy* 16, 6 (1997): 627.

45 Sigurd Burckhardt, "English Bards and APSR Reviewers," *The American Political Science Review* 54, 1 (1960): 158.

46 Stanley Eugene Fish, *Is There a Text in This Class? The Authority of Interpretive Communities* (Cambridge: Harvard University Press, 1980), 23; Parker, *How to Interpret Literature: Critical Theory for Literary and Cultural Studies*, 28 and 279.

47 Fish, *Is There a Text in This Class? The Authority of Interpretive Communities*, 48.

48 Again Fish, *Is There a Text in This Class? The Authority of Interpretive Communities*, 3.

49 Parker, *How to Interpret Literature: Critical Theory for Literary and Cultural Studies*, 279.

50 Stow, *Republic of Readers? The Literary Turn in Political Thought and Analysis*, 52. Emphasis in the original.

51 Stow, *Republic of Readers? The Literary Turn in Political Thought and Analysis*, 51.

52 Baron, "Law, Literature, and the Problems of Interdisciplinarity," 1070.

53 Stow, *Republic of Readers? The Literary Turn in Political Thought and Analysis*, 50.

54 Porter H. Abbott, *The Cambridge Introduction to Narrative*, 2nd ed. (Cambridge; New York: Cambridge University Press, 2008), 89–90.
55 Stow, "Written and Unwritten America: Roth on Reading, Politics and Theory," 81. Emphasis in the original.
56 Stow, *Republic of Readers? The Literary Turn in Political Thought and Analysis*, 148–9.

Chapter 4

1 Lisle, *The Global Politics of Contemporary Travel Writing*, 93. Ottmar Ette, however, presents a different view, pointing out, for instance, that Roland Barthes speaks of four phases: leaving, traveling, arriving, and staying. See Ette, *Literatur in Bewegung: Raum und Dynamik grenzüberschreitenden Schreibens in Europa und Amerika*, 81.
2 Lisle, *The Global Politics of Contemporary Travel Writing*, 35.
3 Nel, "The Poet in Transit: Travel Poems and Liminality in *Lykdigte* (Elegies) and *Ruggespraak* (Consultation) by Joan Hambridge," 226–7.
4 Freese, *Die Initiationsreise: Studien zum jugendlichen Helden im modernen amerikanischen Roman*.
5 Kaplan, "Contested, Constructed Home(lands): Diaspora, Postcolonial Studies and Zionism," 86.
6 The typology starts at Freese, *Die Initiationsreise: Studien zum jugendlichen Helden im modernen amerikanischen Roman*, 139.
7 For the typology described in the following paragraph see Ette, *Literatur in Bewegung: Raum und Dynamik grenzüberschreitenden Schreibens in Europa und Amerika*, 63–77.
8 Werner Schlögel, "Kartenlesen, Augenarbeit. Über die Fälligkeit des *Spatial Turn* in den Geschichts- und Kulturwissenschaften," in *Was sind Kulturwissenschaften? 13 Antworten*, ed. Heinz Dieter Kittsteiner (München: Wilhelm Fink Verlag, 2004), 274–5.
9 Brauner, *Philip Roth*, 42, Bella Brodzki, "Reading Himself and Others: *The Professor of Desire*," in *Profils Américains: Philip Roth*, eds. Paul Lévy and Ada Savin (Montpellier: Presses de l'Université Paul-Valéry Montpellier III, 2002), 79.
10 Russell E. Brown, "Bruno Schulz and World Literature," *The Slavic and East European Journal* 34, 2 (1990): 238–40.
11 Russell E. Brown, "Bruno Schulz and World Literature," 238.
12 Edward W. Said, "Zionism from the Standpoint of Its Victims," *Social Text*, 1 (1979): 18.
13 Brauner, *Philip Roth*, 43.
14 Andrew Furman, "A New 'Other' Emerges in American Jewish Literature: Philip Roth's Israel Fiction," *Contemporary Literature* 36, 4 (1995): 636; Levinson and Zoline, "Impact of Summer Trip to Israel on the Self-Esteem of Jewish Adolescents," 94.
15 Akhil Gupta and James Ferguson, "Beyond 'Culture': Space, Identity, and the Politics of Difference," *Cultural Anthropology* 7, 1 (1992): 10–11.
16 Erik H. Cohen, *Youth Tourism to Israel: Educational Experiences of the Diaspora*, eds. Mike Robinson and Alison Phipps, vol. 15, Tourism and Cultural Change (Clevedon, Buffalo, Toronto: Channel View Publications, 2008), 7–8. For a more personal description of such a trip, cf. Levinson and Zoline, see "Impact of Summer

Trip to Israel on the Self-Esteem of Jewish Adolescents." For a very vivid impression of the effects of a so-called "Birthright Israel" tour, see the graphic novel *How to Understand Israel in 60 Days or Less* (New York: Vertigo/DC Comics, 2010) by Sarah Glidden.

17 Cohen, *Youth Tourism to Israel: Educational Experiences of the Diaspora*, 116 and 194.

18 On the stylistic playfulness see Posnock, *Philip Roth's Rude Truth: The Art of Immaturity*, 125–6.

19 Edward W. Said, "Invention, Memory, and Place," *Critical Inquiry* 26, 2 (2000): 180.

20 Derek Parker Royal, "Texts, Lives, and Bellybuttons: Philip Roth's *Operation Shylock* and the Renegotiation of Subjectivity," *Shofar* 19, 1 (2000): 55; Whitebrook, *Identity, Narrative and Politics*, 43.

21 The case of Ivan Demjanjuk (in the U.S. press referred to as John Demjanjuk, since he adopted an English name) gained notoriety again in spring 2009, when he was extradited to Germany. He died in March 2012 in Germany, where the Landgericht in Munich had condemned him to five years in prison. At the time of his death, his defense was appealing the case. The trial witnessed by Roth ended in 1977 with a death sentence, which was, however, repealed by the Israeli Supreme Court. Years after his return to the United States, a court saw it as proven that Demjanjuk had indeed served as a guard in concentration camps. These developments have been extensively covered by the press, cf. for instance the online dossier of the New York Times.

22 Whitebrook, *Identity, Narrative and Politics*, 44 and 55. She furthermore elaborates on the issue of multiple identities and the significance of a double, which are of less interest here.

23 Safer, *Mocking the Age: The Later Novels of Philip Roth*, 56.

24 *Ibid*, 45.

25 André Bleikasten, "'Improvisations on a Self': Les aléas de l'identité chez Philip Roth," in *Profils Américains: Philip Roth*, eds. Paule Lévy and Ada Savin (Montpellier: Presses de l'Université Paul-Valéry Montpellier III, 2002), 15.

26 Royal, "Texts, Lives, and Bellybuttons: Philip Roth's *Operation Shylock* and the Renegotiation of Subjectivity," 60.

27 Hat tip towards Adam Zachary Newton, *Facing Black and Jew: Literature as Public Space in Twentieth-Century America* (Cambridge: Cambridge University Press, 1999), 107.

28 Daniel Boyarin and Jonathan Boyarin, "Diaspora: Generation and the Ground of Jewish Identity," *Critical Inquiry* 19, 4 (1993): 723.

29 On the presence of the question of "authenticity" among secular Jews see Alice A. Butler-Smith, "Diaspora Nationality vs Diaspora Nationalism: American Jewish Identity and Zionism after the Jewish State," *Israel Affairs* 15, 2 (2009): 164.

30 Alain Finkielkraut, *The Imaginary Jew*, trans. Kevin O'Neill and David Suchoff (Lincoln, London: University of Nebraska Press, 1994), 169; Nathalie Rachlin, "Alain Finkielkraut and the Politics of Cultural Identity," *SubStance* 24, 76/77 (1995): 77.

31 Finkielkraut, *The Imaginary Jew*, 110–11.; Stuart Z. Charmé, "Varieties of Authenticity in Contemporary Jewish Identity," *Jewis Social Studies* 6, 2 (2000): 145.

32 Finkielkraut, *The Imaginary Jew*, 89–90.

33 Rachlin, "Alain Finkielkraut and the Politics of Cultural Identity," 75.

34 Charmé, "Varieties of Authenticity in Contemporary Jewish Identity," 138, 145–6. See also Rachlin, "Alain Finkielkraut and the Politics of Cultural Identity," 76.

35 On home and its role for identity construction, cf. Catarina Kinnvall, "Globalization and Religious Nationalism: Self, Identity, and the Search for Ontological Security," *Political Psychology* 25, 5 (2004): 747.
36 Scott Donaldson, "Philip Roth: The Meanings of 'Letting Go.'" *Contemporary Literature* 11, 1 (1970): 21–35.
37 Bergmann, *And Then the Child Becomes a Woman. Weibliche Initiation in der amerikanischen Kurzgeschichte 1865–1970*, 37–8.
38 Severs, "'Get Your Map of America': Tempering Dystopia and Learning Topography in *The Plot Against America*," 231.
39 Ette, *Literatur in Bewegung: Raum und Dynamik grenzüberschreitenden Schreibens in Europa und Amerika*, 26–7.
40 Liisa Malkki, "National Geographic: The Rooting of Peoples and the Territorialization of National Identity among Scholars and Refugees," *Cultural Anthropology* 7, 1 (1992): 26.
41 Again Liisa Malkki, "National Geographic: The Rooting of Peoples and the Territorialization of National Identity among Scholars and Refugees," 26.

Chapter 5

1 Julia Faisst, "'Delusionary Thinking, Whether White or Black or in Between': Fictions of Race in Philip Roth's the Human Stain," *Philip Roth Studies* 2, 2 (2006): 122.
2 Homi K. Bhaba, *The Location of Culture* (London: Routledge, 2003), 1–2.
3 Danièle Kahn-Paycha, *Popular Jewish Literature and Its Role in the Making of an Identity*, vol. 21, Jewish Studies (Lewiston, Queenston, Lampeter: The Edwin Mellen Press, 2000), 23.
4 The expression was common in the United States between 1890 and 1920 to describe Americans with a rather recent migrant background. Theodore Roosevelt referred to these "hyphenated Americans" in a speech held on 12 October 1915, claiming that "[t]here is no such thing as a hyphenated American who is a good American." Woodrow Wilson would later add that "[a]ny man who carries a hyphen about with him carries a dagger that he is ready to plunge into the vitals of this Republic." See Kay Deaux, "To Be an American: Immigration, Hyphenation, and Incorporation," *Journal of Social Issues* 64, 4 (2008): 935.
5 Michele Byers, "Material Bodies and Performative Identities: Mona, Neil, and the Promised Land," *Philip Roth Studies* 2, 2 (2006): 113.
6 Matthew Wilson, "Reading the Human Stain through Charles W. Chesnutt: The Genre of the Passing Novel," *Philip Roth Studies* 2, 2 (2006): 139.
7 Steven J. Belluscio, *To Be Suddenly White: Literary Realism and Racial Passing* (Columbia and London: University of Missouri Press, 2006), 9–10; Werner Sollors, *Neither Black nor White yet Both: Thematic Explorations of Interracial Literature* (New York: Oxford University Press, 1997), 247. Both Belluscio and Sollors explore a wide range of novels on passing, yet go beyond the literary aspect of the theme by covering social and legal issues connected to passing.
8 Allen Guttmann, "The Conversions of the Jews," *Wisconsin Studies in Contemporary Literature* 6, 2 (1965); Sander L. Gilman, *Multiculturalism and the Jews* (New York and London: Routledge, 2006), 142–3.

9 Victoria Aarons, "American-Jewish Identity in Roth's Short Fiction," in *The Cambridge Companion to Philip Roth*, ed. Timothy Parrish (Cambridge: Cambridge University Press, 2001), 12.
10 Barry Gross, "American Fiction, Jewish Writers, and Black Characters: The Return Of 'The Human Negro' in Philip Roth," *MELUS* 11, 2 (1984): 7.
11 Aarons, "American-Jewish Identity in Roth's Short Fiction," 13.
12 Detlef Garz, *Sozialpsychologische Entwicklungstheorien. Von Mead, Piaget und Kohlberg bis zur Gegenwart*, 4th ed. (Wiesbaden: VS Verlag für Sozialwissenschaften, 2008), 45.
13 For the German speaking reader: "I" is translated as "Ich" and "me" as "ICH."
14 Byers, "Material Bodies and Performative Identities: Mona, Neil, and the Promised Land," 108.
15 Van Gennep, *Übergangsriten*, 78.
16 Elizabeth Tonkin, "Masks and Powers," *Man* 14, 2 (1979): 240. She also elaborates on the ancestral spirit believed to be invoked by masks.
17 Gilman, *Multiculturalism and the Jews*, 127.
18 Beth Widmaier Capo, "Inserting the Diaphragm in(to) Modern American Fiction: Mary McCarthy, Philip Roth, and the Literature of Contraception," *The Journal of American Culture* 26, 1 (2003): 119.
19 Cf. Gilman, *Multiculturalism and the Jews*, 45.
20 Gérard Genette, *Paratexte. Das Buch vom Beiwerk des Buches*, trans. Dieter Hornig (Frankfurt am Main: Suhrkamp, 1989), 94–5.
21 Marie Maclean, "Pretexts and Paratexts: The Art of the Peripheral," *New Literary History* 22, 2 (1991): 273–4.
22 The beginning of frame analysis in media studies and political studies can be traced back to Erving Goffman, *Frame Analysis: An Essay on the Organization of Experience* (Cambridge, MA: Harvard University Press, 1974).
23 Byers, "Material Bodies and Performative Identities: Mona, Neil, and the Promised Land," 106.
24 Gilman, *Multiculturalism and the Jews*, 127.
25 Debra Shostak, "Return to the Breast: The Body, the Masculine Subject, and Philip Roth," *Twentieth Century Literature* 45, 3 (1999): 329.
26 Gross, "American Fiction, Jewish Writers, and Black Characters: The Return of 'The Human Negro' In Philip Roth," 8.
27 Andrew Furman, "Immigrant Dreams and Civic Promises: (Con-)Testing Identity in Early Jewish American Literature and Gish Jen's *Mona in the Promised Land*," *MELUS* 25, 1 (2000): 212.
28 Gilman, *Multiculturalism and the Jews*, 142–3.
29 Here and in the following Aarons, "American-Jewish Identity in Roth's Short Fiction," 18 and 10.
30 Bleikasten, "'Improvisations on a Self': Les aléas de l'identité chez Philip Roth," 12.
31 Thomas H. Frank, "The Interpretation of Limits: Doctors and Novelists in the Fiction of Philip Roth," *The Journal of Popular Culture* 28, 4 (1995): 69.
32 In 1903 in "The Soul of Black Folk"; cf. Lisa A. Kirby, "Shades of Passing: Teaching and Interrogating Identity in Roth's *The Human Stain* and Fitzgerald's *The Great Gatsby*," *Philip Roth Studies* 2, 2 (2006): 153.
33 Central theme of Gilman, *Multiculturalism and the Jews*.

34 Belluscio, *To Be Suddenly White: Literary Realism and Racial Passing*, 9–10 and 149; Sollors, *Neither Black nor White yet Both: Thematic Explorations of Interracial Literature*, 249.
35 Sollors, *Neither Black nor White yet Both: Thematic Explorations of Interracial Literature*, 223.
36 Belluscio, *To Be Suddenly White: Literary Realism and Racial Passing*, 134.
37 Sollors, *Neither Black nor White yet Both: Thematic Explorations of Interracial Literature*, 249.
38 An overview is provided by Randall Kennedy, "Racial Passing," *Ohio State Law Journal* 62, 1145 (2001): 1–28.
39 Belluscio, *To Be Suddenly White: Literary Realism and Racial Passing*, 240.
40 Françoise Kral, "F(r)ictions of Identity in *The Human Stain*," *Philip Roth Studies* 2, 1 (2006): 47.
41 Ette, *Literatur in Bewegung: Raum und Dynamik grenzüberschreitenden Schreibens in Europa und Amerika*, 244–5.
42 For years, it has been assumed that Roth had actually been inspired by Broayard, see for instance Brett Ashley Kaplan, "Anatole Broyard's Human Stain: Performing Postracial Consciousness," *Philip Roth Studies* 1, 2 (2005): 125. As Roth himself explained in a blog entry at *The New Yorker Online* in 2012, he instead took his inspiration from an incident that besmirched the reputation of his friend Melvin Tumin, a Princeton sociologist. Tumin had inquired about the whereabouts of two African-American students with the very same words Roth would later have Silk use. See Roth, "An Open Letter to Wikipedia."
43 On the symbols of purity and purification in *The Human Stain*, cf. Kinzel, *Die Tragödie und Komödie des amerikanischen Lebens. Eine Studie zu Zuckermans Amerika in Philip Roths Amerika-Trilogie*, 173–4.
44 Kaplan, "Anatole Broyard's Human Stain: Performing Postracial Consciousness," 183.
45 R. Goldman, "The Psychological Impact of Circumcision," *BJU International* 83, 1 (1999): 93.
46 Kral, "F(r)ictions of Identity in *The Human Stain*," 50; Patrice D. Rankine, "Passing as Tragedy: Philip Roth's *The Human Stain*, the Oedipus Myth, and the Self-Made Man," *Critique: Studies in Contemporary Fiction* 47, 1 (2005): 104.
47 Faisst, "'Delusionary Thinking, Whether White or Black or in Between': Fictions of Race in Philip Roth's *The Human Stain*," 123.
48 Timothy Parrish, "Roth and Ethnic Identity," in *The Cambridge Companion to Philip Roth*, ed. Timothy Parrish (Cambridge: Cambridge University Press, 2007), 139.
49 See Chapter 6.

Chapter 6

1 On the artistic representation of Chimera, see Anne Roes, "The Representation of the Chimaera," *The Journal of Hellenic Studies* 54 (1934): 21–5.
2 Cf. Chapter 4.
3 Cottam et al., *Introduction to Political Psychology*, 224.
4 Judith Nagata, "Beyond Theology: Toward an Anthropology of 'Fundamentalism,'" *American Anthropological Association* 103, 2 (2001): 482; Carla Pasquinelli,

"Fundamentalisms," *Constellations* 5, 1 (1998): 11; Malise Ruthven, *Fundamentalism: A Very Short Introduction* (Oxford, New York: Oxford University Press, 2007), 5–6.

5 Barrie Paskins, "Fanaticism in the Modern Era," in *Fanaticism and Conflict in the Modern Age*, ed. Matthew Hughes and Gaynor Johnson (London and New York: Frank Cass, 2005), 7 and 13.

6 Jeff Victoroff, "The Mind of the Terrorist: A Review and Critique of Psychological Approaches," *Journal of Conflict Resolution* 49, 1 (2005): 11.

7 David Simpson, "Telling It Like It Isn't," in *Literature after 9/11*, ed. Ann Keniston and Jeanne Follansbee Quinn (New York, London: Routledge, 2008), 218.

8 Sara Upstone, "A Question of Black or White: Returning to Hanif Kureishi's *The Black Album*," *Postcolonial Text* 4, 1 (2008): 15.

9 Flaminia Nicora, "An Imperfect Resistance: Kureishi's Rhetorical Strategies as Critique in the Short Story 'My Son the Fanatic,'" in *Literary Encounters of Fundamentalism. A Case Book*, eds. Klaus Stierstorfer and Annette Kern-Stähler, *Anglistische Forschungen* (Heidelberg: Universitätsverlag Winter, 2008), 91 and 94. With recourse to Paul Watzlawick's theory on communication, Nicora analyzes on one level the contents of the communication between Parvez and Farid, and then on a second level the communication as a negotiation of the interpersonal relationship that connects the subjects involved in the exchange.

10 More in depth on the tension between his roles as an actor and as an immigrant: Bradley Buchanan, *Hanif Kureishi*, New British Fiction (Hampshire and New York: Palgrave Macmillan, 2007), 45 and 151

11 Upstone, "A Question of Black or White: Returning to Hanif Kureishi's *The Black Album*," 8.

12 Buchanan, *Hanif Kureishi*, 58.

13 Frederick M. Holmes, "The Postcolonial Subject Divided between East and West: Kureishi's *The Black Album* as an Intertext of Rushdie's *The Satanic Verses*," *Papers on Language and Literature* 37, 3 (2001).

14 Nicora, "An Imperfect Resistance: Kureishi's Rhetorical Strategies as Critique in the Short Story 'My Son the Fanatic,'" 90.

15 Pinaki Chakravorty, "The Rushdie Incident as Law-and-Literature Parable," *The Yale Law Journal* 104, 8 (1995): 2215–6.

16 Recall the structure of *The Counterlife* as explained in Chapter 4.

17 Furman, "A New 'Other' Emerges in American Jewish Literature: Philip Roth's Israel Fiction," 644.

18 Victoroff, "The Mind of the Terrorist: A Review and Critique of Psychological Approaches," 35.

19 Aaron T. Beck, "Prisoners of Hate," *Behaviour Research and Therapy* 40 (2002): 212; Jerrold M. Post, "When Hatred Is Bred in the Bone: Psycho-Cultural Foundations of Contemporary Terrorism," *Political Psychology* 26, 4 (2005): 617; Victoroff, "The Mind of the Terrorist: A Review and Critique of Psychological Approaches," 22.

20 Arie W. Kruglanski and Shira Fishman, "The Psychology of Terrorism: 'Syndrome' versus 'Tool' Perspectives," *Terrorism and Political Violence* 18, 2 (2006): 194.

21 Beck, "Prisoners of Hate," 211.

22 Here and in the following Robert S. Robins and Jerrold M. Post, *Die Psychologie des Terrors: Vom Verschwörungsdenken zum politischen Wahn*, trans. Christiana Goldmann (Ulm: Droemer, 2002), 131, 99–100 and 138.

23 Beck, "Prisoners of Hate," 212.
24 Nagata, "Beyond Theology: Toward an Anthropology of 'Fundamentalism,'" 485.
25 See also for other rhetorical figures used automatically in Political Science and politics in general: Seth Thompson, "Politics without Metaphors Is Like a Fish without Water," in *Metaphor: Implications and Applications*, eds. Jeffrey Scott Mio and Albert N. Katz (Mahwah, NJ: Lawrence Erlbaum Associates, 1996), 186.
26 Post, "When Hatred Is Bred in the Bone: Psycho-Cultural Foundations of Contemporary Terrorism," 618.
27 Post, "When Hatred Is Bred in the Bone: Psycho-Cultural Foundations of Contemporary Terrorism," 622.
28 Axel Stähler, "The 'Aesthetics' of Fundamentalism in Recent Jewish Fiction in English," in *Fundamentalism and Literature*, eds. Catherine Pesso-Miquel and Klaus Stierstorfer (New York: Palgrave McMillan, 2007), 63.
29 Martha Crenshaw, "Explaining Suicide Terrorism: A Review Essay," *Security Studies* 16, 1 (2007): 153.
30 Alice LoCicero and Samuel J. Sinclair, "Terrorism and Terrorist Leaders: Insights from Developmental and Ecological Psychology," *Studies in Conflict and Terrorism* 31, 3 (2008): 246.
31 Buchanan, *Hanif Kureishi*, 73; Nicora, "An Imperfect Resistance: Kureishi's Rhetorical Strategies as Critique in the Short Story 'My Son the Fanatic,'" 95–6.
32 Upstone, "A Question of Black or White: Returning to Hanif Kureishi's *The Black Album*," 2.
33 Buchanan, *Hanif Kureishi*, 148.
34 Nicora, "An Imperfect Resistance: Kureishi's Rhetorical Strategies as Critique in the Short Story 'My Son the Fanatic,'" 92.
35 Upstone, "A Question of Black or White: Returning to Hanif Kureishi's *The Black Album*," 17.
36 Cottam et al., *Introduction to Political Psychology*, 225; Kinnvall, "Globalization and Religious Nationalism: Self, Identity, and the Search for Ontological Security," 763.
37 Barry Asker, "Fighting for What's Fundamental: Leo Tolstoy, V. S. Naipaul, Nadine Gordimer and John Updike (with References to Salman Rushdie and Alexander Solzhenitsyn)," in *Literary Encounters of Fundamentalism. A Case Book*, eds. Klaus Stierstorfer and Annette Kern-Stähler, *Anglistische Forschungen* (Heidelberg: Universitätsverlag Winter, 2008), 70.
38 Michiko Kakutani, "John Updike's 'Terrorist' Imagines a Homegrown Threat to Homeland Security," *New York Times Online*, 6 June 2006.
39 Asker, "Fighting for What's Fundamental: Leo Tolstoy, V. S. Naipaul, Nadine Gordimer and John Updike (with References to Salman Rushdie and Alexander Solzhenitsyn)," 71–2.
40 Banerjee suggests that *Terrorist* is less a psychograph of the titular protagonist, but of the author himself and of the political climate during the time of the book's publication: Mita Banerjee, "'Whiteness of a Different Color?' Racial Profiling in John Updike's Terrorist," *Neohelicon* 35, 2 (2008): 15.
41 John Updike, "Talk of the Town," *The New Yorker*, 24 September 2001, online.
42 Sandra Kumamoto Stanley, "'Mourning the Greatest Generation': Myth and History in Philip Roth's American Pastoral," *Twentieth Century Literature* 51, 1 (2005).
43 Timothy Parrish, "The End of Identity: Philip Roth's *American Pastoral*," *Shofar* 19, 1 (2000): 91.

44 Kinzel, *Die Tragödie und Komödie des amerikanischen Lebens. Eine Studie zu Zuckermans Amerika in Philip Roths Amerika-Trilogie*, 137.
45 See also Part I.
46 Posnock, *Philip Roth's Rude Truth: The Art of Immaturity*, 110.
47 Freese, *Die Initiationsreise: Studien zum jugendlichen Helden im modernen amerikanischen Roman*, 138–9.
48 Kinzel, *Die Tragödie und Komödie des amerikanischen Lebens. Eine Studie zu Zuckermans Amerika in Philip Roths Amerika-Trilogie*, 124; Parrish, "The End of Identity: Philip Roth's *American Pastoral*," 92.
49 My translation. Kinzel, *Die Tragödie und Komödie des amerikanischen Lebens. Eine Studie zu Zuckermans Amerika in Philip Roths Amerika-Trilogie*, 151. Cf. also Parrish, "The End of Identity: Philip Roth's *American Pastoral*," 95.
50 Parrish, "The End of Identity: Philip Roth's *American Pastoral*," 93.
51 Brauner, *Philip Roth*, 164.
52 Observations by Brauner, *Philip Roth*, 17.
53 Arthur Saltzman, "*Leviathan:* Post Hoc Harmonies," in *Beyond the Red Notebook: Essays on Paul Auster*, ed. Dennis Barone (Philadelphia: University of Pennsylvania Press, 1995), 163; Aliki Varvogli, *The World That Is the Book: Paul Auster's Fiction* (Liverpool: Liverpool University Press, 2001), 143.
54 Richard Glejzer, "Witnessing 9/11: Art Spiegelman and the Persistence of Trauma," in *Literature after 9/11*, eds. Ann Keniston and Jeanne Follansbee Quinn (New York, London: Routledge, 2008), 101.
55 Tyler Cowen, "Terrorism as Theater: Analysis and Policy Implications," *Public Choice*, 128 (2006): 233.
56 Varvogli, *The World That Is the Book: Paul Auster's Fiction*, 153.
57 For a relatively new, extensive and highly accessible introduction to her work see Anne Sauvageot, *Sophie Calle, l'art caméléon* (Paris: Presses Universitaires de France, 2007). Sauvageot explains Calle's artful dissolution of fact and fiction on the basis of the project *Des histoires varies*, starting at 133.
58 Michael Rothberg, "Seeing Terror, Feeling Art: Public and Private in Post-9/11 Literature," in *Literature after 9/11*, eds. Ann Keniston and Jeanne Follansbee Quinn (New York; London: Routledge, 2008), 125.
59 Holmes, "The Postcolonial Subject Divided between East and West: Kureishi's *The Black Album* as an Intertext of Rushdie's *The Satanic Verses*"; Upstone, "A Question of Black or White: Returning to Hanif Kureishi's *The Black Album*," 10.

Chapter 7

1 Breanna Fahs, "Second Shifts and Political Awakenings," *Journal of Divorce & Remarriage* 47, 3 (2007): 43–4.
2 Jon A. Krosnick and Duane E. Alwin, "Aging and Susceptibility to Attitude Change," *Journal of Personality and Social Psychology* 57, 3 (1989): 416–25; Duane E. Alwin and Jon A. Krosnick, "Aging, Cohorts, and the Stability of Sociopolitical Orientations over the Life Span," *The American Journal of Sociology* 97, 1 (1991): 169–95.

3 M. Kent Jennings and Gregory B. Markus, "Political Involvement in Later Years: A Longitudinal Survey," *American Journal of Political Science* 32, 2 (1988): 302–16.
4 Robert H. Binstock, "Older People and Voting Participation: Past and Future," *The Gerontologist* 40, 1 (2000): 18–31.
5 Stephanie Cherolis, "Philip Roth's Pornographic Elegy: *The Dying Animal* as a Contemporary Meditation on Loss," *Philip Roth Studies* 2, 1 (2006): 14.
6 Cherolis, "Philip Roth's Pornographic Elegy," 22; Aristie Trendel, "Master and Pupil in Philip Roth's *The Dying Animal*," *Philip Roth Studies* 3, 1 (2007): 60.
7 Trendel, "Master and Pupil in Philip Roth's *The Dying Animal*," 60.
8 *Ibid*, 59.
9 Isabel Coixet, "Elegy," (USA: Samuel Goldwyn Films, Lakeshore Entertainment, Sony Pictures Entertainment (SPE) Worldwide Acquisitions Group, 2008).
10 Brauner, *Philip Roth*, 219.
11 Volker Hage, *Philip Roth. Bücher und Begegnungen* (München: Carl Hanser Verlag, 2008), 130.
12 Volker Hage, "'Alter ist ein Massaker.' Ein Interview mit Philip Roth," *Spiegel Online*, 27 August 2006, online.
13 Hage, *Philip Roth. Bücher und Begegnungen*, 137–8.
14 Claudia Roth Pierpont, "The Great Enemy," *The New Yorker*, 1 May 2006, online.
15 Briefly on Colerdige: Abbott, *The Cambridge Introduction to Narrative*, 197.
16 Brauner, *Philip Roth*, 219.
17 Posnock, *Philip Roth's Rude Truth: The Art of Immaturity*, 12 and 87.
18 See Part I. Instead of recapitulating many, cf. Marcus, "What Is an Initiation Story?," 222.
19 Carl Benson, "Conrad's Two Stories of Initiation," *PMLA* 69, 1 (1954): 50.
20 Cf. also Sam Bluefarb, "The Sea – Mirror and Maker of Character in Fiction and Drama," *The English Journal* 48, 9 (1959): 504.
21 Cf. Part I. Benson, "Conrad's Two Stories of Initiation," 50.
22 Cesare Casarino, "The Sublime of the Closet; or, Joseph Conrad's Secret Sharing," *boundary 2* 24, 2 (1997): 201.
23 Michel Foucault, "Of Other Spaces," *Diacritics* 16, 1 (1986): 27.
24 Benson, "Conrad's Two Stories of Initiation," 50.
25 Michael C. Kotzin, "The Fairy Tale and Fiction: Enchantment in Early Conrad," *Folklore* 91, 1 (1980): 15–6.
26 Alexis Kate Wilson, "The Ghosts of Zuckerman's Past: The Zuckerman Bound Series," in *Philip Roth: New Perspectives on an American Author*, ed. Derek Parker Royal (Westport, CT and London: Praeger, 2005), 105.
27 Brauner, *Philip Roth*, 29.
28 Cf. Steven Milowitz, *Philip Roth Considered: The Concentrationary Universe of the American Writer* (New York: Garland Publishing, 2000), 28.
29 See again Milowitz, *Philip Roth Considered: The Concentrationary Universe of the American Writer*, 37.
30 Van Gennep, *Übergangsriten*, 143.
31 See van Gennep, *Übergangsriten*, 76.

32 Stian Stang Christiansen ("Zuckerman versus Kliman: Boundaries between Life and Literature in the Zuckerman Novels," *Philip Roth Studies* 5, 2 [2009]) goes further by suggesting that "some characters" in *Exit Ghost* "function as repetitions of characters in *The Ghost Writer*: Jamie becomes Amy, while Kliman appears as the young Zuckerman" (219). He then, however, outlines how Kliman and Zuckerman stand for very different approaches to the tenuous relationship between life and literature, the factual and fiction.

Sources

Novels and other writings by Philip Roth

American Pastoral. London: Vintage, 2005.
The Anatomy Lesson. London: Vintage, 2005.
The Breast. New York: Vintage International, 1994.
"The Conversion of the Jews." In *Goodbye, Columbus*, 105–20. London: Vintage, 2006.
The Counterlife. London: Vintage, 2005.
Deception. London: Vintage, 2006.
The Dying Animal. London: Vintage, 2002.
"Eli, the Fanatic." In *Goodbye, Columbus*, 185–221. London: Vintage, 2006.
Everyman. London: Jonathan Cape, 2006.
Exit Ghost. London: Jonathan Cape, 2007.
The Facts: A Novelist's Autobiography. New York: Vintage International, 1997.
The Ghost Writer. London: Vintage, 2005.
Goodbye, Columbus. London: Vintage, 2006.
The Great American Novel. London: Vintage, 2006.
The Human Stain. London: Vintage, 2001.
The Humbling. London: Jonathan Cape, 2009.
I Married a Communist. London: Vintage, 1999.
Indignation. Boston, New York: Houghton Mifflin Company, 2008.
Letting Go. New York: Vintage International, 1997.
My Life as a Man. New York: Vintage International, 1993.
"An Open Letter to Wikipedia." *The New Yorker*, 7 September 2012, http://www.newyorker.com/online/blogs/books/2012/09/an-open-letter-to-wikipedia.html.
Operation Shylock. A Confession. New York: Vintage International, 1994.
Our Gang (Starring Tricky and His Friends). London: Vintage, 2006.
Patrimony. A True Story. London: Vintage, 1999.
The Plot Against America. New York: Vintage International, 2004.
Portnoy's Complaint. London: Vintage, 1999.
The Prague Orgy. New York: Vintage International, 1996.
The Professor of Desire. New York: Vintage International, 1994.
Reading Myself and Others. New York: Vintage International, 2001.
Sabbath's Theater. London: Vintage, 1996.
Shop Talk: A Writer and His Colleagues at Work. New York: Vintage International, 2002.
"The Story Behind 'The Plot Against America.'" *The New York Times*, 19 September 2004, http://query.nytimes.com/gst/fullpage.html?res=9500E7DB1338F93AA2575AC0A9629C8B63.
When She Was Good. New York: Vintage International, 1995.
Zuckerman Unbound. New York: Vintage International, 1995.

Works by other authors and artists

Anderson, Sherwood. *Winesburg, Ohio*. New York: Signet Classics, 2005.
Auster, Paul. *Leviathan*. London: faber and faber, 2001.
Bellow, Saul. *The Adventures of Augie March*. London: Penguin Books, 2001.
Calle, Sophie. *Double Game*. London: Violette Editions, 2007.
Coixet, Isabel. "Elegy." 108 min. USA: Samuel Goldwyn Films, Lakeshore Entertainment, Sony Pictures Entertainment (SPE) Worldwide Acquisitions Group, 2008.
Conrad, Joseph. *Lord Jim*. London: Wordsworth Classics, 2002.
— *The Shadow-Line. A Confession*. Oxford: Oxford University Press, 2003.
Ellison, Ralph. *Invisible Man*. New York: Vintage Books, 1995.
Glidden, Sarah. *How to Understand Israel in 60 Days or Less*. New York: Vertigo/DC Comics, 2010.
James, Henry. "The Middle Years." In *Tales of Henry James*, edited by Christof Wegelin and Henry B. Wonham, 221–28. New York: W.W. Norton & Company, 2003.
Jen, Gish. *Mona in the Promised Land*. New York: Vintage Books, 1997.
Johnson, James Weldon. *The Autobiography of an Ex-Colored Man and Other Writings*. New York: Barnes & Noble Classics, 2007.
Kureishi, Hanif. *The Black Album*. London: faber and faber, 2000.
— *The Buddha of Suburbia*. London: faber and faber, 1990.
— *My Son the Fanatic*. Stuttgart: Philipp Reclam jun., 2007.
Larsen, Nella. *Passing*. New York: Penguin Books, 2003.
Lewis, Sinclair. *It Can't Happen Here*. New York: Signet Classics, 2005.
Miller, Arthur. *Focus*. London: Methuen, 2002.
Ozick, Cynthia. *The Messiah of Stockholm*. New York: Vintage Books, 1988.
Rushdie, Salman. *Imaginary Homelands. Essays and Criticism 1981–1991*. London: Granta Books and Penguin Books, 1992.
Spiegelman, Art. *In the Shadows of No Towers*. New York: Phaeton Books, 2004.
Updike, John. *Terrorist*. New York: Ballantine Books, 2007.

Academic sources

Aarons, Victoria. "American-Jewish Identity in Roth's Short Fiction." In *The Cambridge Companion to Philip Roth*, edited by Timothy Parrish, 9–21. Cambridge: Cambridge University Press, 2001.
Abbott, Porter H. *The Cambridge Introduction to Narrative*. 2nd ed. Cambridge, New York: Cambridge University Press, 2008.
Alwin, Duane E., and Jon A. Krosnick. "Aging, Cohorts, and the Stability of Sociopolitical Orientations over the Life Span." *The American Journal of Sociology* 97, 1 (1991): 169–95.
Aponte, Barbara B. "El rito de la iniciación en el cuento hispanoamericano." *Hispanic Review* 51, 2 (1983): 129–46.
Asker, Barry. "Fighting for What's Fundamental: Leo Tolstoy, V.S. Naipaul, Nadine Gordimer and John Updike (with References to Salman Rushdie and Alexander Solzhenitsyn)." In *Literary Encounters of Fundamentalism. A Case Book*, edited by Klaus Stierstorfer and Annette Kern-Stähler, 53–74. Heidelberg: Universitätsverlag Winter, 2008.

Bachelard, Gaston. *Poetik des Raumes*. Übers. Kurt Leonhard. 7. Aufl. Frankfurt am Main: Fischer Taschenbuch Verlag, 2003.

Banerjee, Mita. "'Whiteness of a Different Color?' Racial Profiling in John Updike's Terrorist." *Neohelicon* 35, 2 (2008): 13–28.

Baron, Jane B. "Law, Literature, and the Problems of Interdisciplinarity." *The Yale Law Journal* 108, 5 (1999): 1059–85.

Bassler, Moritz. "Einleitung: New Historicism – Literaturgeschichte als Poetik der Kultur." In *New Historicism*, Hrsg. Mario Bassler, 7–28. Tübingen; Basel: Francke/ Uni-Taschenbücher, 2001.

Beck, Aaron T. "Prisoners of Hate." *Behaviour Research and Therapy* 40 (2002): 209–16.

Belfiore, Eleonora, and Oliver Bennett. "Rethinking the Social Impacts of the Arts." *International Journal of Cultural Policy* 13, 2 (2007): 135–51.

Belluscio, Steven J. *To Be Suddenly White: Literary Realism and Racial Passing*. Columbia and London: University of Missouri Press, 2006.

Benson, Carl. "Conrad's Two Stories of Initiation." *PMLA* 69, 1 (1954): 46–56.

Bergmann, Ina. *And Then the Child Becomes a Woman. Weibliche Initiation in der amerikanischen Kurzgeschichte 1865–1970*. Vol. 110, American Monograph Series. Heidelberg: Universitätsverlag Winter, 2003.

Berti, Anna Emilia. "Children's Understanding of Politics." In *Children's Understanding of Society*, edited by Martyn and Eithne Buchanan-Barrow Barrett, 69–104. Hove, England: Psychology Press, 2005.

Bhaba, Homi K. *The Location of Culture*. London: Routledge, 2003.

Binstock, Robert H. "Older People and Voting Participation: Past and Future." *The Gerontologist* 40, 1 (2000): 18–31.

Bleikasten, André. "'Improvisations on a Self': Les aléas de l'identité chez Philip Roth." In *Profils Américains: Philip Roth*, éd. Paule Lévy et Ada Savin, 11–24. Montpellier: Presses de l'Université Paul-Valéry Montpellier III, 2002.

Bloom, Claire. *Leaving a Doll's House. A Memoir*. Boston, New York, Toronto, London: Little, Brown and Company, 1996.

Blotner, Joseph. *The Political Novel*. Reprint ed. Westport, Conn: Greenwood Press, 1979.

Bluefarb, Sam. "The Sea–Mirror and Maker of Character in Fiction and Drama." *The English Journal* 48, 9 (1959): 501–10.

Boyarin, Daniel, and Jonathan Boyarin. "Diaspora: Generation and the Ground of Jewish Identity." *Critical Inquiry* 19, 4 (1993): 693–725.

Brauner, David. *Philip Roth*. Manchester and New York: Manchester University Press, 2007.

Brodzki, Bella. "Reading Himself and Others: *The Professor of Desire*." In *Profils Américains: Philip Roth*, éd. Paul Lévy et Ada Savin, 77–88. Montpellier: Presses de l'Université Paul-Valéry Montpellier III, 2002.

Brown, Russell E. "Bruno Schulz and World Literature." *The Slavic and East European Journal* 34, 2 (1990): 224–46.

Buchanan, Bradley. *Hanif Kureishi*. New British Fiction. Hampshire and New York: Palgrave Macmillan, 2007.

Buckingham, David. "News Media, Political Socialization and Popular Citizenship: Towards a New Agenda." *Critical Studies in Mass Communication* 14, 4 (1997): 344–66.

Burckhardt, Sigurd. "English Bards and APSR Reviewers." *The American Political Science Review* 54, 1 (1960): 158–66.

Burwick, Frederick. "'Art for Art's Sake' and the Politics of Prescinding: 1790s, 1890s, 1990s." *Pacific Coast Philology* 34, 2 (1999): 117–26.

Butler-Smith, Alice A. "Diaspora Nationality vs Diaspora Nationalism: American Jewish Identity and Zionism after the Jewish State." *Israel Affairs* 15, 2 (2009): 159–79.

Byers, Michele. "Material Bodies and Performative Identities: Mona, Neil, and the Promised Land." *Philip Roth Studies* 2, 2 (2006): 102–20.

Camps-Robertson, Régine. "Les seuils infranchissables dans *Portnoy's Complaint*." In *Profils Américains: Philip Roth*, éd. by Paul Lévy et Ada Savin, 63–75. Montpellier: Presses de l'Université Paul-Valéry Montpellier III, 2002.

Caplan, Jane. "Postmodernism, Poststructuralism, and Deconstruction: Notes for Historians." *Central European History* 22, 3/4 (1989): 260–78.

Carter, Amy, and Ryan L. Teten. "Assessing Changing Views of the President: Revisiting Greenstein's 'Children and Politics.'" *Presidential Studies Quarterly* 32, 3 (2002): 453–62.

Casarino, Cesare. "The Sublime of the Closet; or, Joseph Conrad's Secret Sharing." *Boundary 2* 24, 2 (1997): 199–243.

Chaffee, Steven H., Clifford I. Nass, and Seung-Mock Yang. "The Bridging Role of Television in Immigrant Political Socialization." *Human Communication Research* 17, 2 (2006): 266–88.

Chakravorty, Pinaki. "The Rushdie Incident as Law-and-Literature Parable." *The Yale Law Journal* 104, 8 (1995): 2213–47.

Charmé, Stuart Z. "Varieties of Authenticity in Contemporary Jewish Identity." *Jewish Social Studies* 6, 2 (2000): 133–55.

Cherolis, Stephanie. "Philip Roth's Pornographic Elegy: *The Dying Animal* as a Contemporary Meditation on Loss." *Philip Roth Studies* 2, 1 (2006): 13–24.

Chodat, Robert. "Fictions Public and Private: Philip Roth." *Contemporary Literature* 46, 4 (2005): 688–719.

Christiansen, Stian Stang. "Zuckerman versus Kliman: Boundaries between Life and Literature in the Zuckerman Novels." *Philip Roth Studies* 5, 2 (2009): 219–25.

Cohen, Eileen Z. "Alex in Wonderland, Or 'Portnoy's Complaint.'" *Twentieth Century Literature* 17, 3 (1971): 161–68.

Cohen, Erik H. *Youth Tourism to Israel: Educational Experiences of the Diaspora*. Edited by Mike Robinson and Alison Phipps. Vol. 15, Tourism and Cultural Change. Clevedon, Buffalo, Toronto: Channel View Publications, 2008.

Connell, Raewyn W. "Political Socialization in the American Family: The Evidence Re-Examined." *The Public Opinion Quarterly* 36, 3 (1972): 323–33.

Conner, Marc C. "Fathers and Sons: *Winesburg, Ohio* and the Revision of Modernism." *Studies in American Fiction* 29, 2 (2001): 209–38.

Cook, Timothy E. "The Bear Market in Political Socialization and the Costs of Misunderstood Psychological Theories." *The American Political Science Review* 79, 4 (1985): 1079–93.

Cooper, Alan. "It Can Happen Here, or All in the Family Values: Surviving *The Plot Against America*." In *Philip Roth: New Perspectives on an American Author*, edited by Derek Parker Royal, 241–53. Westport, Connecticut, London: Praeger, 2005.

Cottam, Martha, Beth Dietz-Uhler, Elena Mastors, and Thomas Preston. *Introduction to Political Psychology*. Mahwah, NJ: Lawrence Erlbaum Associates, 2004.

Cowen, Tyler. "Terrorism as Theater: Analysis and Policy Implications." *Public Choice*, 128 (2006): 233–44.

Crenshaw, Martha. "Explaining Suicide Terrorism: A Review Essay." *Security Studies* 16, 1 (2007): 133–62.

Deaux, Kay. "To Be an American: Immigration, Hyphenation, and Incorporation." *Journal of Social Issues* 64, 4 (2008): 925–43.
Donaldson, Scott. "Philip Roth: The Meanings of 'Letting Go.'" *Contemporary Literature* 11, 1 (1970): 21–35.
Douthat, Ross. "It Didn't Happen Here." *Policy Review*, February/March (2005), http://www.hoover.org/publications/policyreview/3431551.html.
Dudley, Robert L., and Alan R. Gitelson. "Political Literacy, Civic Education, and Civic Engagement: A Return to Political Socialization?" *Applied Developmental Science* 6, 4 (2002): 175–82.
Easton, David, and Jack Dennis. "The Child's Acquisition of Regime Norms: Political Efficacy." *The American Political Science Review* 61, 1 (1967): 25–38.
— *Children in the Political System*. New York: McGraw-Hill Book Company, 1969.
Easton, David, and Robert Hess. "The Child's Political World." *Midwest Journal of Political Science* 6, 3 (1962): 229–46.
Eliade, Mircea. *Das Mysterium der Wiedergeburt – Initiationsriten, ihre kulturelle und religiöse Bedeutung*. Zürich: Rascher, 1961.
Ette, Ottmar. *Literatur in Bewegung: Raum und Dynamik grenzüberschreitenden Schreibens in Europa und Amerika*. Weilerswist: Velbrück Wissenschaft, 2001.
Fahs, Breanna. "Second Shifts and Political Awakenings." *Journal of Divorce & Remarriage* 47, 3 (2007): 43–66.
Faisst, Julia. "'Delusionary Thinking, Whether White or Black or in Between': Fictions of Race in Philip Roth's *The Human Stain*." *Philip Roth Studies* 2, 2 (2006): 121–37.
Finkielkraut, Alain. *The Imaginary Jew*. Translated by Kevin O'Neill and David Suchoff. Lincoln, London: University of Nebraska Press, 1994.
Fish, Stanley Eugene. *Is There a Text in This Class? The Authority of Interpretive Communities*. Cambridge: Harvard University Press, 1980.
Fishman, Ethan. "Saul Bellow's 'Likely Stories.'" *The Journal of Politics* 45, 3 (1983): 615–34.
Flanagan, Constance, and Leslie S. Gallay. "Reframing the Meaning of 'Political' in Research with Adolescents." *Perspectives on Political Science* 24, 1 (1995): 34–41.
Fludernik, Monika. "*Winesburg, Ohio*: The Apprenticeship of George Willard." *Amerikastudien/American Studies* 32, 4 (1987): 431–52.
Foucault, Michel. "Of Other Spaces." *Diacritics* 16, 1 (1986): 22–7.
Frank, Thomas H. "The Interpretation of Limits: Doctors and Novelists in the Fiction of Philip Roth." *The Journal of Popular Culture* 28, 4 (1995): 67–80.
Freese, Peter. *Die Initiationsreise: Studien zum jugendlichen Helden im modernen amerikanischen Roman*. Tübingen: Stauffenburg-Verlag, 1998.
Fridkin, Kim L., Patrick J. Kenney, and Jack Crittenden. "On the Margins of Democratic Life: The Impact of Race and Ethnicity on the Political Engagement of Young People." *American Politics Research* 34, 5 (2006): 605–26.
Furman, Andrew. "Immigrant Dreams and Civic Promises: (Con-)Testing Identity in Early Jewish American Literature and Gish Jen's *Mona in the Promised Land*." *MELUS* 25, 1 (2000): 209–26.
— "A New 'Other' Emerges in American Jewish Literature: Philip Roth's Israel Fiction." *Contemporary Literature* 36, 4 (1995): 633–53.
Fussell, Edwin. "*Winesburg, Ohio*: Art and Isolation." In *Sherwood Anderson: A Collection of Critical Essays*, edited by Walter B. Rideout, 39–48. Englewood Cliffs, NJ: Prentice-Hall, Inc., 1974.

Garz, Detlef. *Sozialpsychologische Entwicklungstheorien. Von Mead, Piaget und Kohlberg bis zur Gegenwart*. 4. Aufl. Wiesbaden: VS Verlag für Sozialwissenschaften, 2008.
Geller, Jeffrey L. "*Indignation: A Novel*. Book Review." *Psychiatric Services* 59, 12 (2008): 1476.
Genette, Gérard. "Fictional Narrative, Factual Narrative." *Poetics Today* 11, 4 (1990): 755–74.
— *Palimpseste. Die Literatur auf zweiter Stufe*. Übers. Wolfram Bayer und Dieter Hornig. Frankfurt a.M.: Suhrkamp, 1993.
— *Paratexte. Das Buch vom Beiwerk des Buches*. Übers. Dieter Hornig. Frankfurt am Main: Suhrkamp, 1989.
Gilman, Sander L. *Multiculturalism and the Jews*. New York and London: Routledge, 2006.
Glass, Jonathan M. "Religious Circumcision: A Jewish View." *BJU International* 83, 1 (1999): 17–21.
Glejzer, Richard. "Witnessing 9/11: Art Spiegelman and the Persistence of Trauma." In *Literature after 9/11*, edited by Ann Keniston and Jeanne Follansbee Quinn, 99–119. New York, London: Routledge, 2008.
Glick, Leonard B. "Jewish Circumcision. An Enigma in Historical Perspective." In *Understanding Circumcision: A Multi-Disciplinary Approach to a Multi-Dimensional Problem*, edited by George C. Denniston, Frederick Mansfield Hodges and Marylin Fayre Milos, 19–54. New York, Boston, Dordrecht, London, Moscow: Kluwer Academic/Plenum Publishers, 2001.
Goffman, Erving. *Frame Analysis: An Essay on the Organization of Experience*. Cambridge, MA: Harvard University Press, 1974.
Goldman, Ronald. "The Psychological Impact of Circumcision." *BJU International* 83, 1 (1999): 93–102.
Gooblar, David. *The Major Phases of Philip Roth*. London and New York: Continuum, 2011.
Gottfried, Alex, and Sue Davidson. "Utopia's Children: An Interpretation of Three Political Novels." *The Western Political Quarterly* 15, 1 (1962): 17–32.
Grasseni, Cristina. "Taxidermy as Rhetoric of Self-Making: Charles Waterton (1782–1865), Wandering Naturalist." *Studies in History and Philosophy of Biology and Biomedical Sciences* 29, 2 (1998): 269–94.
Grimes, Ronald L. *Deeply into the Bone: Re-Inventing Rites of Passage*. Berkeley, Los Angeles and London: University of California Press, 2000.
Gross, Abraham. "The Blood Libel and the Blood of Circumcision: An Ashkenazic Custom That Disappeared in the Middle Ages." *The Jewish Quarterly Review* 86, 1/2 (1995): 171–74.
Gross, Barry. "American Fiction, Jewish Writers, and Black Characters: The Return of 'The Human Negro' in Philip Roth." *MELUS* 11, 2 (1984): 5–22.
— "Seduction of the Innocent: *Portnoy's Complaint* and Popular Culture." *MELUS* 8, 4 (1981): 81–92.
Gross, John. "A Constant Reader." *The New York Review of Books*, 14 May 2009, 8–10.
Gupta, Akhil, and James Ferguson. "Beyond 'Culture': Space, Identity, and the Politics of Difference." *Cultural Anthropology* 7, 1 (1992): 6–23.
Guttmann, Allen. "The Conversions of the Jews." *Wisconsin Studies in Contemporary Literature* 6, 2 (1965): 161–76.
Gwinn Wilkins, Karin. "The Role of Media in Public Disengagement from Political Life." *Journal of Broadcasting and Electronic Media* 44, 4 (2000): 569–80.
Hage, Volker. "'Alter ist ein Massaker.' Ein Interview mit Philip Roth." *Spiegel Online*, 27. August 2006, http://www.spiegel.de/kultur/literatur/0.1518.433535.00.html.

— *Philip Roth. Bücher und Begegnungen*. München: Carl Hanser Verlag, 2008.
Hanne, Michael. *The Power of the Story: Fiction and Political Change*. Providence: Berghahn Books, 1994.
Harrington, Charles. "Sexual Differentiation in Socialization and Some Male Genital Mutilations." *American Anthropologist* 70, 5 (1968): 951–56.
Haskins, Ekaterina V. "'Put Your Stamp on History': The USPS Commemorative Program *Celebrate the Century* and Postmodern Collective Memory." *Quarterly Journal of Speech* 89, 1 (2003): 1–18.
Hassan, Ihab. *Radical Innocence: Studies in the Contemporary American Novel*. Princeton, NJ: Princeton University Press, 1961.
Heller, Arno. *Odyssee zum Selbst. Zur Gestaltung jugendlicher Identitätssuche im neueren amerikanischen Roman*. Innsbruck, 1973.
Holmes, Frederick M. "The Postcolonial Subject Divided between East and West: Kureishi's *The Black Album* as an Intertext of Rushdie's *The Satanic Verses*." *Papers on Language and Literature* 37, 3 (2001): 296–314.
Hutchison, Anthony. "Purity is Petrefaction: Liberalism and Betrayal in Philip Roth's *I Married a Communist*." *Rethinking History* 9, 2 (2005): 315–27.
— *Writing the Republic: Liberalism and Morality in American Political Fiction*. New York: Columbia University Press, 2007.
Hyman, Herbert H. *Political Socialization: A Study in the Psychology of Political Behavior*. London: Collier-Macmillan, 1969.
Jaeger, Stephan. "Erzähltheorie und Geschichtswissenschaft." In *Erzähltheorie transgenerisch, intermedial, interdisziplinär*, Hrsg. Vera Nünning und Ansgar Nünning, 237–63. Trier: WVT Wissenschaftlicher Verlag, 2002.
Jaros, Dean. "Children's Orientations toward the President: Some Additional Theoretical Considerations and Data." *The Journal of Politics* 29 (1967): 368–87.
Jennings, M. Kent. "The Intergenerational Transfer of Political Ideologies in Eight Western Nations." *European Journal of Political Research* 12, 3 (2006): 261–76.
Jennings, M. Kent, and Kenneth P. Langton. "Mothers Versus Fathers: The Formation of Political Orientations among Young Americans." *The Journal of Politics* 31 (1969): 329–58.
Jennings, M. Kent, and Gregory B. Markus. "Political Involvement in Later Years: A Longitudinal Survey." *American Journal of Political Science* 32, 2 (1988): 302–16.
Jennings, M. Kent, and Richard G. Niemi. "The Transmission of Political Values from Parent to Child." *The American Political Science Review* 62, 1 (1968): 169–84.
Kahn-Paycha, Danièle. *Popular Jewish Literature and Its Role in the Making of an Identity*. Vol. 21, Jewish Studies. Lewiston, Queenston, Lampeter: The Edwin Mellen Press, 2000.
Kakutani, Michiko. "John Updike's 'Terrorist' Imagines a Homegrown Threat to Homeland Security." *New York Times Online*, 6 June 2006, http://www.nytimes.com/2006/06/06/books/06kaku.html.
Kam, Cindy D., and Carl L. Palmer. "Reconsidering the Effects of Education on Political Participation." *The Journal of Politics* 70 (2008): 612–31.
Kaplan, Brett Ashley. "Anatole Broyard's Human Stain: Performing Postracial Consciousness." *Philip Roth Studies* 1, 2 (2005): 125–44.
—. "Contested, Constructed Home(lands): Diaspora, Postcolonial Studies and Zionism." *Journal of Modern Jewish Studies* 6, 1 (2007): 85–100.
Keen, Suzanne. *Empathy and the Novel*. Oxford, New York: Oxford University Press, 2007.
Kennedy, Randall. "Racial Passing." *Ohio State Law Journal* 62, 1145 (2001): 1–28.

Kinnvall, Catarina. "Globalization and Religious Nationalism: Self, Identity, and the Search for Ontological Security." *Political Psychology* 25, 5 (2004): 741–67.

Kinzel, Till. *Die Tragödie und Komödie des amerikanischen Lebens. Eine Studie zu Zuckermans Amerika in Philip Roths Amerika-Trilogie*. Vol. 137, American Studies Monograph Series. Heidelberg: Universitätsverlag Winter, 2006.

Kirby, Lisa A. "Shades of Passing: Teaching and Interrogating Identity in Roth's *The Human Stain* and Fitzgerald's *The Great Gatsby*." *Philip Roth Studies* 2, 2 (2006): 151–60.

Köhler, Andrea. "Der endlose Strom des Blutes: Philip Roth erzählt von jenseits des Grabes." *Neue Zürcher Zeitung*, 10. Februar 2009, 37.

Kotzin, Michael C. "The Fairy Tale and Fiction: Enchantment in Early Conrad." *Folklore* 91, 1 (1980): 15–26.

Kral, Françoise. "F(r)ictions of Identity in *The Human Stain*." *Philip Roth Studies* 2, 1 (2006): 47–55.

Krosnick, Jon A., and Duane E. Alwin. "Aging and Susceptibility to Attitude Change." *Journal of Personality and Social Psychology* 57, 3 (1989): 416–25.

Kruglanski, Arie W., and Shira Fishman. "The Psychology of Terrorism: 'Syndrome' versus 'Tool' Perspectives." *Terrorism and Political Violence* 18, 2 (2006): 193–215.

Kumamoto Stanley, Sandra. "'Mourning the Greatest Generation': Myth and History in Philip Roth's American Pastoral." *Twentieth Century Literature* 51, 1 (2005): 1–24.

Lane, Robert E. "Fathers and Sons: Foundations of Political Belief." *American Sociological Review* 24, 4 (1959): 502–11.

Lee, Hermione. "Age Makes a Difference. Hermione Lee Talks with Philip Roth about His New Novel, 'Exit Ghost.'" *The New Yorker*, 1 October 2007, http://www.newyorker.com/reporting/2007/10/01/071001fa_fact_lee.

Levine, Caroline. *Provoking Democracy: Why We Need the Arts*. Malden, MA, Oxford and Victoria: Blackwell Publishing Ltd, 2007.

Levinson, Tamar A., and Susan Zoline. "Impact of Summer Trip to Israel on the Self-Esteem of Jewish Adolescents." *Journal of Psychology and Judaism* 21, 2 (1997): 87–119.

Lévy, Ellen. "Non-Genetic Genealogies in *I Married a Communist*." In *Profils Américains: Philip Roth*, éd. Paul Lévy et Ada Savin, 169–79. Montpellier: Presses de l'Université Paul-Valéry Montpellier III, 2002.

Lewis, Charles. "Real Planes and Imaginary Towers: Philip Roth's *The Plot Against America* as 9/11 Prosthetic Screen." In *Literature after 9/11*, edited by Ann Keniston and Jeanne Follansbee Quinn, 246–60. New York, London: Routledge, 2008.

Lisle, Debbie. *The Global Politics of Contemporary Travel Writing*. Cambridge: Cambridge University Press, 2006.

Livezeanu, Irina. "Journal 1935–1944: The Fascist Years." *Holocaust and Genocide Studies* 16, 3 (2002): 451–55.

LoCicero, Alice, and Samuel J. Sinclair. "Terrorism and Terrorist Leaders: Insights from Developmental and Ecological Psychology." *Studies in Conflict and Terrorism* 31, 3 (2008): 227–50.

Maccoby, Eleanor E., Richard E. Matthews, and S. Morton Anton. "Youth and Political Change." *The Public Opinion Quarterly* 18, 1 (1954): 23–39.

Macho, Thomas. *Rituale*. Vol. 1750, Vontobel-Schriftenreihe. Zürich: Vontobel-Stiftung, 2006.

Maclean, Marie. "Pretexts and Paratexts: The Art of the Peripheral." *New Literary History* 22, 2 (1991): 273–79.

Malina, Debra N. *Breaking the Frame: Metalepsis and the Construction of the Subject*. Columbus: The Ohio State University Press, 2002.

Malkki, Liisa. "National Geographic: The Rooting of Peoples and the Territorialization of National Identity among Scholars and Refugees." *Cultural Anthropology* 7, 1 (1992): 24–44.

Mar, Raymond A., Keith Oatley, Jacob Hirsh, Jennifer dela Paz, and Jordan B. Peterson. "Bookworms versus Nerds: Exposure to Fiction Versus Non-Fiction, Divergent Associations with Social Ability, and the Simulation of Fictional Social Worlds." *Journal of Research in Personality* 40 (2006): 694–712.

Marcus, Mordecai. "What Is an Initiation Story?" *The Journal of Aesthetics and Art Criticism* 19, 2 (1960): 221–28.

McDevitt, Michael, and Steven H. Chaffee. "From Top-Down to Trickle-up Influence: Revisiting Assumptions About the Family in Political Socialization." *Political Communication* 19, 3 (2002): 281–301.

McIntosh, Hugh, Daniel Hart, and James Youniss. "The Influence of Family Political Discussion on Youth Civic Development: Which Parent Qualities Matter." *PS: Political Science and Politics* 40, 3 (2007): 495–99.

Merelman, Richard M. "The Adolescence of Political Socialization." *Sociology of Education* 45, 2 (1972): 134–66.

Middleton, Russell, and Snell Putney. "Political Expression of Adolescent Rebellion." *The American Journal of Sociology* 68, 5 (1963): 527–35.

Milowitz, Steven. *Philip Roth Considered: The Concentrationary Universe of the American Writer*. New York: Garland Publishing, 2000.

Mishler, William, and Richard Rose. "What Are the Origins of Political Trust? Testing Institutional and Cultural Theories in Post-Communist Societies." *Comparative Political Studies* 34, 1 (2001): 30–62.

Morinis, Alan. "The Ritual Experience: Pain and the Transformation of Consciousness in Ordeals of Initiation." *Ethos* 13, 2 (1985): 150–74.

Nagata, Judith. "Beyond Theology: Toward an Anthropology of 'Fundamentalism.'" *American Anthropological Association* 103, 2 (2001): 481–98.

Nel, Adéle. "The Poet in Transit: Travel Poems and Liminality in *Lykdigte* (Elegies) and *Ruggespraak* (Consultation) by Joan Hambridge." In *Beyond the Threshold: Explorations of Liminality in Literature*, edited by Hein Viljoen and Chris N. van der Merwe, 223–46. New York: Peter Lang, 2007.

Newton, Adam Zachary. *Facing Black and Jew: Literature as Public Space in Twentieth-Century America*. Cambridge: Cambridge University Press, 1999.

Nicora, Flaminia. "An Imperfect Resistance: Kureishi's Rhetorical Strategies as Critique in the Short Story 'My Son the Fanatic.'" In *Literary Encounters of Fundamentalism. A Case Book*, edited by Klaus Stierstorfer and Annette Kern-Stähler, 89–100. Heidelberg: Universitätsverlag Winter, 2008.

Niemi, Richard G., and Mary A. Hepburn. "The Rebirth of Political Socialization." *Perspectives on Political Science* 24, 1 (1995): 7–16.

Niemi, Richard G., and Barbara I. Sobieszek. "Political Socialization." *Annual Review of Sociology* 3 (1977): 209–33.

Nora, Pierre. "Between Memory and History: *Les lieux de mémoire*." *Representations*, 26 (1989): 7–24.

Nünning, Ansgar. "Welten – Weltbilder – Weisen der Welterzeugung: Zum Wissen der Literatur und zur Aufgabe der Literaturwissenschaft." *Germanisch-Romanische Monatsschrift* 59, 1 (2009): 65–80.

Nussbaum, Martha C. "The Literary Imagination in Public Life." *New Literary History* 22, 4 (1991): 877–910.

— *Poetic Justice: The Literary Imagination and Public Life*. Boston, MA: Beacon Press, 1995.

Owen, Diana. "Service Learning and Political Socialization." *PS: Political Science and Politics* 33, 3 (2000): 638–40.

Pacheco, Julianna Sandell. "Political Socialization in Context: The Effect of Political Competition on Youth Voter Turnout." *Political Behavior* 30 (2008): 415–36.

Pappas, Christine. "'You Hafta Push': Using Sapphire's Novel to Teach Introduction to American Government." *Journal of Political Science Education* 3, 1 (2007): 29–50.

Parker, Robert Dale. *How to Interpret Literature: Critical Theory for Literary and Cultural Studies*. New York, Oxford: Oxford University Press, 2008.

Parrish, Timothy. "The End of Identity: Philip Roth's *American Pastoral*." *Shofar* 19, 1 (2000): 84–99.

— "Roth and Ethnic Identity." In *The Cambridge Companion to Philip Roth*, edited by Timothy Parrish, 127–41. Cambridge: Cambridge University Press, 2007.

Paskins, Barrie. "Fanaticism in the Modern Era." In *Fanaticism and Conflict in the Modern Age*, edited by Matthew Hughes and Gaynor Johnson, 7–18. London and New York: Frank Cass, 2005.

Pasquinelli, Carla. "Fundamentalisms." *Constellations* 5, 1 (1998): 10–17.

Peng, Yali. "Intellectual Fads in Political Science: The Cases of Political Socialization and Community Power Studies." *PS: Political Science and Politics* 27, 1 (1994): 100–08.

Plax, Martin J. "Thoughts on *The Plot Against America*." *Society* 42, 4 (2005): 77–83.

Posnock, Ross. "On Philip Roth's *The Plot Against America*." *Salmagundi: A Quarterly of the Humanities & Social Sciences*, 150/151 (2006): 270–82, http://cms.skidmore.edu/salmagundi/backissues/150-151/index.cfm.

— *Philip Roth's Rude Truth: The Art of Immaturity*. Princeton, NJ: Princeton University Press, 2006.

Post, Jerrold M. "When Hatred is Bred in the Bone: Psycho-Cultural Foundations of Contemporary Terrorism." *Political Psychology* 26, 4 (2005): 615–36.

Pozorski, Aimee. *Roth and Trauma: The Problem of History in the Later Works (1995–2010)*. London and New York: Continuum, 2011.

Rachlin, Nathalie. "Alain Finkielkraut and the Politics of Cultural Identity." *SubStance* 24, 76/77 (1995): 73–92.

Radford, Colin, and Michael Weston. "How Can We Be Moved by the Fate of Anna Karenina?" *Proceedings of the Aristotelian Society* 49 (1975): 67–93.

Randall, William Lowell. *The Stories We Are. An Essay on Self-Creation*. Toronto, Buffalo, Canada: University of Toronto Press, 1995.

Rankine, Patrice D. "Passing as Tragedy: Philip Roth's *The Human Stain*, the Oedipus Myth, and the Self-Made Man." *Critique: Studies in Contemporary Fiction* 47, 1 (2005): 101–12.

Ricœur, Paul. "Life in Quest of Narrative." In *On Paul Ricœur: Narrative and Interpretation*, edited by David Wood, 20–33. London and New York: Routledge, 1991.

Robins, Robert S., and Jerrold M. Post. *Die Psychologie des Terrors: Vom Verschwörungsdenken zum politischen Wahn*. Translated by Christiana Goldmann. Ulm: Droemer, 2002.

Roes, Anne. "The Representation of the Chimaera." *The Journal of Hellenic Studies* 54 (1934): 21–25.

Rosenberg, Shawn W. "Sociology, Psychology, and the Study of Political Behavior: The Case of the Research on Political Socialization." *The Journal of Politics* 47, 2 (1985): 715–31.

Rosenberg, Warren. *Legacy of Rage: Jewish Masculinity, Violence, and Culture*. Amherst, MA: University of Massachusetts Press, 2001.

Roth Pierpont, Claudia. "The Great Enemy." *The New Yorker*, 1 May 2006, http://www.newyorker.com/archive/2006/05/01/060501crbo_books.

Rothberg, Michael. "Seeing Terror, Feeling Art: Public and Private in Post-9/11 Literature." In *Literature after 9/11*, edited by Ann Keniston and Jeanne Follansbee Quinn, 123–42. New York, London: Routledge, 2008.

Roughley, Alan. "Liminal Paperspaces: Writing between Derrida and Joyce and Being and Writing." In *Mapping Liminalities: Thresholds in Cultural and Literary Texts*, edited by Lucy Kay, Zoë Kinsley, Terry Phillips and Alan Roughley, 209–28. Bern: Peter Lang, 2007.

Royal, Derek Parker. "Texts, Lives, and Bellybuttons: Philip Roth's *Operation Shylock* and the Renegotiation of Subjectivity." *Shofar* 19, 1 (2000): 48–65.

Russell, Bertrand. *Why I Am Not a Christian. And Other Essays on Religion and Related Subjects*. London and New York: Routledge, 2008. Reprint, 7.

Ruthven, Malise. *Fundamentalism: A Very Short Introduction*. Oxford, New York: Oxford University Press, 2007.

Safer, Elaine B. *Mocking the Age: The Later Novels of Philip Roth*. Albany: State Univ. of New York Press, 2006.

Said, Edward W. "Invention, Memory, and Place." *Critical Inquiry* 26, 2 (2000): 175–92.

— "Zionism from the Standpoint of Its Victims." *Social Text*, 1 (1979): 7–58.

Saltzman, Arthur. "*Leviathan:* Post Hoc Harmonies." In *Beyond the Red Notebook: Essays on Paul Auster*, edited by Dennis Barone, 162–70. Philadelphia, PA: University of Pennsylvania Press, 1995.

Sánchez, Yvette. *Coleccionismo y literatura*. Madrid: Cátedra, 1999.

Sauvageot, Anne. *Sophie Calle, l'art caméléon*. Paris: Presses Universitaires de France, 2007.

Schlegel, Alice, and Herbert Barry III. "Adolescent Initiation Ceremonies: A Cross-Cultural Code." *Ethnology* 18, 2 (1979): 199–210.

— "The Evolutionary Significance of Adolescent Initiation Ceremonies." *American Ethnologist* 7, 4 (1980): 696–715.

Schlögel, Werner. "Kartenlesen, Augenarbeit. Über die Fälligkeit des *Spatial Turn* in den Geschichts- und Kulturwissenschaften." In *Was sind Kulturwissenschaften? 13 Antworten*, Hrsg. Heinz Dieter Kittsteiner, 261–83. München: Wilhelm Fink Verlag, 2004.

Schocket, Eric. "Redefining American Proletarian Literature: Mexican Americans and the Challenge to the Tradition of Radical Dissent." *The Journal of American Culture* 24, 1–2 (2001): 59–69.

Scott, Daniel G. "Rites of Passage in Adolescent Development: A Reappreciation." *Child and Youth Care Forum* 27, 5 (1998): 317–35.

Sears, David O. "Whither Political Socialization Research? The Question of Persistence." In *Political Socialization, Citizenship Education, and Democracy*, edited by Orit Ichilov, 69–97. New York and London: Teachers College Press, 1990.

Segal, Alan. "*Portnoy's Complaint* and the Sociology of Literature." *The British Journal of Sociology* 22, 3 (1971): 257–68.

Seixas, Peter. "Lutz Niethammer. Posthistoire: Has History Come to an End?" *Historical Studies in Education/Revue d'histoire de l'éducation* 6, 1 Spring/Summer (1994): 121–24.

Severs, Jeffrey. "'Get Your Map of America': Tempering Dystopia and Learning Topography in *The Plot Against America*." *Studies in American Fiction* 35, 2 (2007): 221–39.

Shklar, Judith. *Political Thought and Political Thinkers*. Chicago, IL: University of Chicago Press, 1998.

Shostak, Debra. *Philip Roth: Countertexts, Counterlives.* Columbia, SC: University of South Carolina Press, 2004.

— "Return to the Breast: The Body, the Masculine Subject, and Philip Roth." *Twentieth Century Literature* 45, 3 (1999): 317–35.

Sigel, Roberta S. "Image of a President: Some Insights into the Political Views of School Children." *The American Political Science Review* 62, 1 (1968): 216–26.

— "New Directions for Political Socialization Research: Thoughts and Suggestions." *Perspectives on Political Science* 24, 1 (1995): 17–22.

Sigler, Mary. "Review: A Sneeze and a Cup of Sugar: A Cautionary Tale of Narrative and the Law." *Law and Philosophy* 16, 6 (1997): 617–28.

Simon, James, and Bruce D. Merrill. "Political Socialization in the Classroom Revisited: The Kids Voting Program." *The Social Science Journal* 35, 1 (1998): 29–42.

Simpson, David. "Telling It Like It Isn't." In *Literature after 9/11*, edited by Ann Keniston and Jeanne Follansbee Quinn, 209–23. New York; London: Routledge, 2008.

Sklar, Howard. "Narrative as Experience: The Pedagogical Implications of Sympathizing with Fictional Characters." *Partial Answers* 6, 2 (2008): 481–501.

Smith, Kathy. "The Emptiness of Zero: Representations of Loss, Absence, Anxiety and Desire in the Late Twentieth Century." *Critical Quarterly* 46, 1 (2004): 40–59.

Sollors, Werner. *Neither Black nor White yet Both: Thematic Explorations of Interracial Literature.* New York: Oxford University Press, 1997.

Solomon, Norman. *Judentum: Eine kurze Einführung.* Stuttgart: Reclam, 1999.

Stähler, Axel. "The 'Aesthetics' of Fundamentalism in Recent Jewish Fiction in English." In *Fundamentalism and Literature*, edited by Catherine Pesso-Miquel and Klaus Stierstorfer, 43–77. New York: Palgrave McMillan, 2007.

Steinmetz, Horst. *Literatur und Geschichte.* München: Iudicum Verlag, 1988.

Stouck, David. "*Winesburg, Ohio* and the Failure of Art." *Twentieth Century Literature* 15, 3 (1969): 145–51.

— "*Winesburg, Ohio* as a Dance of Death." *American Literature* 48, 4 (1977): 525–42.

Stow, Simon. *Republic of Readers? The Literary Turn in Political Thought and Analysis.* Albany, NY: State University of New York Press, 2007.

— "Written and Unwritten America: Roth on Reading, Politics and Theory." *Studies in American Jewish Literature* 23 (2004): 77–87.

Thiessen, Elmer John. "Initiation, Indoctrination, and Education." *Canadian Journal of Education/Revue canadienne de l'éducation* 10, 3 (1985): 229–49.

Thompson, Seth. "Politics without Metaphors Is Like a Fish without Water." In *Metaphor: Implications and Applications*, edited by Jeffrey Scott Mio and Albert N. Katz, 185–202. Mahwah, NJ: Lawrence Erlbaum Associates, 1996.

Tolchin, Karen R. *Part Blood, Part Ketchup: Coming of Age in American Literature and Film.* Lanham, MD and Plymouth: Lexington Books, 2007.

Tonkin, Elizabeth. "Masks and Powers." *Man* 14, 2 (1979): 237–48.

Torney-Purta, Judith. "Adolescents' Political Socialization in Changing Contexts: An International Study in the Spirit of Nevitt Stanford." *Political Psychology* 25, 3 (2004): 465–78.

— "Psychological Theory as a Basis for Political Socialization Research: Individuals' Construction of Knowledge." *Perspectives on Political Science* 24, 1 (1995): 23–33.

— "Review: Comparative Perspectives on Political Socialization and Civic Education." *Comparative Education Review* 44, 1 (2000): 88–95.

Torney-Purta, Judith, Carolyn H. Barber, and Britt Wilkenfeld. "Latino Adolescents' Civic Development in the United States: Research Results from the IEA Civic Education Study." *Journal of Youth and Adolescence* 36 (2006): 111–25.

Trendel, Aristie. "Master and Pupil in Philip Roth's *The Dying Animal*." *Philip Roth Studies* 3, 1 (2007): 56–65.

Tsiknaki, Eirini. *Literatur und Persönlichkeitsentwicklung: Eine empirische Untersuchung zur Erfassung des Zusammenhangs zwischen literarischem Lesen und emotionaler Intelligenz*, Forum Europäische Literatur 5. München: M-Press, Meidenbauer, 2005.

Turner, Victor. "Betwixt and Between: The Liminal Period in Rites of Passage." In *Betwixt & Between: Patterns of Masculine and Feminine Initiation*, edited by Steven Foster and Meredith Little Louise Carus Mahdi, 3–19. La Salle, IL: Open Court, 1987.

— *From Ritual to Theatre: The Human Seriousness of Play*. New York: PAJ Publications, 1982.

— *The Ritual Process: Structure and Anti-Structure*. New York: Aldine de Gruyter, 1969.

Updike, John. "Talk of the Town." *The New Yorker* 24 September 2001, http://www.newyorker.com/archive/2001/09/24/010924ta_talk_wtc?printable = true.

Upstone, Sara. "A Question of Black or White: Returning to Hanif Kureishi's *The Black Album*." *Postcolonial Text* 4, 1 (2008): 1–24.

Van Gennep, Arnold. *Übergangsriten*. Übers. Klaus Schomburg und Sylvia M. Schomburg-Scherff. Studienausg. Frankfurt a.M.: Campus, 1999.

Varvogli, Aliki. *The World That Is the Book: Paul Auster's Fiction*. Liverpool: Liverpool University Press, 2001.

Victoroff, Jeff. "The Mind of the Terrorist: A Review and Critique of Psychological Approaches." *Journal of Conflict Resolution* 49, 1 (2005): 3–42.

Viljoen, Hein, and Chris N. van der Merwe. "A Poetics of Liminality and Hybridity." In *Beyond the Threshold: Explorations of Liminality in Literature*, edited by Hein Viljoen and Chris N. van der Merwe, 1–26. New York: Peter Lang, 2007.

Ward, Ian. *Law and Literature: Possibilities and Perspectives*. Cambridge: Cambridge University Press, 1995.

Waugh, Patricia. *Metafiction: The Theory and Practice of Self-Conscious Fiction*. London: Routledge, 1984.

Wernli, Boris. "La transmission intergénérationnelle de l'orientation idéologique en Suisse dans les familles à plusieurs générations." *Swiss Political Science Review* 13, 2 (2007): 237–59.

Whalan, Mark. "Dreams of Manhood: Narrative, Gender, and History in *Winesburg, Ohio*." *Studies in American Fiction* 30, 2 (2002): 229–48.

White, Hayden. "Introduction: Historical Fiction, Fictional History, and Historical Reality." *Rethinking History – The Journal of Theory and Practice* 9, 2/3 (2005): 147–57.

— "The Value of Narrativity in the Representation of Reality." *Critical Inquiry* 7, 1 (1980): 5–27.

White, Hayden V. *Metahistory: The Historical Imagination in Nineteenth-Century Europe*. 4. printing ed. Baltimore, MD: Johns Hopkins University Press, 1983.

— In *Metzler Lexikon: Literatur- und Kulturtheorie. Ansätze – Personen – Grundbegriffe*. 4. Hrsg. Ansgar Nünning, 764–65. Stuttgart, Weimar: Verlag J.B. Metzler, 2008.

Whitebrook, Maureen. "Compassion as a Political Virtue." *Political Studies* 50, 3 (2002): 529–44.

— *Identity, Narrative and Politics*. London: Routledge, 2001.

— *Real Toads in Imaginary Gardens: Narrative Accounts of Liberalism*. Lanham, Maryland etc: Rowman & Littlefield, 1995.

Widmaier Capo, Beth. "Inserting the Diaphragm in(to) Modern American Fiction: Mary McCarthy, Philip Roth, and the Literature of Contraception." *The Journal of American Culture* 26, 1 (2003): 111–23.

Widmann, Andreas Martin. *Kontrafaktische Geschichtsdarstellung. Untersuchungen an Romanen von Günter Grass, Thomas Pynchon, Thomas Brussig, Michael Kleeberg, Philip Roth und Christoph Ransmayr*. Vol. 4, Studien zur historischen Poetik. Heidelberg: Universitätsverlag Winter, 2009.

Wilcox, John. "The Beginnings of L'Art Pour L'art." *The Journal of Aesthetics and Art Criticism* 11, 4 (1953): 360–77.

Wilson, Alexis Kate. "The Ghosts of Zuckerman's Past: The Zuckerman Bound Series." In *Philip Roth: New Perspectives on an American Author*, edited by Derek Parker Royal, 103–17. Westport, CT and London: Praeger, 2005.

Wilson, Matthew. "Reading *The Human Stain* through Charles W. Chesnutt: The Genre of the Passing Novel." *Philip Roth Studies* 2, 2 (2006): 138–50.

Winther, Stefanie. *Weibliche Initiation in den Romanen von Virginia Woolf und Doris Lessing*, Universität Trier. Trier: WVT Wissenschaftlicher Verlag Trier, 2005.

Weintraub Austin, Erica, and Bruce E. Pinkleton. "The Role of Parental Mediation in the Political Socialization Process." *Journal of Broadcasting and Electronic Media* 45, 2 (2001): 221–40.

Wolbrecht, Christina, and David E. Campbell. "Leading by Example: Female Members of Parliament as Role Models." *American Journal of Political Science* 51, 4 (2007): 921–39.

Yuval-Davis, Nira. "Belonging and the Politics of Belonging." *Patterns of Prejudice* 40, 3 (2006): 197–214.

Zerilli, Linda M. G. "Machiavelli's Sisters: Women And 'The Conversation' of Political Theory." *Political Theory* 19, 2 (1991): 252–76.

Ziewacz, Lawrence E. "Holden Caulfield, Alex Portnoy, and Good Will Hunting: Coming of Age in American Films and Novels." *The Journal of Popular Culture* 35, 1 (2001): 211–18.

Zuckert, Catherine H. "On Reading Classic American Novelists as Political Thinkers." *The Journal of Politics* 43, 3 (1981): 683–706.

— "Why Political Scientists Want to Study Literature." *PS: Political Science and Politics* 28, 2 (1995): 189–90.

Index